IT'S NOT THE
GLORY

THE REMARKABLE FIRST THIRTY YEARS OF US WOMEN'S SOCCER

TIM NASH

Lulu Publishing Services rev. date: 5/10/2016

For my parents

ACKNOWLEDGEMENTS

Cover photo: Tony Quinn
Interior photos: Tony Quinn, Andy Mead and Jeff McCrum
Cover Design: Andrew Wood
Design: Allison Nash
Cody editing: Mary Katherine Cornfield
Editorial Assistance: Jennifer Rottenberg, Allison Nash, Julie O'Keefe
*All information and quotes in this book, with the exception of footnoted passages,
are from books and articles written by Tim Nash and published by JTC Sports
and/or interviews conducted by Tim Nash or through press conferences.*

M.K.
Thank you so much
for your diligent work
to help me complete
this book.
Chance meetings sometimes
work out!
Thank again
You're awesome..

A LITTLE BACKGROUND

By Tim Nash

*I*t was sometime in the late 90s. I'm not sure of the exact year but it was definitely before 1999. The women's national team was in Rochester, my father's hometown and the city where I was born. My parents lived 71 miles down the New York State Thruway in Oswego, New York, where I grew up. My dad grew up playing soccer in Rochester in the 1940 and 50s, joining teams of Italian, German or Irish immigrants on weekends, and he played goalkeeper at the State University of New York at Brockport. With a doctorate in elementary education, he was also the assistant coach for the SUNY Oswego soccer team. In grade school, my brother Marty and I started playing soccer, a sport still so rare to our part of the state, we had to travel 40 miles to find another school to play, but we got plenty of practice chasing balls at Oswego State practices. My mother, a physical education teacher, coached the high school jayvee girls' soccer team. So when the national team came to Rochester, my parents wanted to go watch them practice.

I had moved to North Carolina in 1987, started a sports journalism career and was thoroughly enjoying ACC soccer. I co-authored books with Anson Dorrance and Michelle Akers, and in 1998, I was working on a third with Lauren Gregg, who had been the national team's assistant coach since before the 1989 World Championship. I'd been fortunate enough to conduct a whole lot of interviews with members of the national team for the soccer outlets I worked for at the time – internetsoccer.com, College Soccer Weekly, womenssoccer.com, Soccer News and all the WUSA teams. I often went a couple days early to the city in which the U.S. was playing and did interviews after training, wherever and whenever was allowable, mostly remote corners of hotel lobbies. After I finished an interview with one player, it was not uncommon for her to say, "Who do you need next?"

I knew U.S. training sessions were always open to the public, but I thought it would be a good idea to check and see if it was okay for my parents to come watch in Rochester. Lauren assured me it was fine, and my parents packed up their lawn chairs and headed to Rochester. When they got to the field, they did what they had done for years, set their chairs near the sideline and settled in to watch some soccer.

There may have been a total of five spectators there that day, and here's what happened. During a break, Julie Foudy was gathering some stray balls and noticed a couple in their late-60s sitting on the sideline. She came over and said, "You must be the Nashes." Later, Michelle Akers, Lauren Gregg, Tony DiCicco and others stopped by to say hello and introduce themselves.

Think about that for a minute. They didn't have to do that. How many people would actually take the time to do that? How many people who are training for World Cup would take a few minutes to say hello to two people they don't know sitting on the sideline? And call them by name? It's not like my parents would have left mumbling and disappointed if no one had greeted them.

Throughout this book, you will, I hope, come to understand why they do things like that, why that type of personal interaction is important, and why it was all second-nature to them. I hope I was able to do justice to the story of the first 30 years, and explain the type of people that have made up the U.S. Women's National Team from 1985 to 2015. I believe the story of the USWNT is a remarkable one.

A little over two years ago, due to a combination of boredom and nostalgia, I started writing some long-form features about the national team. At the time, I had no plans to do anything with them. Just a little hobby, I thought. It had been over 10 years since I had written anything, and I was enjoying the process again. I sent a few things to some friends. Their feedback encouraged me finish this book.

Much of the information in this book is through interviews with team members and coaches. I figure the process took me to roughly 25 states. I was fortunate enough to cover 17 years of college soccer, the 1996 Olympics, the 1999 World Cup, the 2000 Olympics, the 2003 World Cup and the three years of the Women's United Soccer Association. For that, I need to thank Pat Millen and Jennifer Rottenberg, two of the people who made it possible for me to write about soccer for a living. Additionally, Tim Crothers provided me with early encouragement after reading a section of what I was trying to put together. Aaron Heifetz, the long-time press officer for the women's national team, helped over the years by setting up interviews. Mary Katherine (MK) Cornfield and her copyediting talents, were a huge help, and my daughter Allison provided design help. I would also like to thank my wife Cheri and my son Ian for simply putting up with me.

But the two people who helped me the most are Lauren Gregg and Anson Dorrance. In helping Lauren write The Champion Within, which came out after 1999, I was able to spend time observing the team and conducting countless interviews with players and the staff. As for Anson, I had no idea at the time, but I found out quickly, that having my name on a book with Anson Dorrance was one of those things that gives careers a huge boost. By co-authoring Training Soccer Champions with Anson, I had the credibility to approach Michelle Akers about writing her book. And through the years, Anson has been an invaluable sounding board and source of historical information, as well as a really fun person to talk with. I should also mention that April Heinrichs and Tracey Leone were very helpful with the section on the early years. They spent a great deal of time with me going over their time as players, and Heather O'Reilly was very accommodating in several instances.

Anyway, I hope you enjoy reading this book as much as I enjoyed writing it. Someone else will have to do the next 30 years.

Tim

FOREWORD

By Lauren Gregg

In 1986, the U.S. Women's National Soccer team won the North America Cup, in Blaine, Minnesota. I remember serving a cross to April Heinrichs who scored the game- and tournament-winning goal in front of a handful of fans. It would serve as the U.S. Women' National team's first tournament win. The relatively obscurity stands in stark contrast to the 2015 Women's World Cup Championship boasting the largest TV audience ever, or the 1999 World Cup Final selling out the Rose Bowl. Yet, as publicly different as these events were, they are intimately joined and inseparable on many levels. The culture that was established in 1985 with the first-ever U.S. Women's National Soccer team courses through each subsequent team and forms the foundation of both the incredible success and broad appeal enjoyed today.

I remember vividly as Anson Dorrance, then the head coach of the U.S. Women's National team turned to me after the Blaine event, "I would do anything to be part of the first-ever Women's World Cup." I quickly agreed and tried to envision that day. Would that ever happen in our lifetime? Neither of us knew, of course, that five years later, we would coach together and bring home the first-ever Women's World Championship, in Quanzhou, China. The tradition of being the best in the world had been founded, an unwavering pursuit of excellence rewarded.

I had the amazing fortune of continuing my tenure coaching with Tony DiCicco, as we went on to capture the Gold at the first-ever Olympic Games for women's soccer in 1996 and the 1999 Women's World Cup. The U.S. Women's National team would transcend relative anonymity over the next 25 years to become heroes and household names. How they did this and who was part of this journey unfolds in story-like fashion in Tim Nash's book, *It's Not the Glory*. Tim cleverly explains the essence of what makes this program so special and successful. He does so by recognizing that our success is intertwined with who these people *are* as much as what they did. Yet, each of us shared common ground – a passion for what we did.

Mark Twain once reflected, "Two of the most important days in your life are the day you were born and the day you find out why." It quickly becomes clear that part of the national team's culture was grounded in people who were lucky enough to find their passion. Although the circumstances around each team and every player differs, their goals -- their willingness to outwork everyone, the winning tradition, incredible leadership, fundamental passion and love of the game -- will forever unite them.

Once, running a four-minute mile seemed humanly impossible. For us, the things that seemed elusive that others either didn't believe in, would only motivate us to make it different for those who followed. Each team and player had to break barriers -- many times fighting for what no one else had done and many couldn't even see.

In the beginning, most of the players grew up playing with boys and emulating famous male professional athletes. There was *no* example or script written. They would write their own destiny. But one thing was common then, as much as it was in 1999 and in the summer of 2015 when the U.S. took home their third World Cup, and every day in between – an unwavering commitment to be the best in the world.

While our history is written on the shoulders of incredible moments, performances and heroes that have become symbolic of our sport, you will come to appreciate that no one player or coach was *the* factor. It was and is always about team. Whether that means coming in fit, playing as hard as you can against your peers, accepting your role on the bench, accepting the role of spokesperson, taking on the role of a leader, playing a new position, speaking to media, being away from family, signing every last autograph, it's all done in the name of the team. The team is where one's success is everyone's, where one's failures are shared by all, where love of each other is unconditional, where paving a path for the next generation is more important than your own.

To be part of this team, this program, is a commitment to something far greater than yourself. It's about wearing the USA crest on your chest and inspiring the next generation to follow their heart. It's about family and friendship. It's about loving what you do and having fun doing it. It's about leaving a legacy strong enough to go on without each of us.

PART I

IT'S NOT THE GLORY

U sually, the beginning is the same for all of them. They get a chance to play their chosen sport at the highest possible level and a chance to wear their country's uniform. Then come the dreams—national anthems, award ceremonies, dramatic wins, Gold medals, world championships. When the dreams are achieved, however, the players finally realize that all along it was the friendships, the hard work, the extreme highs, and even the devastating lows that they remember. They discover that it isn't the glory that's lasting. It's the journey that mattered.

This journey begins in, of all places, Italy. No, not Rome or Milan. Those places would be too glitzy for this part of the story. Not even Naples, or Florence, or Parma, or Genoa, all too well-known for this bunch. This story begins north of Venice, in the small town of Jesolo on the shores of the Adriatic Sea. If Italy is shaped like a boot, Jesolo is the part you hold to pull on the boot. After World War II, Jesolo became popular among tourists, and in 1985, a group of American women showed up to play soccer. The name of their team was the United States Women's National Team. It was the first time women ever represented the U.S. in an official soccer match. The venue was fitting because more than one player on that trip described themselves as naïve tourists.

The early years were not glamorous. Far from it, in fact. To say the program operated on a shoestring budget might be giving the strength of the shoestring a little too much credit. The training, the uniforms, the travel, the lodging, the food were all nowhere near what is considered acceptable today. The 1985 trip to Jesolo was the beginning of what is known today as the most dominant women's soccer program in the world—Gold medals in four of the five Olympics in which women's soccer has been played, and the only nation to own three World Cup titles.

The social impact of the team is not measurable, but it can be seen all over the United States. The minds they helped change about the roles of women in society are countless, and they certainly changed the attitudes about women in sports. It's not possible to measure the impact the U.S. women's national team has had in places like Japan, Brazil, Nigeria, Mexico, and most everywhere else in between, where women are now allowed to be athletes and accepted as competitors. Sure, there are statistics about participation in sports by girls, and there are studies about the benefits of athletics to young girls. There is official data that could help explain that influence, but it will all be lacking. You see, there is no way to be absolutely sure what the full impact of this team has been, and there are two reasons why: First, it's not over yet. Like any good movement, it should never end. It should build on itself constantly, go through cycles, evolve, and spread. The second reason is simple. You can't measure dreams.

Carin Jennings
Photo by Tony Quinn

ORIGINALS

Imagine you just finished your freshman year in college. You had a good year, too, scoring 14 goals in 14 games and earning All-America honors. You learned your team is pretty good and filled with women who love to play soccer nearly as much as you do. It appears the decision to leave Seattle and go to school across the country in Orlando, Florida, was a good one. So now what? You are happy at the University of Central Florida, and the chances to win more games, score more goals, and play the game you love at a high level are very promising. Everything's good.

But wait. What's this you hear about someone putting together a group of players to travel overseas? A guy you know from Seattle has been asked to coach it. It all seems very official. They are even calling it the United States team. You've been asked to go to Italy with them for a tournament. What do you do? If you're Michelle Akers, you say, "Cool. I'll go." In August of 1985, Akers was a member the first-ever U.S. Women's National Team. Coached by Mike Ryan, a long-time youth coach in Seattle, the team ventured to Jesolo, Italy and played four games. Lost three, tied one.

"It was weird," said Akers. "I had no idea what I was doing. I was just playing soccer. I remember all the other teams being so much better—skillful, tactical. We just chased and chased. They fouled a lot, too. They were grabbing, punching, spitting, kicking. Amateurs that we were, we complained to the ref and finally started getting physical ourselves only to get a few cards. It was quite an experience, but I definitely did not feel like I was playing for the USA."

Soon, Akers would become the most important figure in women's soccer globally, and over the next 15 years, she would play a major role in setting a standard for what it meant to play for the USA.

Now, suppose you just finished your college soccer career. You played 85 games and scored a remarkable 87 goals. You have destroyed the myth about women not being competitive. Your coach at the University of North Carolina, Anson Dorrance, marveled at the way you "would never sacrifice your own level of excellence to win the Miss Congeniality Award." In fact, you have almost single-handedly changed the way he approached the way he worked with female athletes. You are leaving the University North Carolina, the school you left Colorado to attend, having accomplished almost everything a team can accomplish. You won the NCAA Championship three times in your four years. You have been named First-Team All-America three times, and the school is going to retire your jersey. And your team ran up a record of 85-3-3. But it's 1986, and you weren't on that first-ever USA team that went to Italy last year. However, your college coach, Anson Dorrance has just replaced Mike Ryan at the helm of what is being called the national team. You are at the top of the list of players he wants to invite to his first training camp. But your knees are bad. Soccer is painful. You don't know how much longer you can do it.

So what do you say? If you are April Heinrichs, you probably use the phrase Dorrance used to describe the way you played, "Give me the ball, and get the hell outta my way." Heinrichs would go on to play a crucial role in making the U.S. Women's National Team the unique and inspiring organization it is today. She had an enormous impact first as a player and later as a coach. What is overlooked, however, is her lasting effect as a captain. "April evolved as a leader," said Shannon Higgins Cirovski, an early teammate. "She didn't worry about how she was playing as much as how the team was playing."

Now think of yourself growing up in California. There are a lot of girls playing soccer, and you take to the sport early. You go to high school at Palos Verdes High and earn All-America honors four times, mostly because you scored an amazing 220 goals in your four years. You choose to stay close to home and go to the University of California Santa Barbara. You set a national collegiate record for career goals with 102. You can do things with the ball no other female player has been able to do. Your teammates marvel at your dribbling prowess. Your opponents shutter when you come at them.

By now it is 1987. You are out of college with your business degree. You have been offered a chance to come to training camp with the U.S. National Team. Would you go? If you're Carin Jennings, you go, and you change the way the game is played with your elegant ball control and your dramatic dribbling.

"She could make the most athletic person look as if walking was something new to them," said Mia Hamm. "She was amazing. The way she could cut the ball as dynamically as she could at full speed was unbelievable. Defenders would fall down a lot. They just couldn't keep up with her. She was faster than a lot of people gave her credit for. She could beat you on the dribble, or she could run past you. I learned so much from watching her. A lot of times when I cut the ball the way I do, it's because I watched her for so long. You could just see how devastating it was to defenders. You could be really fast, and she could find ways to beat you."

Jennings, dubbed "Crazy Legs" and "Gumby" by her teammates, honed her skills with a training partner, the man she was dating and eventually would marry. Jim Gabarra, a U.S. Olympic soccer team member at the time, would go on to coach women in three professional leagues. Playing one-on-one against one of the top male players in the country certainly had its rewards. "I remember trying out for a state team in California, and she was there," said Julie Foudy. "The first time I saw her, I was like, 'Who the hell is that girl?' She was just tearing through teams. She would literally tear through five defenders and score. I was in awe."

Let's not suggest for a minute that the USA was a three-person team. They were, of course, much more than three forwards. Adding those three pieces was crucial, though. When the team took the field in the 1991 Women's World Championship, the USA played with three forwards—Heinrichs on the right, Akers in the middle, and Jennings on the left. "It was a great mix with good chemistry," said Mia Hamm, who observed the three from the right midfield spot she played sporadically. "You had three totally dynamic and different types of front-runners. April was more of a slasher that could get in behind defenses. Michelle was someone that was more of a target player who could play back-to-pressure and shoot from distance. Carin was just a carver. She'd take people on, and cut the ball so dynamically that it just got people off-balance." In 1991, the Chinese media would marvel at the USA attack and dub Heinrichs, Akers, and Jennings "The Triple Edged Sword."

Now imagine you are Michelle Akers, April Heinrichs, or Carin Jennings. Little girls did, at least the ones lucky enough to see them play. And frankly, not enough had that chance. If any of the three came along 10 or 20 years later, their fame would have been magnified to Mia Hamm, Abby Wambach or Alex Morgan-like levels. No regrets, though.

"I wouldn't change my decade for any other decade," said Heinrichs. "I wish I were healthy enough to play every day and play at the highest level. I wish I didn't have the pain in my knee. But it was all about the game. It wasn't about the fame."

WHO IS THIS KID?

She can't legally drive yet, but she's at her first national team training camp. She's in her room with her roommates, and they are irritated with her right now. She won't stop jumping on the bed. "Who is this kid?" wondered April Heinrichs, as close to a grizzled veteran as this team of novices can produce. "She's annoying me when I'm trying to rest."

Take a quick look. It appears the youngster and the veteran couldn't be more different. The Kid, some young phenomena named Mia Hamm, is 15 years old, and she is having the time of her life. April is 21, and she's not. It's just another day at the office. The kid is a rookie, full of energy and nerves and questions about her ability. April, owner of three collegiate national championships, is full of confidence. She's looked to as a leader. She established a new standard for the sport at the University of North Carolina with an all-out-all-the-time style of play. She just wanted to win. And she was very interested in being the one— the one carrying others over the finish line in order to make sure her team was successful, the one scoring the winning goal, the one people depended on. Mia dreaded being the one.

Was there a reason Anson Dorrance, who doubled as coach of the USA and the University of North Carolina, put Mia and April in the same room? Did he also have a reason to put Tracey Bates there, too? Dorrance described Bates as a "Positive Life Force, someone who brightened up your day every time she comes around." Was Mia being exposed or groomed? Or both? Was she being shown a culture where women could be strong, confident, and unapologetic for excellence—a place where they could, in fact, be great?

"I was overwhelmed," said Mia. "I was just this young kid coming into an environment where people knew each other and were pretty comfortable with each other. For me, I just was excited with the fact that there were women who were definitely better than I was—women who loved the game, were just as passionate as I was. So that was cool. But I just remember physically feeling like I was a fish out of water. Being from a small town, there were a couple girls that played at a higher level, but I had mostly competed against boys. I could do stuff with the ball, but I definitely wasn't anywhere close to being as technically sound or as fit as those players were. But from then on, I knew I had a chance to go to college and that I wasn't alone."

And that's why Mia's jumping on the bed. It's because she's 15, and until today, she thought she was all alone. She thought, like just about every 15-year-old, that there was something wrong with her. Other girls weren't interested in the same things she was—getting dirty and sweaty, playing against boys, and competing with everything inside you until you've won. It turns out there were, in fact, others just like her. "In a situation like that, you get to thinking you're the only one doing it," said Hamm. "Then you come in an environment like (the national team). Seeing so many other girls and women competing at such a high level and enjoying what they do made me feel good."

And, can you believe this? Someone had taken the time to invite them all—Carin, Julie, and Joy from California, Michelle from Seattle, Kristine from Connecticut, Tracey from Texas, Wendy from Virginia— to the same place. And they were invited just to play soccer! It gets even better, there's a coach who expects—no, demands—they play hard, compete with each other. To dominate! All of those words have been taboo. Those things have always set Mia apart, made her stand out instead of fit in. But no more. She can even jump on the bed. "It's 6:30 in the morning, and Mia's jumping on the bed," April remembered. "We were all in college and like, 'What are you nuts?' Get out of here.'"

If Mia's smart, she'll let April sleep. More than one national team player described their first training camp like this: "April scared the crap out of me." But Heinrichs and the rest of the players at the U.S. National team training camp have heard all about Mia Hamm since her performance in a regional event, which was unlike anything the coaches had seen. Still, the players wondered what all the fuss was about. April and Tracey were members of the North Texas State team, an invitation-only regional youth team playing under coach John Cossaboom, when they found out. One day, Cossaboom approached them with a request. "He pulled us aside and said, 'This girl Mia Hamm—you just wait. She's only 15, but she is going to be incredible,'" remembered Leone. "We said, 'No problem. We'll take care of her.' First game, she goes out and scores this upper-90 goal. It was just awesome, and I was like 'Wow! Holy Mackerel!' She got instant respect."

April recalled the same play but from a slightly different angle: "I remember this flash where Mia took the ball and started flying toward goal," she said. "I was wide open, and I couldn't believe she wouldn't give me the ball. Then she drilled this rocket into the upper corner, and I thought, 'Okay, good second option.'"

That was on the field. Off the field, Mia was still a shy, skinny kid away from home, scared to death yet having a blast. Soccer, at times, had been frustrating to her. The quality of training sessions seemed to be at the mercy of the effort her club or high school teammates were willing to give. Mia wanted to play, to run, to dribble, shoot, run harder, dribble faster, and shoot some more. At times, she felt out of place, and fitting in had always been a very important part of her life. Her family moved a lot, you see. But through the national team, she would meet a collection of women with whom she would share a life-long bond. They would be among the most important people in her life.

In the summer of 1987, U.S. Soccer held an inter-regional camp at Marquette University. The purpose of the camp was to select a senior national team and an Under-19 national team, both of which would compete in an international event in Blaine, Minnesota. On the youth team was a pair of 16 year olds, Kristine Lilly and Julie Foudy, 19-year-old Joy Biefeld (Fawcett), and 15-year-old Hamm. Dorrance was suddenly presented with exciting possibilities. Rumblings had been heard about a world championship for women to be held as early as 1990. Dorrance set out to build a team that would be able to compete for that title. Lilly, Hamm, Foudy, and Fawcett represented his youth movement.

"I was watching them the entire time—in games and in training," said Dorrance. "It was clear that they were special players. Mia's athleticism and acceleration were just extraordinary. Foudy had this very sophisticated and elegant presence with the ball, and her change of pace struck me immediately. Kristine was like the Tasmanian devil. I was just stunned at her work rate. She never stopped running. I remember thinking, 'This kid is going to have a heart attack by the time she's 30.' Joy had to grow on you. Her speed and skill were there, but her smoothness washed away any spectacular nature of her game. I watched her several times as a youth player, and she blended in with the team so well that she didn't jump out at me."

Hamm remembered, "It was funny because everyone got called in at different times. I think I was the last choice. I think Joy was the first one. Kristine might have been second, and Jules third. I was definitely the last. The first thing that shocked me was how intense it was. I really didn't know what intense soccer was till I joined that team."

For their entire lives up until now, Foudy, Biefeld, Hamm, and Lilly had been big fish. Now, all of a sudden, their pond became gigantic. "Everyone was great. I had to find my little niche to contribute—doing what I could do and not what I dominated doing in other leagues," remembered Lilly. "But in my first practice, I thought I was going to faint. Everyone was so fast and so good. I thought I was going to die from nerves and anxiety."

Foudy said, "For two years, it was constantly this questioning 'Do I belong with this group? Am I good enough?' But it was a good experience. I had to learn to fight through that. Once I realized 'Yeah, I can do this,' then it was about keeping that consistency of confidence."

Important lessons learned: First, there is a thing called the U.S. Women's National Team. Second, you are good enough to play on it. Third, you are going to have to challenge yourself. Fourth, training is intense, and fifth, don't wake up college-age players at 6:30 in the morning.

The Blaine event also served as a preparation for a trip to China on which they would embark less than three weeks later. All the youngsters were invited to go, but Foudy didn't want to. "It seemed I was always calling home, 'Mom, I got invited to another camp. I need more money.' Finally, Anson came to me and said, 'Julie, do you understand what I'm asking you?' I said, 'Yeah, I should probably go, huh?'"

"I was like 'well, I don't know if I can go to China unless I ask my parents,'" Lilly said. "I had to call home." After having secured permission from her parents to travel to China, Lilly brought her stuffed animal with her. "She carried around a lion or something like that," said Heinrichs. "We used to steal it all the time and hang it."

The youngsters' expectations for the future were not high. They were just excited about what was happening to them at the moment. "For me, it was just to play soccer," Lilly said. "It was just an opportunity to play the game that I loved and at the highest level. I just wanted to play." Foudy had a similar objective. "Just to get better," she said. "And to learn. I was so young. I was like a sponge."

While Lilly and Foudy's ambitions revolved around the field, Hamm and Biefeld simply hoped to stay on it. "To not throw up at fitness—that was my goal," said Hamm. For Fawcett, ambitions went beyond any one aspect of training. It touched them all. "To survive," she recalled with a laugh. "To survive and stay on the team. That was my goal. I was just such a scared kid, and I was scared of everyone and everything. I just didn't want to get cut."

The trip to China was unlike anything any of the players had experienced. In July of 1987, China lifted Martial Law in Taiwan opening the possibility of free elections and better relations between China and the United States. Less than a month later, the U.S. women's national team arrived in China for two matches over a 10-day period. "We were among the first Americans to get into the country," said Carin Jennings (Gabarra). "That was pretty strange. They told us not to dress in bright colors and not to wear shorts because women always wore long pants or dresses, even though it was 95 degrees. I mean, this is a country with two million bicycles, and they're all the same color. A lot of the Chinese people had never seen Americans before, and the kids were scared to death of us.

We would give them balloons and food, and they were astonished. Adults would come up to us, especially to the blonde players, and grab our hair. They'd yank it because they couldn't believe it was real. They had never seen blonde hair."

When the team traveled, it gave them a chance to bond, to learn about each other, and to hopefully, create some chemistry. But chemistry is a tricky subject. Mix the wrong elements together, and you have an explosion on your hands. Dorrance and his assistant coaches, Lauren Gregg and Tony DiCicco, knew their science pretty well, though. The elements they were mixing together—the most talented female soccer players in the country—were sure to create some sort of explosion. The challenge was to harness it to create something positive. The opposite effect was also possible. The eruption could destroy the entire project.

Part of the effort to organize positive team chemistry was to initiate a big-sister program, where an older player would take a youngster under their wing. Lori Henry was Mia's big sister, while Jennings took charge of Lilly, and April Heinrichs's little sister was Joy. "She scared the crap out of me," said Joy. "I don't think I said two words. It was more off the field. On the field, I would definitely yell at her to come back on defense."

"That's why Joy is so quiet now," joked Julie Foudy, someone who has never been accused of being quiet. "April traumatized her. Mia and Kristine were initially quiet, and then they opened up, but Joy stayed really quiet. Joy was always reading like she does now. And she's always steady. Nothing rattles her."

The players who were with the team before the four teenagers arrived—all competitive, skilled, and experienced players—could have easily bristled at the new kids. If they did, it didn't show. The opportunity to improve the team seemed to outweigh any personal agendas, even when four of them lost their jobs to Facwett, Lilly, Foudy, and Hamm. "A lot of the players on that team were great teammates," said Joy Fawcett. "None of them showed any bitterness towards us. I'm sure they were bummed about not playing, but they never looked at it as a personal thing."

NO WHINING

Funny thing about a group of women—they usually do not take themselves too seriously, nor do they look at any given situation on the field as life or death. "Women have the superior understanding that their relationships are more important than the game itself," said Dorrance. So, if the relationships off the field are rock-solid, the bond will carry over into games, right? The chemistry experiment worked. Trips abroad helped create a strong bond between the players, mostly because of things that happened off the field.

"There's someone in every era with a dark, sick sense of humor," said April Heinrichs. "Someone else feeds off it, and then they milk it, and it becomes a joke and a story that's told years later. In those days, it was Lori Henry and Kim Maslin, Amy Allmann."

Heinrichs and Lori Henry, a towering central defender from the University of North Carolina, were the team captains. They established the standard for leadership, both verbally and by the example they set, for all future captains. "I think Henry was a big team person," said Brandi Chastain, a reserve forward on the 1991 team. "She wanted you to do the right thing, and if you didn't, she was in your face. She was just very deliberate about the way she conducted herself. Fifteen minutes before the game, you had to be there and ready to go—which was a struggle for me. She went to practice every day to play her hardest. It might be a five-v-two drill, and she would be diving at your ankles or getting in your face. I remember practicing corner kicks in China, and she was in front of the goal winning headers and yelling at us because we weren't trying hard enough."

Human nature says that a group will tolerate much more than an individual will. And vice-versa. Everything depends, of course, on the particular group. A collection of sour pessimists will, without a doubt, struggle in challenging circumstances. Those types of players never lasted very long with the U.S. women. At UNC, Dorrance required all his seniors to read a book by Viktor Frankl. The book, titled *Man's Search for Meaning*, is about life in an Auschwitz concentration camp during World War II. Frankl's point, the one Dorrance hoped his players would grasp, is that the one thing that is truly under your control is your attitude. Each American player knew this for sure—an attitude can make or break just about any experience. "If you have a positive attitude, you are going to have a positive experience," said Tracey Bates (Leone). "And anyone would rather have a positive experience than a negative one."

Tracey Bates was key in creating and maintaining the attitude the team needed on their adventures abroad. "Tracey is just very positive as a person, and she is always working hard," Joy Fawcett said. "She would never get bitter about anything. I think her attitude definitely helped set the tone." Helping the situation was that no one missed an opportunity to remind someone of the attitude they had adopted as a team. A teammate could easily be snapped back to a positive frame of mind by hearing a quick "No whining" from a teammate.

Now, when players talk of the travel or the food, they laugh. The memories are funny, not disgusting. Amy Allmann remembered vividly a trip to Italy. "We flew on a cargo plane—Tower Air," she said. "We didn't know what to expect. We were worried it wouldn't have seats. It had seats but it was so big it took two runways to take off."

"Flights were always an adventure," said Shannon Higgins (Cirovski). "In China, we were taking off, and the whole inside of the exit door fell off onto this woman. We didn't fly more than a mile high the whole time. I thought we were dodging cows and stuff we were so low. It was a propeller plane, and you'd be thinking, 'At any time, this thing can go down.' I remember riding on coal trains in the middle of the afternoon. It was hot so the windows were open, and the smoke would come in the windows. We rode 17 hours on a coal train in rural China, and by the time we arrived, coal was stuck to our faces. Down the aisle, there was a little hole in the corner of the room. That was the bathroom—just this little hole, and it would go right out onto the tracks. It definitely made us stronger as people. We learned the value of what we had."

But true to their adopted team motto of "Deal with It," the team embraced the challenges—never were they called "sacrifices," always "challenges." They made the most of the experiences and got a great deal out of them. "In Sardinia (Italy), we played on dirt field and stayed in a place with nothing around it at all—nothing," said Tracey Leone. "We joked about the field. It was perfectly flat, graded dirt."

The 1989 trip to Italy was Mary Harvey's first with the national team. A standout goalkeeper at the University of California-Berkeley, Harvey was in goal for a 0-0 draw against Poland in Sardinia. "It was beautiful there, but kind of, well, rustic," Harvey remembered. Lauren Gregg, the team's assistant coach, remembered going to the hotel where the team was staying and the players seeing a gravel field out the window of the bus. "Hey, I bet that's where we're playing," they joked. When they pulled up to that same field the next day for training, the joke became funnier. "After two workouts on the field, everyone's shoes had lost all their cleats," said Harvey. "They looked like cycling shoes." The players, however, found the bright side. "Well, the game field has to be better than this," they said. It was. It was dirt.

"I remember doing 120s (a series of full-field sprints), and literally three yards away from the end line was the fence, so we had to stop right on the end line," recalled Heinrichs. "And when we ran, we would stir up the dust. Everyone was coughing the whole time. Our mottos were 'Deal with It' and 'No whining.' We said that all the time."

Lori Henry was what Foudy called, "A real nutter." But she made the food in China more fun. "Henry would eat anything," remembered Foudy. "After she tested the food, she might start barking to let us know what it was. I dropped down to 118 pounds after the first China trip. I had a parasite or something. I remember some of the parents joking that they wished they got a parasite and could lose 12 pounds. The players had to face facts; there were some Chinese delicacies they just couldn't stomach. "There would be a whole fish on the plate with the eyes, or a pig head, or turtle soup with a turtle claw in the soup," said Lilly. "And you are like, 'What the heck is this?' I remember the shrimp had heads. We would eat the shrimp and give the heads to Henry. She would put the heads on her fingers and give a puppet show."

"Henry was definitely the taste-tester," said Heinrichs. "I was the one trying to get people to eat things. You know, 'Hey, pass that snake over here.'" The next time the U.S. team went to China, they brought their own chefs. Pete Dorrance, Anson's brother, and Greg Overbeck, Carla Werden's future husband, were partners in a restaurant in Chapel Hill, where some of the players worked as waitresses. They travelled with the team to China.

Leone added, "We had to make the best of it. We had to bond, and I think it was good for us as a team to go through those crazy things that don't happen in five-star hotels. It's not like we could watch TV all day, so we would find things to entertain ourselves. It wasn't like in a week we were going to be leaving for another trip. This was it. Trips were few and far between. Those kinds of situations really pulled the team together. And we were all so excited about going to all these remote places."

On August 3, 1987, the USA defeated China 2-0 in Tianjin, both goals coming from Carin Jennings. The starting lineup that day was Amy Allmann in goal, Lori Henry, Linda Hamilton, and Debbie Belkin as defenders, Tracey Bates and Shannon Higgins as center midfielders, Kristine Lilly at left midfielder, and Joy Fawcett at right midfielder. The forward line had April Heinrichs, Carin Gabarra, and Mia Hamm. The team would use variations of that lineup throughout 1987 and the first half of 1988 until Foudy met Dorrance's defensive requirements. At that point, a crucial adjustment was made. "Basically, all my California players were in interceptor mode, and I was telling them in player meetings that there was another way to get the ball other than waiting for the other team to hand it to you," said Dorrance. "Joy emerged first. Initially, I played Akers next to Shannon Higgins in center midfield, and it was at some foreign tournament, where Foudy emerged. That gave me permission to separate Shannon and Michelle, who were very similar—unbelievably unselfish, great vision, great speed of play. With those two, we had the same kind of players playing in midfield, which you don't want. But Foudy was a little different. She was a galloping, penetrating midfielder. She wanted to get through midfield with her acceleration, sort of galloping through. Higgins and Akers wanted to get through with a quick one-two passes forward. The nice thing about Foudy emerging was that our midfield became less predictable. That gave me permission to use Michelle at forward. In the early days after she moved to forward, Michelle was like a midfielder playing on the front line. We wanted Michelle to be more selfish. There was nothing wrong with her decision-making, but they were the decisions of a play-making midfielder. Up front, you want more of a selfish personality, and slowly but surely, Michelle converted herself into this attacking personality that wanted the ball."

The team played just once in 1989, bringing their total number of international matches played to 31. By comparison, Norway had played 68 by the beginning of 1987, and Italy, which started a women's program in 1968, had well over 100 international matches behind them. In 1989, it appeared that FIFA, soccer's world governing body, would hold a world championship for women. Not a World Cup, mind you. That name was for the men's event only. FIFA wanted to be sure the women's event didn't tarnish the image of the World Cup. When Dorrance took over as head coach of the national team, he was challenged by the U.S Soccer Federation to be completive in our region. The qualifying rounds for the CONCACAF region, the North and Central Americas and the Caribbean region would be held the following year.

# YOUTH SOCCER BOOM

The base of players that would rise to the national team was being formed in youth soccer programs, in which girls were beginning to participate in record numbers. Dads, whether or not they knew anything about the sport, began coaching their daughters. And, of course, you can't underestimate the power of a father who wants a field, a program, or some additional resources for his daughter and her friends. And the future success of the national team program would be the beneficiary of it.

In 1990, outside Detroit in Bloomfield Hills, Michigan, a four-foot, 11-inch, 85-pound forward named Kate Sobrero was getting ready for her sophomore season at Detroit Country Day High School. In Memphis, Tennessee, 13-year-old Cindy Parlow was preparing to enter Brentwood High, where she would spend just three years before jumping to UNC to accelerate her rise to the national team. Abby Wambach was 10 years old and taking regular poundings in Rochester, New York, from her seven older siblings. Eight-year-old Cat Reddick was playing boom-ball soccer and learning to be a Southern Belle in Alabama. Lindsay Tarpley was seven years old in Michigan, and Heather O'Reilly was five in New Jersey. In San Jose, California, Aly Wagner entered a juggling contest that served as a fundraiser for her youth soccer league. As others tried to keep the ball up, Aly went about her business. After 20 minutes, Aly was told to stop. She had juggled the ball 1,500 times and was declared the winner. She was 10.

That year, the Americans played six matches, winning all six by a combined score of 26-3. The Heinrichs-Akers-Jennings combination on the front line was clicking, to say the least. In the six games in 1990, the trio combined for 19 goals. Jennings had four, Heinrichs popped in six, and Akers scored a remarkable nine times. Mia Hamm, playing mostly as a front-line sub or as a right midfielder, scored four times in the six matches. In the fourth game of the year, an 8-0 thrashing of the Soviet Union in Blaine, 21-year-old Carla Werden (Overbeck), a recent graduate from the University of North Carolina, started her first international match. Over the next 10 years, the national team would rarely take the field without her. In her four-year UNC career, Werden's Tar Heels went 89-0-6. In her sophomore year, the Werden-led defense allowed just two goals in 25 games. Her Tar Heel teammate Wendy Gebauer likes to point out that one of those two goals was actually scored by Carla, an own goal.

"Carla came onto the team as a skinny, scrawny girl, but she developed herself into a fitness machine," said Michelle Akers. "She is very strong, has incredible endurance, and her mental tenacity is that of someone extremely intense and focused. Carla became a great leader, too. She is someone who makes you want to live up to her standards, which are exceptional."

"Okay. Thanks. We'll give you a call when we can get together again. Oh, and by the way, you better be fit." That was the message from the coaches on August 11, 1990, the day of the team's last game until April of 1991. In the meantime, the players were expected to work out on their own for eight months. When the team was called in together again, they were expected to be in top condition. The culture of training on your own was born.

"We didn't have all the opportunities players have today," said Tracey Leone. "ODP (Olympic Development Program) was just beginning, and the youth national teams were paper teams. European trips were not even considered. But I think there were many benefits to our situation. I went out with my older sister or by myself every day and played with the ball for hours—in the backyard or against a wall (our poor neighbors) just making things up and loving it. There weren't as many organized practices back then, maybe two-to-three times a week, so we played indoor soccer at the recreation center down the street with neighborhood kids every day after school and every day in the summer. Even before practice. Many of our friends were guys, so we played with and against guys growing up, many of them older. The Bates girls and some of our friends were the only girls. We played soccer tennis at night under lit tennis courts. It was a social event for me and my sisters. There was nothing I would have rather been doing. All that really helped my technical ability and speed of play."

Carin Jennings was working out on her own as well with her future husband, a U.S. Olympic team member. But the player who set the standard was Akers, who trained regularly with her then-husband Robby Stahl, owner of Post-to-Post Soccer Camps. Her routine of striking ball after ball for hours, running, heading, and working on all technical aspects of the game was legendary. She rehabilitated her many injuries on a squash court, knocking the ball of a wall, receiving it, turning, and knocking it off another wall.

The U.S National team at the CONCACAF
Qualifying tournament in Haiti.
Front to Back: Kim Maslin, Megan McCarthy, Debbie Belkin,
Wendy Gebauer, Joy Biefeld, Kristine Lilly, Carin Jennings,
Julie Foudy, Michelle Akers, Mia Hamm, Amanda Cromwell,
Tracey Bates, Brandi Chastain, Keri Sanchez, Carla Werden,
Shannon Higgins, Amy Allman, April Heinrichs

Photo by Tony Quinn

DOMINATION IN QUALIFYING

Let's move on to Haiti. Yes, Haiti. An important part of this story happens there. The regional qualifying tournament for the world championship was held in in the depressed, chaotic, Caribbean nation.

Not only did the U.S. women establish unquestionable supremacy in their region, but they left with a strong sense of confidence that would carry through to the 1991 World Championship. Perhaps most importantly, the players further crafted the attitudes and standards that would become normal, accepted behavior for every team that came after. At the team hotel in Haiti, the rooms had running water and electricity for just one hour each day. Deal with it. "You have one flush for the day," laughed Leone. "Those are the things that bond you."

"We would just play cards by candlelight for hours and hours and hours until the candle would burn completely down," remembered Heinrichs. "We would be sitting in our bras and underwear because it was so hot. We basically bathed in the pool. The pool was pretty gross by the time we left."

A simple game of cards was never played by the U.S. women's national team. In fact, they never played a simple game of anything. Everything was a competition that required a winner. Even showers in Haiti became a personal competition – you vs. the water supply. "We had an hour to take showers," said Leone. "If you took too long, the water and electricity would cut off. We would hear a scream and knew that someone got caught."

If the U.S. was bothered by the conditions, it certainly didn't show on the field. The Americans destroyed their regional foes. First Mexico fell 12-0, Martinique followed by the same margin. Trinidad & Tobago were pounded 10-0, as was Haiti. The USA finished up qualifying with a 5-0 win over Canada. When it was all over, the Americans had scored 49 goals and allowed none. Of the 49 goals, Akers had 11, Heinrichs eight, and Gabarra five. Brandi Chastain came off the bench in three games and scored six goals, five of them coming against Mexico in the opener. The first step toward the 1991 title had been accomplished. In the most dominate way, the USA had qualified for the first-ever women's world championship to be held in China in November of 1991.

Guess what? People in the soccer community were starting to pay attention to the women's team. And they were even willing to listen. After the qualifying tournament, Michelle Akers was invited to speak at the annual meeting of the Soccer Industry Council of America (SICA). "I got up and told them about qualifying and about the upcoming world championship in China," Michelle remembered. "I told them how we had all been fired from our jobs and how we made $10 a day, and that we needed monetary support. I had no idea what I was doing at the time, but I knew we needed support, and these were the people that could provide it."

Having blasted through CONCACAF, the U.S. still wasn't sure how they would stack up against the rest of the world. Dorrance thought they would be competitive, but he knew the team needed more seasoning. To accomplish that, the USA needed to play some European teams, but that cost money. The United States Soccer Federation came through, putting together an aggressive schedule for 1991, by far the most competitive to date. The USA played 12 matches between the end of qualifying and the kickoff of China '91. Twenty days after leaving Haiti, the Americans were in France to begin a 12-day trip that would take them to Holland, Germany, and Denmark. Their 20-day tour of Europe provided better tests and perhaps a more accurate measuring stick. After beating England 3-1 on goals from Heinrichs, Akers, and Jennings, the USA lost 4-3 to Holland, and then defeated Germany 4-2 before losing to Denmark 1-0—the first time the Americans had been shutout since that 0-0 draw with Poland on the dirt field of Sardinia 349 days earlier.

Dorrance's staff included 29-year-old Lauren Gregg. Any discussion of women's soccer pioneers is incomplete with a thorough mention of Gregg, who over the next 25 years would add a list of "firsts" to be any description of her. At UNC, she helped lead the Tar Heels to the first NCAA soccer championship for women. She helped the USA win the first ever Women's World Cup, the first ever Olympic soccer gold medal, and as a coach at the University of Virginia, she was the first female coach to led a team to the Final Four and she was the first woman to be named the collegiate coach of the year by the National Soccer Coaches Association of America.

Assistant coach is a sometimes thankless job. Being comfortable in the background is one of the primary skills needed. At the same time, the coach depends on you to voice your opinion, articulate your point of view, and support whatever decision is made whether you agree or not. Lauren Gregg did the job expertly from 1989 to 2000. She played for Dorrance at UNC and played for the national team from 1986 to 1989. Then Dorrance asked her to be his assistant. At the time, though, neither knew there would be a world championship for women, but they often talked about how much they would love to be involved in it, even half-joking that they would serve as equipment managers if that's what it took.

With Gregg as assistant in 1991, Dorrance knew, and DiCicco would later discover, the team would be prepared. Her scouting reports breaking down the opponents' strengths and weaknesses in exhaustive detail were invaluable, her input during games always spot-on.

Twenty-four years after China '91, Dorrance received the prestigious Werner Fricker Builder Award from the U.S. Soccer Federation. In his speech, he said: "I appreciate this public forum to thank Lauren Gregg, my brilliant and loyal assistant. As Tony DiCicco knows, Lauren made the most important tactical decision for us during that championship run and her love and loyalty is felt to this day."

"WE WERE NAÏVE, BUT WE WERE SPECTACULAR"

So here you are. As little as four or five years ago, some of you didn't even know there was such a thing as the U.S. Women's National Team. Now you are on the other side of the world, literally, getting ready to play for a world championship.

Just how good are you? In your country's history, the team has played 59 games. By comparison, European countries—Italy, Sweden, Norway—have played more than twice that number. Still, of the 59 games you have won 35, lost 18, and tied six. Pretty good so far. However, nearly half of your games have been played against just three teams—China eight times, and Norway and Canada seven times each.

Recent results have been good. You destroyed the competition in the regional qualifying tournament, and a subsequent trip to France produced positive, confident-building results. Leading up to the World Championship, you have won 15 games, lost six, and tied one. Are you ready? Who knows. There are certainly reasons to be concerned. First, your leading scorer, Michelle Akers, seems to be competing with herself to see which she can get more of—goals or injuries. Her medical chart lists injuries to feet, toes, knees, shoulders, a concussion or two, and several instances when she had to spit out broken teeth. Her latest? She tore up her kneecap after losing a battle with a sprinkler head, suffered a week earlier while working a soccer camp. Why, you might ask, would someone a week away from the biggest tournament of her life slide for a ball in a pointless game at a soccer camp?

"When I first started coaching her, I was always afraid she would hurt herself," said Dorrance. "I just couldn't get her to be more careful. But isn't it a wonderful problem to have as a coach when you have a player who lists her greatest weakness as 'I take too many physical risks'?"

Next, your captain is playing in pain, a lot of pain. Her knees are deteriorating. Ice bags are attached to Heinrichs whenever she is off the field. If your team goes all the way to the final, it will be six games in 13 days. If that's not enough to test your confidence, your central midfielder, Shannon Higgins, the player who so smoothly starts the attack and dictates the pace and flow of the game, has a bone fracture in her foot. Is she going even be able to play? She'll play, but she will wear a sneaker on one foot. Wait, what? That's right. She wore a soccer shoe on her left foot and a sneaker on her right. Oh, by the way, she's right-footed.

So three of your most important players are, let's say, less than 100 percent. How confident are you now? Oh, one more thing. Just before you left for China, Megan McCarthy, your starting right defender in the 3-4-3 formation that Dorrance employed, tore her ACL. You and your teammates, however, are adamant that McCarthy will be allowed to travel with the delegation that went to China. "I remember it was very important to us that Megan came with us to China, even though she was injured and couldn't play," said Brandi Chastain. "The team insisted that she go, and that says a lot about how close that team was."

Your right back spot is open. Now what? No problem, you say. You can use the youngest player on your roster, 19-year-old Mia Hamm. That's what Dorrance did to make a brave adjustment to his lineup, a switch that would impact the team into the next century. Joy Biefeld (Fawcett) was one of the most effective flank midfielders in the international game. A tireless worker with breakaway speed, Biefeld was an attacking force at right midfield. But Dorrance moved her back to play right defender and put Hamm at right midfield.

In the years after the '91 title, both Dorrance and his successor, Tony DiCicco, would try to move Fawcett back into the midfield with no success. The problem, they both said, was that they didn't have another player good enough to replace her at defender. In essence, the problem was that there was just one Joy Fawcett. "I remember being shocked that I had to go back and play defense," remembered Joy, a chronic doubter of her own ability and the security of her place on the team. "I had always been a forward or a midfielder. That was my first shot at playing defender, and I have never been able to get out."

"I only started because Megan McCarthy got injured," said Hamm. "I had played a little midfield growing up, but in our system, I had more defensive responsibility than I realized. Anson was great about it. Because we were so dynamic up front, he told me not to worry about getting into the attack. He said my main responsibility was defensive."

Okay, so how do you feel about your team now? As usual, you look to your captain. What does she think? "To a certain extent, we did know a little bit about how good some of the other teams were," said Heinrichs. "We weren't one of the European countries that played each other all the time, but from '85 on, we had a yardstick to measure ourselves by. In '85, we were a little bit behind, but we knew we had closed the gap by '91. And we felt we were prepared and confident. I think by nature Americans are confident athletically, but the training sessions we had gave us more confidence. And the work every player put in on their own time gave us a confidence that there weren't a lot of countries out there that were doing all the things we were doing."

No one would know it by watching or listening to Anson Dorrance, but he, too, was unsure how good the Americans were. Concerned about injures and inexperience in the international game, Dorrance let none of it show. "Anson made us feel that we were the best team and had the best players," remembered Kristine Lilly. "That added to the way we played, as well. We knew we had great talent, but he instilled that in us every time we stepped on the field."

Dorrance is also not someone who leaves things to chance, especially something as critical as confidence. "I remember having a meeting with the team," he said. "I asked them a rhetorical question. I told them there are two ways to go into this World Cup: One is to sneak in on cat's paws and surprise everyone; the other way is to go in with your flag flying, trumpets blaring, and say 'We are the best.' I think it was very clear the way I wanted to go in. I knew we were capable of some amazing things. I was not a cat's paws kind of guy. I wanted to go in and say, 'Here we are. Give us your best shot.' It was a wonderfully powerful mentality that we went in with."

"We didn't go in shy, that's for sure," said Brandi Chastain. Julie Foudy added, "Anson was great at that. He got you to the point where you wanted to rip their heads off. He's the best motivator in the world."

Flags flying, imaginary trumpets blaring, the USA entered the first-ever women's world championship on November 17th in Panyu, China. There were 14,000 people that showed up—only a handful of Americans and most of them parents and relatives of the players. Before the team played their first match, Heinrichs called another meeting. "April got us together in a players-only meeting," said Leone. "She even had tournament brackets drawn up, but she didn't complete the bracket. It wasn't like, 'If we beat this team, then we play the winner of this game.' It was blank. It helped us stay in the moment and take one game at a time, and that was really important. This was our first world event. We were all pretty clueless. We had been to a few tournaments as a team, but not that many. We had certainly never done anything like this. I think that was a key moment for our team when we came together and got on common ground. I remember the team coming out of the meeting with an extraordinary level of focus. The coach can always say those things and should always say those things, but there is something different when the captain takes that responsibility. It was an open forum too, and we were able to discuss everything. There were no lines drawn. I thought it was great."

Now you have all your bases covered. You're confident. You're mentally prepared. You feel you are good enough to win. The only thing lacking, as it turns out, is your inability to take your foot off the gas pedal. And it almost costs you. Your first opponent, Sweden, is not a pushover, despite what the scoreboard says with under 20 minutes remaining in the game. The two goals by Jennings surrounding halftime and a third goal by Hamm with 18 minutes left in the game sure seemed like enough at the time. "Thank God that game ended," said Foudy, who had a hip-pointer from a collision with Carla Werden. "That's the game I remember most, even more than the final. I felt I was going to die."

"We were beating Sweden 3-0 and kept attacking," explained Dorrance. "Most sophisticated teams will go up a few goals and protect a lead. Against Sweden, we were up 3-0 and still trying to get a fourth. And so the Swedes got two goals and almost won the game. I remember saying in the press conference that if the game was any longer, Sweden would have won. We were naïve, but we were frigging spectacular. We thrilled the fans."

MORE BRAZILIAN THAN BRAZIL

"Sell the game." If women's soccer was going to go anywhere with the general public, Dorrance believed it was up to the players. Play with flair, play with style, win with grace, and lose with grace. And attack. The age-old criticism of soccer is that there aren't enough goals. Teams play to not lose instead of playing to win. It's too defensive, they say. Dorrance's idea of playing to not lose was to score bunches of goals as possible as quickly. The ideal score to some coaches is 3-0, and 4-0 is an excessive bonus. To Dorrance, 9-0 is a good day. In a world championship tournament, 5-0 would do just fine.

Playing on just two days of rest, the USA met Brazil on November 19th. The Brazilians, the standard bearers for "Jogo Bonito" or the beautiful game because of the flair, freedom, and creativity with which Brazilian players played, won a less-than-beautiful opening match 1-0 over Japan. A Brazil goal in the fourth minute was followed by, well, not much else. The U.S. game would be worse. Behind two goals from Heinrichs, and one each from Akers, Jennings, and Hamm, the USA thumped the Brazilians 5-0. "The greatest compliment I've ever received as a coach, came from the Brazil coach," said Dorrance. "I was telling him how much I admired the Brazilian game, and the coach said, 'Of all the teams in this tournament, your team plays most like Brazil.'"

At the center of the American attacking spectacle was what the Chinese media dubbed the Triple Edged Sword—Heinrichs, Akers, and Jennings. After two matches, the sharpest edge of the sword was Jennings. "She played in front of me most of the time," recalled Lilly. "I remember catching myself just watching her. She could really cut the ball in front of the defender. She would show them the ball and then cut it away and they could never touch it. I remember giving her the ball and saying to myself, 'Okay, I'm just going to watch this.' It was just precision."

Watching from the bench was Wendy Gebauer, who had to deal with the conflicting emotions of wanting to get on the field and supporting the starters. Gebauer saw action in three games in Bulgaria tournament, and she scored three goals. A goal a game would seemingly be good enough to earn you a starting spot. Unless, that is, the player starting ahead of you is scoring two a game. She got her chance when Dorrance decided to rest Heinrichs for the team's last game of the Group stage against Japan. A pair of goals by Akers made it 2-0, and Gebauer scored just before halftime. This time, the USA avoided any dramatic comebacks and won 3-0.

"One of the things that was so good about the 1991 World Cup was that FIFA realized, 'Oh my God, we have an exciting product,'" said Dorrance. "Look at the way the Americans attack. Look at the aggressive way they play. Look at the way they relentlessly go forward."

Five goals. Three in the first half, two in the second half. That's not what the USA scored against Chinese Taipei in the quarterfinals. That's what Michelle Akers scored against Chinese Taipei, bringing her tournament-leading total to eight goals in six games. Foudy and Joy Biefeld also scored, and the USA stormed into the semifinals, boosted by a 7-0 win. All is good, right? Well, not quite.

"There was a very critical meeting between the quarterfinals and semifinals," remembered Heinrichs. "We had a little ruffle in the water, and a couple people were upset about an issue. We had a players-only meeting, and one or two players aired out what they wanted to say, and one player slept. Everyone bonded together. The meeting allowed one or two players to say what was on their mind, and it allowed everyone to realize we were all in it for the right reasons. We were all in it together. It was a positive meeting in the end. I came out of that meeting knowing that we were going to win, and then we played Germany. That's when it changed from 'I want to win, I think we can win, I hope we win,' to 'I know we are going to win.' When you look back, you can always say that. But after that meeting in '91 I knew we were going to win."

Germany hadn't allowed a goal in their first three games of the tournament, and it wasn't until Denmark scored on a penalty kick 25 minutes into the quarterfinals that recently unified Germany, was scored upon. But that was of no interest to the confident Americans. In 1988 and 1990, the USA had defeated West Germany, 2-1 and 3-0. The teams had played just once after East and West Germany united, and the U.S. took a 4-2 win on May 30, 1991, in Kaiserslautern. Akers and Jennings each had two goals that day, and the 1991 semifinals nearly six months later would see Akers score twice and Jennings record the hat-trick.

"Her goals were amazing," said Chastain of Jennings's performance. "She spun this one girl into the ground. She did this outside of the foot, outside of the foot, outside of the foot, and oh my gosh, the girl just fell down."

Dorrance still marvels at the strike Jennings hit against Germany. "She got the ball near the mid-stripe," he explained. "After beating a couple players, she just hit this screaming 30-yarder on a rope to the upper corner. That goal was truly remarkable."

"She was the best player in the world in '91—there was no question," said Heinrichs. "Her domination when she got the ball in any situation was remarkable."

Leadership moments are tough to define. They aren't planned. They can't be rehearsed. They have to stem from someone's character, and they have to be spontaneous. Heinrichs came up with two more to help drive her teammates to the title. The Americans admit that the Norway game was not their best match of the tournament. Norway was an equal opponent, and the five previous matches had taken their toll on the U.S. players, especially Heinrichs. "I even said to Anson before the final, if you want to sit me, I understand," said Heinrichs. "If I couldn't play my best, I didn't want to put a coach in a position of having angst over using somebody else who could help us win. So I went to Anson and said, 'If you want to play someone else, play someone else.'"

"Anson made the right decision," said Tracey Leone. "We could just not take her off the field. She was too much of a leader. You knew she was going to help the team win, only if she had one leg. There are not many people at this level that you can say that about. He made the right decision. She was the emotional spirit of our team. And that's not to mention all the things she could do on the field. She was strong and powerful. One of those 'Get out of my way' players. She would run by you, dribble by you, or plow by you. Whatever it took."

Heinrichs's team needed her now, as much as ever. Norway was giving the U.S. all they could handle. The Americans could not hold possession of the ball and were chasing the Norwegians in what seemed like a fruitless effort. "It was not a pretty game," recalled Higgins. "We were just running. We couldn't get a hold of the ball. We couldn't string more than two passes together, and I remember April getting us all together during a stoppage of play and saying, 'Listen, we're good! Think about it. We're good!' And I remember going back and saying, 'Yeah, we are good. We aren't showing it right now, but we're good.' You can't let your lack of confidence kill you. April was telling us to emerge."

Two more goals by Akers gave the United States the first-ever women's world championship in a 2-1 win over Norway. Higgins, wearing a soccer shoe on her right foot for the first time in the tournament, set up both. "Michelle's first goal against Norway was the perfect example of how dominant she was in the air," said Dorrance. "She was being marked by perhaps the second greatest header in the world, Heidi Store. When you watch the replay, you see Michelle jumping up over everyone and heading it so hard that the goalkeeper, literally, does not move as the ball is going into the net."

Heinrichs has a way of getting right to the point. In fact, when asked to identify the key moment of the '91 final, she said, "When Michelle scored the second goal." With time running out, Akers chased a Higgins pass toward the Norwegian goal. She beat a defender to the ball and cut around the charging goalkeeper and calmly set herself up. The U.S. players didn't know how much time was left, but they were certain it wasn't much. "I remember thinking, 'Hurry up and shoot it already,'" said Foudy. "It seemed like it took her forever." There were less than two minutes remaining in regulation when Akers slid the ball into the empty net.

"There is a lot of protocol with FIFA, especially in something like a World Cup final," said Dorrance. "They actually sent some of their tournament organizers to speak to us. They let us know that there is a protocol after you win. One of the things you don't do is run out on the field to celebrate. I remember thinking, 'Guess what … we do.' I'm not going to hold players back from running out on the field. In our culture, you don't stand on the sideline and give a little golf clap."

At the final whistle, the Americans on the bench raced past Dorrance onto the field and a wild celebration ensued. The players hugged, cried, and waved American flags. And they went to the area in front of their families, who were seated on a small platform behind the bench. There were over 65,000 people in the stands that day, but very few Americans. Family and friends were the only ones with whom the players would be able to celebrate. But it was enough. A small band of supporters—almost entirely parents, siblings, and other relatives—followed the team in the early days, and they provided a comfort zone for the team. While the players were developing a culture—expectations, standards, and codes of behavior to which future generations of players would adhere—the parents were doing the same.

Kristine Lilly's father was easy to spot among the 65,000 fans in the stands. The spattering of Americans certainly stood out. If the players needed any help finding them, the American flags waving served as a landmark. And Lilly's dad was smack in the middle of the U.S. section. "I looked over at my dad, and I have never seen his face like that," said Kristine. "It was just pure joy. He had an American flag painted on his face, and I have never seen him so happy. It made me cry. To think that I could do something that would make him so happy—it was just incredible."

At the post-tournament banquet honoring the world champions, China brought out the very best it had to offer—snake soup, pigeon, ox, and some little vegetables that resembled broccoli. "Our head of delegation told us that China was a very poor country, and they were giving us the best of what they had," said

Amy Allmann. "All we wanted was rice. We begged for rice, but they said that rice was peasant's food, and it would be an insult to serve it to us."

The only media coverage of the event in the U.S. was reports by Soccer America on a weekly basis, and *USA Today* was running a journal written by Akers. The accomplishment went virtually unnoticed. The newly crowned world champions boarded a flight home. It would be more than 50 hours before they landed at JFK airport in New York City and returned to obscurity. The team certainly did not arrive home with flags waving and trumpets blaring. They arrived, sneaking in on cat's paws, but not by choice. Six people met them at the airport. One was the bus driver. Did they complain, feel slighted, or disrespected? No. They just dealt with it.

"Where have you been?" a Stanford classmate asked Julie Foudy.

"I was in China winning the world soccer championship."

"Cool," the classmate said. "Have you studied for chemistry?"

Not exactly a ticker-tape parade, or an appearance on Letterman, or being honored at the ESPY's. But you have to start somewhere. And there was no victory tour. The world champs played two games in 1992.

"I'm not one of these people who think we were victims or exploited or under-appreciated," said Dorrance. "I understood where our Federation was in those days. I loved the fact that we had a training camp before the World Cup. I loved the fact they bought us plane tickets to go to the World Cup. I'm not one of these people who think we weren't treated well. I knew we didn't have any money, and I thought we were treated great. We just went back to whatever we were doing. It wasn't like we were an on-going team with an active roster. We were like, 'Okay, no money. Let us know when you have some money, and we'll get the gang together again.'"

If a team is a reflection of its coach, the UNC Tar Heels are a reflection of their coach's driving style—go as fast as possible until you reach your destination. On any given day, Anson Dorrance can tell you his current record for traversing the 18 miles from his office in Chapel Hill to the Raleigh Durham International Airport, parking spot to parking spot.

But on a foggy morning in Chapel Hill, Dorrance, driving slowly, went by a local park trying to determine if he was seeing what he thought he was. There was someone out there with a soccer ball. All he could really tell at first was that the person was dribbling, shooting, chasing the ball, and doing it all again, then doing 120-yard sprints. But the silhouette—the one with the pony tail flapping as she ran, arms extended away from her body, and the thumb and index finger on her right hand forming an O—was unmistakable. It was the same figure the Women's United Soccer Association, the first fully professional women's league, would use on its logo years later.

Dorrance drove away at normal speed, his normal speed anyway. He couldn't wait to get to the office. He was a note-writer, you see. He would send notes of inspiration, encouragement, and instruction to his players on a regular basis. He knew exactly what he was going to send that morning. "Dear Mia. A champion is someone drenched in sweat, bent over, at the point of exhaustion when no one else is watching." Mia never said anything to Dorrance about the note. But it was on the first page of her book, *Go for the Goal*, a few years later.

"The nature of the team in those days was it was assembled for an event and then disassembled," said Dorrance. "We didn't have opportunities to meet on a regular basis. We developed this team with what we called self-coaching. So, if we had one event a year, you coach yourself the rest of the time. We had a self-coaching manual that we mailed out to all the players. The players were all self-motivated and disciplined. And anyone who wasn't, we let go. Today, you don't have to be intrinsically self-motivated to survive."

CHANGE

It's been 10 months since the U.S. defeated Norway in China. The USA has played their Scandinavian rival twice since then—and lost both times, 3-1 in Medford, Massachusetts and 4-2 in New Britain, Connecticut. The team featured just two players from the '91 championship team -- Mia Hamm and Mary Harvey. But several newcomers are beginning to emerge. One is Saskia Webber in goal. Another is Stanford product Sarah Rafanelli. Also getting their feet wet are Tisha Venturini in midfield and Tiffeny Milbrett at striker. In 1992, Milbrett, a five-foot-two dynamo with natural goal-scoring ability, was second in the nation in scoring with 30 goals and 15 assists at the University of Portland. Playing next to her on the Pilots' front line was 18-year-old Shannon MacMillan. She scored 19 goals that season to be the highest scoring freshman in the country. Across the continent in Chapel Hill, Mia Hamm put together her greatest season as a collegiate—32 goals, 33 assists. Kristine Lilly added 23 goals and 19 assists for the Tar Heels, and Venturini had 14 goals and 18 assists for the 25-0-0 national champs.

The country's youth and collegiate systems were producing plenty of young talent. A 15-year-old in San Ramon, California, Tiffany Roberts, was beginning to catch the eye of youth national team coaches. Gone, however, were the some of the players who formed the heart of the early teams—including Heinrichs, Leone, and Henry. "People get out of the game for different reasons, and April's reason was her knee," explained Tracey (Bates) Leone. "She could have played at that level longer but her knee wouldn't allow it. For me, my time was just up. I was hanging on as it was. It became time to say there are better players and that's that. I am honored to have had the time that I had."

In Point Pleasant, New Jersey, Christie Pearce (Rampone) was the point guard on her high school basketball team, the striker on her soccer team, and the star of her field hockey team. She led the conference in scoring in all three sports. The following year, she headed off to tiny Monmouth College to play basketball and soccer. Down the Jersey turnpike in Delran, a nine-year-old named Carli

Lloyd was in her fourth year playing recreation soccer with boys. Outside of Rochester, New York, Matthew Wambach watched as a neighborhood boy stayed on the ground groaning after being tackled in a neighborhood football game by his 11-year-old kid sister Abby.

Little happened on the field for the USA in 1992, but it was a crucial year in the growth of women's soccer. In addition to serving as the assistant the U.S. National team, Lauren Gregg was in her sixth year as the head coach of the University of Virginia. Heinrichs became the head coach of Princeton University, the first of several from the '91 team to be hired at major Division I universities. Debbie Belkin soon signed on to coach Fairfield University and later began the women's soccer program at the University of Michigan. Joy Biefeld became the coach at Long Beach Community College then went to coach UCLA. Lori Henry landed at the University of North Carolina Greensboro then went to Ohio State. Shannon Higgins started coaching at George Washington and moved on to the University of Maryland. Tracey Bates Leone took the assistant coaching job at Creighton before building a national contender at Clemson. Several others served as assistants at colleges near their hometowns, and the trickle-down effect begun in earnest. Heinrichs and Leone would go on to coach national teams, April with the full team and Tracey several youth national teams.

"Going from a player to a college coach—which is a great job, secure, you're your own boss, good living, you get to have an influence on players—then on to the national team, was great," said Heinrichs. "If I played in today's era, it wouldn't be the same path. It would be a more circuitous path. If Tracey and I would have come along later, I'm not sure we would be national team coaches. I didn't have any trouble coaching against North Carolina and Anson, but coaching against Tracey when she was at Clemson was horrible. The best thing about our generation was we had our time and we moved on. I wouldn't change it for the world."

There was a spotlight on the sport, though, and it shined on Akers. Even those who paid little attention to the team found it difficult to not notice her 10 goals in six world championship games, except for the woman sitting next to her on the plane trip home from China. The woman inquired why Akers was in China.

"I was playing for the United States in the world championship," replied Akers. "And we won!"

"That's nice," said that woman, and that was the end of the conversation.

WANTED: NEW EDGE FOR A THREE-SIDED SWORD

Fortunately, the U.S. did not have to place a want ad when Heinrichs retired. That kid, who five years ago was jumping on her bed, could fill in just fine. Mia Hamm replaced Heinrichs on the front line, becoming the third edge of the Triple Edged Sword. As Akers struggled with her health, Hamm was emerging as one of the world's top players. The national team finished their 1993 schedule in August, and the bulk of the team went back to school. That season, Hamm finished her collegiate career by scoring 26 goals and handing out 16 assists.

It's early on the afternoon of November, 21, 1993. The sky is clear blue, the type of day which a long time ago prompted some North Carolinians to proclaim that if God was not a University of North Carolina fan, how come He made the sky Tar Heel blue? Plenty around the state can argue with that, but no one will argue the fact that the greatest women's college soccer player in history ended her NCAA career a day earlier. It ended right out there on Fetzer Field on the campus of UNC. It was Mia Hamm's fourth NCAA championship, and she was determined to enjoy it. All she wanted to do was watch, but not from the sidelines. No, she had to be on the field. Her collegiate career was remarkable, featuring staggering numbers. Her team was 94-1 when she wore a Tar Heel jersey. She scored 103 goals in those 95 games, handed out 72 assists, set UNC, ACC, and NCAA records for goals, assists, and points. She didn't care, though. Not yesterday anyway. Maybe someday she'll think about it and say, "That's pretty good." Yesterday, all she wanted to do was watch.

Over there is the Hut, the tiny, run-down, three-room structure that serves as UNC's locker room, meeting room, coach's office, and source of a million memories for countless championship teams. Too small and too impractical to be known by anything else, the Hut doesn't bear anyone's name like the rest of the athletic facilities on campus—not Carmichael, or Smith, or Keenan, or Koury. It is, however, where the players laughed and cried and celebrated. It's the place they dragged themselves in and out of during pre-season. It's where they heard the motivational brilliance of their coach, Anson Dorrance. And Mia has spent her last days there. In six years, the Hut will be torn down and replaced with a glittering new office building, locker room, meeting facility that has a name on it—The McCaskill Soccer Center. The Hut was where Mia threw up occasionally before a game, grabbing the closest waste paper basket when nerves and self-imposed pressure tossed her stomach through a couple of 360s. It was where she and the other seniors were asked to leave yesterday so Dorrance could tell the underclassmen how much the seniors had meant to the program, and how much he wanted to send them out winners. And why they should, too. He told them how they should play the game of their lives to make sure Mia and the other seniors go out the way they came in—champions. The Hut is from where all those kids came charging, wiping tears from their eyes to win for Mia and the seniors, deathly afraid that a loss would be the most devastating experience of their lives.

Six. That's how many goals the Heels put past George Mason All-American goalkeeper Skye Eddy yesterday. How impressive was it that UNC put six past Eddy? She was named the Defensive MVP of the tournament for her efforts on the other half-million shots the Tar Heels unloaded at her. As the clock ticked down, Mia wandered off toward the sideline, the one closest to the crowd, the one 70 yards away from her teammates on the bench.

Today, she's going to talk about it, explain it the best she can. She's sitting in the stands, a view of Fetzer Field she only sees when the UNC men's team plays. Yesterday, 5,721 tickets were counted. Another 300 or so people watched from over fences, adjacent buildings, roofs, and windows. More saw it on ESPN. The field is empty now, except for the NCAA logos still painted on the grass and some guy jogging on the track. "I just wanted to experience as much of it as I could," she said, looking at the field, nostalgia setting in after less than 24 hours. "I wanted to get a sense of the excitement when everyone rushes on to the field for the celebration. I wanted to see it."

The celebration, you see, is her favorite moment in sports. So she became a guest at her own going-away party. She saw her friends running around hugging each other. She saw it on their faces—the sense of accomplishment, sense of relief, maybe even a sense of history. She saw pure joy and tears and goofy smiles and people falling all over each other. "The championship rings and awards are great," she said. "But the reason I play is to see the smiles on their faces and the tears in their eyes, and to see how hard they embrace. When it's a group of your friends, people that you care so much about, it makes it even better."

It was the fifth time she experienced it. Her first was in 1989 with UNC, then again in 1990. Then she took a year off from UNC to win a world championship in '91 with the national team in China. Then back to Chapel Hill for titles in '92 and '93. There would be many more before she's finished, more chances to celebrate with her friends. But in November of 1993, there was no way to know any of that. Nor was there any way to accurately predict that Mia would become one of those names everyone knew. There were, however, hints of big things. There were clues that Mia was capable of doing whatever it took to bring her sport the attention it needed, like the Italian TV station that waited for her yesterday. There are indications that she was ready to give it her best, but there were also hints she was dreading it somewhat. But she had something to say, and she took the opportunity to say it.

"I wanted to not only tell people what this game has done for me and how much I appreciate it, but you never know what it can do for someone else," she said that day. "If it can get exposure about soccer to some girl or boy who never thought about playing, and it ends up being their calling or their forte, then I have done my job. I always take it with a very serious attitude, because we are still in the process of selling our game. To an extent, we all have a responsibility."

She gave us a peek, though, a look at what is to become an on-going struggle inside her. Not the kind of struggle that sends her searching for a trash can before a game, but the kind that takes a lifetime to work through and a lifetime to make work.

"I don't push myself into interviews, and I don't push myself into the limelight," she explained. "But if I'm put there, I want to make the most of that opportunity because our chances are so few and far between. How many times do you get a chance to speak about the things you love to do and have it printed all over the country? It's a responsibility that I take very seriously. Every time I talk about my success or our team's success and the elements involved, I want it to be as positive as possible. It's generally how I like to look at life. I want to take all the positive things that I can out of it."

It has something to do with the way she was raised. The Hamm children, all five of them, saw more than their share of the world growing up. There's the time they lived in Italy, when Mia saw her first soccer game and started kicking everything in sight. There are the stints in Wichita Falls, Texas, San Antonio, Burke, Virginia. Her mom, Stephanie, was a ballet dancer and dance instructor. She intended to be a nun and planned to enter the convent until she met Bill, an Air Force fighter pilot. Let's take a short break and think about that for a minute. If you want to mix together some genetic and psychological qualities to come up with a goal-scorer, don't you think ballerina and fighter pilot would produce something special?

Of the Hamm children much was expected. Of course, it wasn't without a few moans or a groans that the kids worked at a soup kitchen, or cleaned a home for unwed mothers, or organized a church rummage sale, or performed any other of countless services Stephanie found. And Mia would rebel up to a point, the end-point being when she heard her mom say, "You're going to do it." There were always new schools, new teams, and new teammates. New places to fit in and being the new kid also brought something Mia couldn't stand—attention.

With four siblings, you are never the star, never the one in demand. In a family that spends family time serving, you learn humility. When your big-hearted family of seven is on the move seemingly every time you get comfortable in your new surroundings, you learn to fit in. When people are calling you the best player in the world, you learn, well, what exactly do you learn? First, you learn you don't like it too much. "The only time I get uncomfortable doing interviews is when they depict me as someone I'm not," she said, still gazing at Fetzer Field. "I don't like articles that put me on a pedestal like I'm on top of the mountain, try to knock me off."

There will be plenty of those articles to come, and each year the number of people who read them will multiply.

CAPTAIN CARLA

Heinrichs's departure left an important role to be filled—captain. That job fell to Carla Overbeck. Her leadership style, while different from that of Heinrichs, was just as effective. Leadership, beginning with Heinrichs and moving through Overbeck to Foudy and Fawcett, to Lilly, Wambach, and Rampone, has always been the strength of the team.

"The common dominator for all our captains has been performance, consistency, competitiveness, and buying into what the coach is saying," said Heinrichs. "Our captains were some of the highest performing, most consistent, and most competitive players. Our standards were unwavering and demanding."

Overbeck's standards carried over to every aspect of national team life. There was a way you acted in public because "You never know who is watching," the team would often say. And in training sessions, you pushed past your comfort zone and your limits, using as a standard Dorrance's claim that you will pass out before you died. A common trait of the team's captains throughout the years is that they always wanted to do what was best for the team, and everyone understood that.

"She has the exceptional ability to lead with intensity, yet support players at the same time. It's something that's usually difficult to do," said Anson Dorrance, who coached Overbeck at the University of North Carolina and for seven years with the national team. "Often, players' emotions spill over and comments are negative, but Carla communicates intensity without hurting the feelings of others."

Just how did she lead? Maybe it was the tone of Overbeck's voice, the clear, concise way she spoke that left little doubt she was being demanding and compassionate at the same time. Maybe it was the way she carried herself, the body language that screamed confidence. She moved with a purposefully stride of someone who knew exactly where she was going and why. Maybe it was the professionalism with which she approaches training, setting standards for dedication and consistency. Competitiveness definitely figures into the mix. To say she hated to lose would be an understatement. You feel safe predicting there are six games she remembers most from her 95-game college career at North Carolina. And that's because her team, 89-0-6 in her four years, never lost. Most likely, though, it's all of the above … and more.

"I think you really have to know each player and how to get to them, how to get them fired up," said Carla. "During the course of a game, if someone does something well, you encourage them by letting them know what they just did is what is going to help our team win. The other side of that—and I think this is where some people in leadership roles run into problems—is they are too negative too often. It's okay to get after someone for doing something wrong, but when they do something right, you have to let them know, too. People know your personality off the field, as well. Maybe if you say something to them that isn't nice, they know you are just trying to make them better. They can take the bad things easier if there is something good in there, too. I'm a pretty compassionate person, and when people make mistakes, it's not my job as a player to jump all over them. That's what the coach is there to do. Obviously, the players know when they've made a mistake. They know they messed up, and they don't want someone jumping all over them. So I'm the first to say, 'It's okay. Do better next time.' Everyone is human, and certainly everyone is going to make mistakes, especially yourself. I'm much harder on myself than I am on anyone else."

"She leads very positively, and she is always upbeat," said Tony DiCicco, who took over for Dorrance before the 1995 World Cup. "When someone makes a mistake, she is always the first one to tell them to forget about it. She helps a lot of the players, especially the young ones."

DiCicco learned early about Carla's leadership abilities. In one of his first training camps as head coach, the team just finished one drill, and DiCicco sent them for water. Overbeck walked with her usual deliberate, all-business stride to the sideline, got her drink, and headed back to the field.

"And, of course, the whole team follows her," said DiCicco. "It can create some awkward moments if they are ready before me. I learned right away that you don't have to call this group out on the field for the next drill. They all follow Carla out there. It's in the way she presents herself. She is very intense and focused in practice."

Obviously, if people follow you, you're a pretty good leader.

NEW CHALLENGES

It was a strange sight for those in San Antonio that day in 1993. And scary. Michelle Akers, always a picture of fitness, strength, and power, collapsed during a match at the National Sports Festival. There were symptoms that something wasn't right as early as 1992, but she didn't have time for that. There were more important things to do. When she returned from China two years earlier, opportunities popped up in front of her. The Soccer Industry Council and the National Soccer Coaches Association wanted her to speak at their conventions. Youth soccer clubs from all over the country wanted her to give speeches and clinics, and thousands of young girls found out there was something called the U.S. Women's National Team.

People were listening; important people were paying attention. Her message was simple—we need your help. "At the National Soccer Coaches Association of America annual convention, they gave me a microphone, shoved me on stage, and said, 'Talk to everyone,'" recalled Michelle. "I told them about my team and about our hardships. I did okay, but I had no clue what I was doing. It felt weird having people listen to me."

Mick Hoban was in the audience that day. He offered Akers an endorsement contract with Umbro, and she became the first female soccer player to sign such a deal. The impact was felt throughout the team. Umbro gave Michelle soccer shoes and other training gear, but it conflicted with the official sponsor of the U.S. national teams program, Adidas. Under the contract with Adidas, national team players were required to wear all Adidas gear, including what they wore on their feet. When Michelle showed up at a national team training camp wearing Umbro shoes, shorts, and T-shirts, it became an issue with the U.S. Soccer Federation.

"I remember it being really exciting, but I also remember there were issues because there was a new thing to deal with," said Lilly. "We didn't know how to handle it. With U.S. Soccer, we were shoes up, and we were fighting for our feet. We learned from it. It was new ground like everything else."

At the time, the national team players were required to pay for their Adidas training gear. When Akers was told she couldn't wear Umbro and that she would have to wear Adidas gear, she said, "Give it to me, and I will." Soon, a new deal was struck that enabled the women to wear Adidas from the ankles up. Unless a player was signed to an endorsement contract by a company other than Adidas, they were required to wear Adidas shoes. And they received free training gear. By the time of the 1996 Olympics, all non-collegiate players were signed to deals by either Adidas, Umbro, Nike, Fila, or Reebok.

At an early clinic in California put on by Umbro, over 300 kids—girls and boys—turned out to see Akers. "The connection between young girls and Michelle was something I had never seen before," Hoban said in Akers' book *Standing Fast*. "Young girls had an absolute adulation for her. They finally had a hero of their own. She took it upon herself to fight for resources and recognition for the women's game. She became the point person, and she became very good at it."

But the travel, combined with her relentless personal training regimen, was exhausting. It was not, however, something she couldn't handle, she thought. It was certainly not enough to make her collapse on the soccer field. She was worn out. Her close friends worried about her, but the stubborn nature that made her unstoppable on the field made her unstoppable off it, as well. Finally, in a match during the National Sports Festival in San Antonio, Texas, late in 1993, she collapsed during a match.

At first, she was told she had mono. If she rested, the doctors said, she would be fine. That didn't work. She rested and felt the same, if not worse. She was then diagnosed with the Epstein Barr Virus, which she was convinced she could beat. In reality, however, Akers had Chronic Fatigue Immune Dysfunction Syndrome (CFIDS). In a cruel and ironic twist, CFIDS gets worse the more you exercise. For Akers, rehabilitation had always meant she needed to work harder. And when healthy, she maintained a personal regimen that was unmatched by any of her teammates. She spent hours every day working on fitness and honing the skills that made her famous in 1991. Now, however, she had to monitor her every move in order to conserve energy for soccer. "I had to make changes," she said. "It became obvious that I couldn't continue the way I trained before the illness. I began to do just what the team did, sometimes less depending on how I felt."

Still, though, she was struggling more than any of her teammates realized. She was determined not to allow her illness to become an issue within the team. Never one to look for, or even tolerate, sympathy, Michelle didn't want to be a distraction. She missed team meetings and functions because she needed to save all her energy for training sessions and matches. Her choices were simple—go to the movies or play soccer, go out to dinner or play soccer? Soccer won every time. "She put her social life aside to do what was best for the team—that's a true teammate," said Carla Overbeck, who, as captain, was aware of Michelle's condition and helped ensure the rest of the team knew as much as they needed to know.

Akers had to hatch a plan that would to get her to 1995, and she had to be sure to follow it. Her teammates slowly began to understand. Sometimes she was unable to drive herself home or cook for herself. Carla Overbeck, Kristine Lilly, and Julie Foudy would call to check on her, and Amanda Cromwell would often take her home and make her meals, often having to help her into the house.

"I don't know how I will get through this World Cup," she wrote in her journal a few days before leaving for Sweden. "All I can do is pray. God will get me through it in the way he wants. I hope it's a fun World Cup, not a terrible struggle. I'm sick of fighting uphill. I am terrified and excited at the same time."

As the 1995 World Cup drew closer, Michelle became increasingly concerned with her ability to perform to her own high expectations. The "Road to Sweden Tour" would be a stern test of her health and resolve. Beginning on April 28 in Decatur, Georgia, the team would play six games in 24 days. They would go from Decatur to Davidson, North Carolina to Tacoma, Washington to Portland, Oregon to Dallas and to Edmonton. They would play Finland, Brazil, and Canada twice each. Michelle and Tony DiCicco, who was named head coach when Dorrance resigned in 1995, devised a plan to gradually build her strength and match fitness. More accurately, DiCicco came up with the plan and Michelle reluctantly agreed to it. "Before the World Cup, there was a lot of concern about my health," she said. "There were times, I never thought I would make it. Just two months before the World Cup, I played my first full game in two years, so I was fairly nervous about the level I would be at in June."

If Michelle's ability to score goals was effected, the Road to Sweden tour didn't show it. In the six matches, she played in five and scored six goals. Hamm had five, Gabarra had four, and Tiffeny Milbrett had three. On June 1, 1995, the USA arrived in Sweden to defend their world title. Their first match was five days away. "With Mia playing as well as she was, and with Carin and Michelle playing well, we expected great things," said Carla Overbeck.

SWEDEN '95

So FIFA decided that it was okay to have an official Women's World Cup after all. Using the name "World Cup" for women wouldn't be as embarrassing as they first thought when they insisted the 1991 event be called a world championship. They decided to have another one. It would be held in Sweden in 1995.

The USA lost three of their first four matches of 1993, but then put together a nine-game winning streak, during which they outscored their opponents—rivals that included Germany, Japan, Canada, and Australia—37-1. Akers and Gabarra were still the marquee players in the U.S. attack, but several other players were beginning to shoulder more and more of the scoring load. During the nine-game winning streak, Akers scored three goals, and Gabarra had two. Mia Hamm struck nine times, while Kristine Lilly added seven, and Tisha Venturini got four.

Brandi Chastain was not on the team. The USA's glut of forwards left Brandi on the outside, but her love of the game had her looking for other opportunities. In the '90s, there were few places for American women to play after college. Brandi was now three years past her graduation from Santa Clara University and desperate for a competitive place to play. So she went to Japan, which had a professional league that paid decent money and was allowing foreign players to join teams. Brandi played the 1993 season for Skiroki Serena and earned the team MVP honors.

"It was a bit of a culture shock in the beginning because the players never asked questions, rarely talked, and kept their heads down in a very submissive way when the coach was speaking," explained Brandi. "I was the opposite, and I think it initially caused some waves, but the staff, players, and I finally worked some things out and our team did fairly well. I think I was a good example for my teammates, helping give their thoughts, feelings, and ideas merit, and I think they helped me realize that I couldn't always have an opinion, or to trust a bit more. It was a give-and-take scenario."

College soccer was proving to be a tremendous training ground for the national team. North Carolina produced more than its share, but Stanford and Cal also contributed. Now, it was the University of Portland's turn. Tiffeny Milbrett was beginning to emerge as the fourth edge of the Triple-Edge Sword, playing much the same role Wendy Gebauer did in 1991. And the University of Massachusetts sent a goalkeeper, Briana Scurry, into the USA nets. Scurry had an interesting college career at UMass. During her first three seasons, she split time with another keeper, Skye Eddy, who was one year ahead of Scurry. When Scurry wasn't in goal, she played on the field, and since she was more athletic than Eddy, she saw less time in goal. In her junior season, Bri emerged as the starting goalkeeper, and with Eddy gone to George Mason the following season, Scurry became one of the nation's top keepers, leading the Minutewomen to the 1993 Final Four.

Qualifying rounds for the 1995 World Cup were held in Canada from August 13th through August 21st. Prior to leaving for Canada, the USA played a three-game tournament in the USA, called the Chiquita Cup. On July 30th, the night before the opening match against Germany, Dorrance informed the team that he was resigning, and that assistant coach Tony DiCicco would be taking over. Long-time assistant Lauren Gregg would remain as DiCicco's assistant. Dorrance was finding it more and more difficult to balance his national team duties with his job at UNC and still spend enough time with his wife and three children. He said he decided to resign well before the Chiquita Cup but delayed making the announcement so that U.S. Soccer would have no choice but to name DiCicco as his replacement. It was just 14 days before the national team kicked off in qualifying and less than a year from the 1995 World Cup in Sweden.

The U.S. defeated China in the second match of the Chiquita Cup, 1-0, on a goal by Foudy and a shutout by Scurry. The third and final match was on August 7, 1994, against Norway in Worcester, Massachusetts, and it was the first U.S. women's national team game ever to be shown live on American television. In the broadcast booth was Wendy Gebauer. She explained a 4-1 U.S. win and described two goals by Hamm, one by Akers, and an own-goal by Norway.

Qualifying went mostly as expected. Perhaps the only surprise was that Joy Fawcett played. Less than three months before the qualifying tournament began, Joy and Walter Fawcett welcomed their first child, Katelyn Rose, on May 17, 1994. Joy was actually back in the starting lineup on July 31st against Germany, a remarkable 75 days after giving birth. Katey became a fixture at national team training camps, traveling with Walter to team hotels and going to practices, where Joy would sometimes slip quietly away to breastfeed her. Joy was initially nervous about how the team and coaching staff would respond to having a small child around. "It was like Katey had 20 aunts," said Joy, who gave ample credit to her mother, sisters, and Walter for making the situation work. "Everyone always asked to watch her, and she just loved them all."

Joy played two of the four qualifying matches, and the United States breezed through their regional competition, outscoring opponents 36-1. The USA's attack was more balanced than it had ever been. Akers and Hamm led the team in scoring during the four games of qualifying, tallying six goals each. Lilly and Gabarra each had five goals, while Venturini and 16-year-old Tiffany Roberts scored three times. Despite her youth, Roberts had become one of the most talked-about players in the country. Her athleticism, tenacity, and speed made her a valuable part of the USA's midfield, and she won a starting spot alongside Foudy, Venturini, and Lilly.

"I was in Florida trying out for the under-17 national team, and Clive Charles was the coach," recalled Tiffany. "One day, Clive called me over and told me that I was supposed to stay over with the full national team. I couldn't believe it. I actually went back to him and said, 'I'm sorry, can you repeat what you just said?' So he brought me over to Anson and said that I didn't believe him. Everything happed so quickly. I remember telling Lauren Gregg that I didn't have enough clothes for another week, and then they gave me all this gear, and I thought, 'Cool!'"

As the national team prepared for the '95 World Cup, they were playing under an old contract that was becoming more and more outdated. Unable to make a living playing soccer, the players, especially those out of college, were dependent on part-time jobs and financial help from families. The team was in the process of negotiating a new deal with the United States Soccer Federation in early 1995, when Julie Foudy made a trip to Boston to take part in a round-table discussion organized by sports equipment and apparel leader Spalding. Also serving on the panel was tennis legend Billie Jean King.

"We were complaining that we weren't being treated well—we weren't getting paid, the hotel stuff, food, travel, a whole laundry list of stuff," said Julie. "Billie Jean said, 'Well, what are you doing about it?' I told her we were trying to get the team administrator to help us, but she worked for the Federation, and it wasn't working. Billie Jean said, 'So, do it yourself.' She told us to demand the changes and stick together as a team. She was always saying, 'Think about the next generation. What do you want for them, what's your legacy for them?' That's what I love about that woman. She's my hero because she just doesn't give back to tennis. She just doesn't give back to her sport. She constantly is checking in with athletes to see how things are going. She was the one in 1995 that said, 'Get off your butt and do it yourself! You keep relying on someone else to do it for you. You as a team have to do it.'"

Foudy listened, thought about it, and then it hit her. "It was like this epiphany," she said. "I was on the plane home, and it was just before we were supposed to sign the new contract with the Federation that paid us like $10 a day and gave us basically no rights. I remember I was like on this high— 'She's right, we've got to do something!' We came back and said, 'We aren't signing this thing.' We weren't saying that we should be getting what the men were getting. We told them that they should be treating us fairly. We were bringing money in for them, and we should be treated with respect."

MAY 19, 1995, THE COLLISION

Tell April and Tracey that their roommate back in '87, the one jumping on the bed, would one day be in commercials for shampoo and sports drinks. Tell them that she will do a hugely popular Nike commercial with that guy from UNC who left Carolina the same year April did, that Jordan kid. See if they believe that in 15 years, people will start naming their baby girls Mia, and it will become the 10th most popular girls name in the U.S. Oh, and she'll guest host the Today Show. Dare them to believe there will be a Soccer Barbie Doll modeled after her. It never would have entered their minds. Tell them that in 2004 Michael Wilbon, an ESPN analysis and writer for the Washington Post, will name Mia "Perhaps the most important athlete of the last 15 years." This kid? The shy one with the bangs? You're kidding, right?

But we knew it was coming—the collision between the shy Mia who just wanted to play soccer and be a good teammate, and the Mia who would one day be named to *People* Magazine's list of the 50 Most Beautiful People. At the time of the collision, April Heinrichs was the assistant coach with the national team preparing to play in the '95 World Cup. She witnessed the explosion.

"I can put my finger on the exact date," she said nine years removed from the collision. "It was the day we were in Dallas playing Canada (May 19, 1995). I believe the score was 9-1. I was an assistant with the team, and I remember clearly the social change that was occurring. It was one of the largest crowds we'd had up to that point (6,145). They were introducing all the players, and when they introduced Mia, the crowd went absolutely crazy. The octave of the crowd was that high-pitched, little-girl scream. It was the first time I had ever heard it. And after the game, we are standing around talking in the middle of the field, and one of the little girls called out to Sarah Rafanelli, 'Number 7! Come over here!' And Sarah was like, 'Oh, they want my autograph.' It was one of the first times she had been asked for an autograph. And the little girl says, 'Can you get Mia Hamm's autograph for me?'"

The question was posed in *Sports Illustrated*. It's in a cover story written by Gary Smith, the guy who wrote about Ali and Agassi, Tiger and Tyson, those one-name-is-all-you-need athletes, a class which Mia was entering. Smith writes fascinatingly in-depth articles that ask questions at the heart of the subject. You need to supply the answers. In "The Secret Life of Mia Hamm," the best Mia Hamm story ever written, Smith asked "Did the face launch the movement or did the movement launch the face?" It's the type of chicken-and-egg question people love to debate. Ask Mia, and you'll be told that the face was just a small part of the movement. There were so many faces before and during her time that deserved much more credit than they got. Like Michelle and April, and Carin, and Kristine Lilly, who was Mia's annual pick for best player in the world. "What's hard is talking about myself," she said. "And usually people put you in the environment where they throw out superlatives: 'You're the best. You're this. You're that.' And ever since I was little, I never felt that way."

Whether it was the movement or the face, two things are certain. One, The Movement had started. And two, Mia was The Face of it. If the face launched the movement, it was commercials that launched the face. Pert, Gatorade, Mattel, and Nike all featured the face while most other players on the team were still relatively anonymous. The face learned to accept the movement, and the two discovered how to co-exist. Mia lent the face, which included a set of eyes that could be sympathetic, emotional, frightening, and determined. Those eyes signaled sincerity to reporters and fans, genuine concern to her teammates, as well as send chills down opponents' spines. The movement provided the platform, the podium from which Mia would send her message to millions of young girls about confidence and athletics, teamwork, and friendships. The movement enabled her to tell kids about the Marianne Williamson poem team, the one that made her realize it wasn't failure that scared her and caused her to hold back. No, it was success that frightened Mia. Just how good could she be?

"Our deepest fear is not that we are inadequate," the poem begins. "Our deepest fear is that we are powerful beyond measure. It is our light, not our darkness that most frightens us. We ask ourselves, 'Who am I to be brilliant, gorgeous, talented, fabulous?' Actually, who are you not to be? You are a child of God. You're playing small does not serve the world. There is nothing enlightened about shrinking so that other people won't feel insecure around you. We are all meant to shine, as children do. We were born to make manifest the glory of God that is within us. It's not just in some of us; it's in everyone. And as we let our own light shine, we unconsciously give other people permission to do the same. As we are liberated from our own fear, our presence automatically liberates others."

Mia scored twice that day in Dallas. So did Akers, so did Lilly, and so did Gabarra. Tiffeny Milbrett scored once. But none of them sent the crowd into frenzy like Mia's goals. All of a sudden she was famous, and the players began to understand the kind of impact they could have. Hamm led the way, reluctantly. She signed autographs, and signed, and signed. Never wanting to put herself above the team, or to put the team in an awkward situation, Mia had to balance her fame with her desire to be a good teammate and friend. The way she handled the increase in her popularity, in many ways set the tone for the explosion that was rapidly approaching. Women's soccer, especially among those nations with rich traditions in the sport around the world, was not an acceptable form of the sport. And women's team sports in the U.S. were far from popular.

But it certainly wasn't a Hamm-led charge into the public's consciousness. For years the team had adopted a "Come watch us play and then decide" approach to both potential fans and vocal critics. If someone came and watched a game, the players figured, they would be hooked. In 1995, people started getting hooked. They watched dynamic, attractive, athletic women play a team sport with tremendous passion and skill. And they played it with a fire that destroyed the stereotypical view of women as lesser competitors. Then the fans were greeted with a smile and an autograph. "It became important," said Kristine Lilly. "It wasn't that you could say, 'Oh, I'm not going to sign today.' It was just something you did, like putting your shoes on."

So they played soccer, and they sold the game. Michelle Akers' illness forced her to cut back on appearances and lessened her ability to promote her sport. Hamm became the most recognized face in soccer, and with it came the tag of "best player in the world." "It's funny," said Akers. "People wonder what I think of Mia because they think I feel she stole something from me. It's not like that at all. I am so proud of her. She has worked so hard for it. People need to understand that whatever one of us accomplishes, it's a reason for all of us to celebrate. Mia's success is our success."

Hamm is the first one to share credit for everything she has ever done. If she beat three players and ripped a shot into the upper corner, she would tell the media what a great pass one of her teammates gave her to start the run. She would often—and rather deftly—turn the attention from herself to speak about what a great job a certain teammate did, something that not everyone would notice. And it was sincere.

And with the success of the 1994 Men's World Cup, hosted by the United States, combined with an influx of cash and resources from a new sponsorship deal with Nike, the U.S. Soccer Federation had more resources than ever before. The women were able to play more and more matches, and their popularity was slowing gaining momentum around country. From the start of 1993 to the end of 1995, the USA played 53 games. And not one was in Blaine, the site of so many of their previous home matches. Before 1993, the national team had played only in Blaine, Connecticut, Massachusetts, and Virginia. But from 1993 to the start of the 1995 World Cup, Georgia, Ohio, Michigan, New York, New Jersey, Florida, North Carolina, Washington State, Oregon, and Texas hosted matches. Crowds were ranging between 3,000 and 6,000 per game, and it seemed as if all the fans got together beforehand to synchronize their screeches of "MEEEEyaaaaaaaaaaaaaaaaaa."

Hamm, though, wasn't the only star people came to see. Akers was still the team's go-to player, and she was carrying the label of "World's Best Player" with her to every game and every appearance. "The respect was surprising to me," Akers said. "I didn't crave it or desire it, but it was nice to be appreciated. Still, I had to prove myself each and every game. But refs were asking me for autographs and photos after games. Aren't they supposed to be immune to that? The fact that people were giving me that kind of respect was amazing to me."

SIX MINUTES

What no one expected happened. Six minutes into the USA's match with China, Michelle Akers went up for a header at the top of China's penalty area. A Chinese defender, Fan Yunjie, who would later play for the San Diego Spirit in the WUSA, went up with her. Jumping from behind Michelle, Fan put her full force into the attempted header, but instead she drove her forehead into the back of Michelle's head. Akers was unconscious before she hit the ground.

Initially, the U.S. players didn't realize the extent of the damage. They had seen Michelle go down in a heap countless times, the victim of reckless tackles or futile stabs at limiting her effectiveness. Ironically, Amy Allmann, Michelle's teammate from 1991 and college roommate at the University of Central Florida, was in the broadcast booth as the color commentator for ESPN2. It was her job to describe the replays. "When they showed the replay, it was the first time I'd seen it," remembered Amy. "I couldn't say a word. J.P. (Dellacamera, the play-by-play voice) had to tap me on the shoulder to get me to say something. Everybody who was watching was probably thinking, 'I wonder how they U.S. is going to play without her.' I was thinking, 'I hope she's not paralyzed.'"

Tiffeny Milbrett, four months' shy of her 23rd birthday, watched from the sidelines. "Usually, Michelle gets whacked and bounces right back up," recalled Tiffeny. "But this time, she didn't even move. I was worried for her, saying to myself, 'C'mon Mish, get up!' And then horror set in when I heard Tony say, "Milbrett, warm up.' I was like 'Holy crap! I'm going in!'" As Milbrett hurriedly prepared to enter the game, Michelle slowly got to her feet, and as had become her custom, waved off the stretcher. But she was done. Because she was unconscious before she hit the ground, she landed badly on her right leg and sprained her MCL.

The USA responded to Michelle's absence well. Tisha Venturini put the Americans ahead 1-0 four minutes after the game resumed. Then Milbrett proved she was ready to contribute by putting the USA up 2-0 in the 34th minute. China's Wang Liping cut the lead to 2-1 by beating her future WUSA teammate,

Briana Scurry, seven minutes before halftime. Hamm made it 3-1 in the 51st minute, and it appeared the USA would survive the difficult day. China, however, scored two late goals to escape with a 3-3 draw.

Akers slept for 24 straight hours. "I had never seen anything like it," said Amanda Cromwell, Michelle's roommate in Sweden. "I was devastated for her." When she finally woke up, Michelle found stuffed animals, notes, and cards all over her bed and even on top of her. Her teammates had written notes of encouragement and also messages expressing their admiration for her. "I was overwhelmed," Michelle said, admitting that she had been unaware of what her teammates thought of her until then. "I talked to April about it, and I'll always remember what she said— 'Maybe it takes someone to be knocked down before others feel like they can tell them how they really feel.' I'll never forget that."

While Milbrett scored after Akers' injury, she was still stressed about the situation in which she found herself. She expected to see some playing time, but mostly coming off the bench to rest Akers or Gabarra in games that had already been decided. "Her injury scared the heck out of all of us," Milbrett said. "Personally, I was very scared. Because of her injury, I was playing far sooner than I or anyone had expected. But Michelle helped me a lot more than she knew. She was just the same Mish with me, and being a rookie in my first World Cup, it helped knowing that however I played, she would always be consistent with me. I would ask questions, and she would help me, same as always. All I remember is that through all her hell and all her pain, she displayed complete strength. Support for the team was her first concern. Her injury knocked the wind out of the whole team, but that's nothing compared to what it did to Michelle. She had worked so hard for so long just to be able to play in the World Cup, and it all came crashing down."

It took nine minutes for the USA to score against Denmark in their second match of the World Cup. Playing without Akers gave the U.S. extra incentive to get the job done quickly and efficiently. Kristine Lilly got the team started strong. Milbrett got her second goal of the tournament four minutes into the second half, and this time the USA held onto the lead and walked away with a morale-boosting 2-0 win. The win, however, was not without tension. With a comfortable 2-0 lead in the second half, Tony DiCicco set out to give some players a rest. He replaced Linda Hamilton and her ailing knees with the young, speedy Thori Staples in the 53rd minute, and inserted Debbie Keller for Milbrett in the 61st. Teams were only allowed a total of three substitutions, but DiCicco wanted to rest Carin Gabarra, who was struggling with back pain. If the U.S. used its final substitution too early, they would run the risk of playing shorthanded in the event of an injury. With a two-goal lead, DiCicco replaced Gabarra in the 85th minute with Sarah Rafanelli.

Coaches play out countless scenarios in their heads during the game, but it's unlikely DiCicco, Gregg, and Heinrichs could ever have dreamed this one up. Shortly after Rafanelli entered the match, U.S. goalkeeper Briana Scurry brought the ball to the top of the penalty area to punt it. Referee Mamadouba Engage Camara blew his whistle. "I guess I stepped out of the box," said Bri who at first couldn't understand what the whistle was for. "The ball was already gone. The referee was already up the field. He came running back and just gave me a red card. Actually, in my opinion, what happened was is that he gave the other goalkeeper a yellow in the first half, didn't mark down which goalkeeper he had given it to, and I think he assumed that was my second. Therefore, he just went to the red and tossed me out. And they got the subsequent free kick right there outside the box."

The U.S. was suddenly reduced to 10 players, facing a free kick from 19 yards, and their goalkeeper had just been kicked out of the game. To make matters worse, they could not put their backup keeper, Saskia Webber, into the match because they had used all their allotted subs. A field player would have to finish the game in goal. "They called me over to the bench and said, 'We need you to go in goal,'" said Mia Hamm. "I said, 'What about a real goalkeeper?' So I put on Bri's jersey and gloves, which were a bit too big."

If Hamm thought the gloves were big, she was shocked when she got into the goal. "When you are shooting at it, the goal seems tiny," she says. "But once you are it in, it's huge. I mean huge! Right away, I had to face a direct free kick 19 yards away. Denmark had this girl who could really strike a ball, and Carla said I was hiding behind the wall. I asked Bri never to do that again. She promised she wouldn't."

Previously, her career as a goalkeeper had been limited to practice. "Tish and I would mess around in practice whenever we did this one particular drill," she said. "Bri and Saskia would give us their gloves, and we'd fly around and try to save balls. It was a little different in the game. But I made a couple saves. One was a cross. It was one of those plays where the defender doesn't want to give up a corner kick, so Tish let the girl cross it. Then she remembered that I was in goal. She felt so bad. I had to do a front smother, and it started squeaking out under my arm. I took all the goal kicks and the punts were okay, not like Bri can hit them. It's just one of those things that you are glad turned out the way it did. The fact that we were up 2-0 with only about five minutes left definitely took some of pressure off me."

After the Mia-in-goal incident, the U.S. began training emergency goalkeepers—just in case. "I think the rules have changed, but we didn't have a jersey with my name on it," said Mia. "I actually wore Bri's jersey. In the 2003 World Cup, I think there were three or four of us that actually had keeper jerseys.

I had one, I think Cindy (Parlow) had one. We actually had a practice one day with all the potential goalkeepers."

The USA's final game of group play was against Australia in Helsingborg. At the same time, China was playing Denmark in Vaesteras. The Americans needed to beat Australia by a margin larger than by the margin China beat Denmark. Tony DiCicco was receiving regular updates on the China match, and the USA was struggling with Australia. Lisa Casagrande put Australia ahead 1-0 early in the second half before Julie Foudy tied it up in the 69th minute. At that time, China and Denmark were tied 1-1. Joy Fawcett made it 2-1 USA with 18 minutes left, but Sun Wen put China ahead of Denmark 2-1 four minutes later. "We need one more," DiCicco would yell from the bench after Sun Wen's goal. But China scored again in the 90th minute, "Two more!" DiCicco yelled. Two minutes into injury time Carla Overbeck nailed a penalty kick, but the USA still needed another to win their group. In the 94th minute, Debbie Keller, who came on for Milbrett 16 minutes earlier, scored to give the USA a 4-1 win to finish as the top team in Group C.

As winners of Group C, the USA advanced to the quarterfinals, where they would meet Japan. Lilly scored in the ninth minute, then again in the 42nd minute. Milbrett made it 3-0 before halftime and Tisha Venturini added a fourth 10 minutes before the final whistle. Even without Akers, the U.S. was playing well. Since the 3-3 draw with China in the opening match, they had outscored their three opponents 10-1. Meanwhile, Akers was working furiously to get back for the semifinal or final. After her injury, the team began writing #10 or "Mufasa" on their sock tape. In the team huddle before the Denmark game, Carla Overbeck told the team, "If you get tired out there, I want you to look over at Michelle. She never gives up, and we won't either."

Akers felt fortunate that she was wearing sunglasses because her eyes were filling with tears. The team, however, certainly wasn't treating Michelle with kid gloves. Admittedly gullible, Akers was often the target of practical jokes. On a train trip between venues, Michelle was standing on the station platform holding her bag. Kristine Lilly, often the mastermind behind jokes against Akers, came over the asked Michelle to hold her bag, too. Then one by one, the entire team started piling their bags on Akers. Bags were hanging off her neck, arms, and shoulders as the team stood by laughing at her. "There's Michelle with about 30 bags hanging off her," said Mary Harvey. "It was hilarious. She looked like a coat tree."

Akers never felt closer to her teammates, and it drove her to work even harder to get back on the field. The remnants of her concussion were gone, but the knee was far from healed. She worked her knee to the point where she would be able to play against Norway in the semifinals. But in the days preceding the match, she was wary of how much she could contribute. Norway went up early on a header by Ann Kristin Aarones, another future WUSA player. The U.S. spent most of the remaining time pushing for a goal that never came, but they came agonizingly close when Joy Fawcett rung two shots off the crossbar, and shots by Venturini and Milbrett where tipped over the bar by Norwegian goalkeeper Bente Nordby.

"When Michelle went down in that first game, I think we were able to hold it together for a couple of games, but after that we struggled," explained Mia Hamm. "Going into the Norway game, we wanted to have our best player on the field. Michelle stepped on the field, and it was almost like we said, 'Okay, you're here now. You have to do everything for us.' She was playing with a torn MCL. She could barely run or cut. In the first half, in some way, we expected her to lead like she always did. She just couldn't do it physically. In the second half, it was almost too late. We said, 'Look, we've been playing well without her up to this point because we've had to. Everyone can continue to do so.' We just didn't get our breaks."

What happened immediately following that game would set the tone for the rest of the 1990s. And it wasn't just a quote in the *New York Times* from Norway's captain Linda Medallen, saying that it was fun to beat the USA because the Americans get "so upset" when they lose. It was a problem, she said, because it shows weakness. No, the big problem for the U.S. players was "The Train." There is a traditional Norwegian celebration that involves players getting down on all fours, grabbing the ankles of the person in front of them, and moving in a circle like a train. Tradition or not, the U.S. players didn't like it. Not at all. April Heinrichs, an assistant with the team in 1995, took the opportunity to speak with the team. Her speech began with a simple sentence: "Don't ever forget how you feel right now."

"April talked to us while we were watching Norway celebrate," remembered Mia. "She told us that there are things that we can all do. Search inside ourselves, and see how we can improve and get better, both physically and psychologically to make next year's team even better. People did." On June 17th, the USA beat China 2-0 for third place in the 1995 World Cup with Akers back on the bench. Hamm and Venturini scored for the U.S.

Hanging on the inside of the door of a house occupied by Mia Hamm and Tisha Venturini was a picture of the Norwegian Train, a reminder of who took their world championship away. "It was right on our door. Every day when we went to practice, that's what we saw," Mia said. "It was impressive."

Shannon MacMillan
Photo by Tony Quinn

PART II

STYLE MATTERS

In 1985, when the first national team was hastily put together, an eight-year-old girl in Petaluma, California, was playing every sport imaginable. Her second-grade teacher, as second-grade teachers tend to do, gave her class an assignment to draw a picture of "the nicest dream they ever had." Tiffany Roberts (Sahaydak) drew herself with three, yes three, Gold medals, one for gymnastics, one for track and, of course, one for soccer.

In 1990 when the USA was a year away from winning the first world championship, a 16-year-old girl in Escondido, California, was starring on her club soccer team. One day, she announced to her friend's mom that someday not too far in the future she was going to play soccer for the USA in the Olympics. The woman told Shannon MacMillan years later that she was thinking, "Oh, your poor thing. Soccer isn't played in the Olympics."

MacMillan and Roberts would get their chance to play on one of the grandest stages in sports in 1996. "For most of the world, the World Cup is the biggest thing in sports," said Mia. "For Americans, our big event is the Olympics. I remember hearing about Nadia Comeneci in '76 and Mary Lou Retton and thinking that I wanted to be a part of that. I would have loved to just go and watch."

The coaching staff included Tony DiCicco and his assistants Lauren Gregg and April Heinrichs, and for the first time, a sports psychologist, Dr. Colleen Hacker, who quickly became a favorite of the players. Hacker's primary task was to help the players enhance their performance through mental skills training. A soccer coach as well at Pacific Lutheran College in Washington State, Hacker kept her soccer opinions to herself, leaving that to DiCicco, Gregg, and Heinrichs. Her value was in helping the players off the field. When they were on the field in a training session, she was shagging loose balls, collecting cones, and doing whatever needed to be done. Those efforts further endeared her to the players.

"The main thing Colleen Hacker helped with was team chemistry," said Tiffany Roberts. "She played a huge role in how close our team became. We worked in small groups and had to accomplish a goal. Afterward, we realized we never would have gotten that done without teamwork. She taught us what it takes to be supportive. When we would do a team-bonding exercise, Joy Fawcett would really stand out. Joy listened to everyone's opinion, and then she'd put them all together. Through the exercise, everybody got to point out something good about everybody else. It might seem rather trivial that you need somebody to say you did a good job, but everybody needs that. And when it comes from these people, it really means something because they have to count on you every day."

Another part of the team's preparation involved a guest speaker, a former U.S. Olympian who asked the players to think of their most exciting moment in sports. Then he told them to multiply it by 1,000. That, he said, is the Olympics.

Change. Some resist it, others seem to need it whether it's necessary or not. Some avoid it and some recognize when it is needed. At the 1995 World Cup, the USA entered as the defending champions and the favorites to repeat. The third-place finish gave DiCicco permission to change, though. Women's soccer was evolving. Athleticism was still and always will be a key component to winning teams. Just having a bunch of athletes, however, was not enough. Teams were becoming more and more sophisticated, increasingly skillful, and tactical. Norway, under head coach Even Pellerud, had found the right mix in 1995, employing a system being used more and more by men's team. Gone, now, were the days of man-to-man marking and the sweeper. Zonal defending was more reliable and made it easier for teams to transition from defending to attacking.

As the game evolved, DiCicco liked what he was seeing. He believed the U.S. could hang on to the characteristic that made American women stand out—speed, athleticism, relentlessness, pride and work ethic—while employing a more sensible style of soccer. To do that, he figured, he needed skilled players at every position. It was no longer enough for a player to play a role of destroyer. They needed to be able to create as well.

Coming out of college, Shannon MacMillan seemed on the fast track to national team stardom. As a senior at the University of Portland in 1995, she won both major player of the year awards and entered national team training camp with a promising future. Her only liability was the position she played. The USA already had a glut of forwards—Mia Hamm, Tiffeny Milbrett, Carin Gabarra, Michelle Akers, Debbie Keller, Sarah Rafanelli, Cindy Parlow, and sometimes Lilly. And compounding the problem for coach Tony DiCicco was that Olympic rosters were to include just 16 players, four fewer than went to

Sweden for the World Cup and two less than would be allowed in the 1999 World Cup. Shannon was cut.

"It completely devastated me," Shannon said. "But Clive Charles (the University of Portland coach) told me that I had to keep working and keep proving myself until it got to the point where they can't turn me down. I was like, 'Yeah, whatever.' But I walked out of his office and got to thinking that maybe he was right. So I just went back out there and tried twice as hard. I did the little things over and over. A lot of it was mental and a lot has to come from your heart. I worked on my fitness and my ball touch, all the little things. I wanted to make sure that when I got the call to come back in, I would be ready. I didn't want to just hang out and mope around and waste my next chance by going in completely out of shape. I didn't want to give them reason to say, 'See, we were right.' I wanted them to say, 'Well, maybe we need to bring her back in again.'"

The call came. The national team needed players for a January trip to Brazil, and Shannon got her second chance. She scored in the first match, an 8-1 win over Russia before giving way to Carin Gabarra. She got one more goal in the three other matches. She was impressive enough in Brazil to be asked to stick around when the team resumed training in Orlando. But there was a catch. Tony DiCicco asked her to try outside midfield.

"I had played almost 18 years, and I had always been up front," Shannon explained. "I was faster and quicker than most players, so my coaches always put me up front. I think it took getting cut for the coaches to try me at another position and for me to accept it. Because I was so eager to make the team, I was completely open to the switch. You really have to be willing to do anything for the team. You have to put the team ahead of what you want. When Tony approached me and said they needed a flank midfielder, I just said, 'Okay, I'll try it.' It was just a complete learning experience, but it was neat. The first game, I was getting beat all over the place. Fortunately, I had Kristine Lilly playing across from me. I had watched her for years, and I finally figured out that I could learn from watching her because I was playing the same position now. I really had to learn from scratch. I was fortunate because I already had the attacking mentality, so I could focus on the defensive side of the game. I've always had a love for the game. It's never really been all about scoring."

Before the Olympics, the largest crowd to watch the women's national team play in the United States was 8,975 on February 4, 1996—a 2-1 loss to Norway in Jacksonville, Florida. The Jacksonville match was part of a tour of the U.S. the team used to prepare for the Olympics. Like anytime the team hit the road, the tour was a chance to "sell the game." Between the match in Jacksonville on February 4th, and the Olympic opener in Orlando on July 21st, the USA played 13 matches. Total attendance for the 13 games was 56,550, an average of 4,350.

But the crowds were filled with young girls and boys, and the relatively small crowds were capable of a lot of noise. While the girls were shrieking for Mia, they were also discovering other heroes. Post-game autograph seekers were greeted eye-contact, a smile and a short conversation. "Do you play soccer?" the national team players would ask. "What's the name of your team? What position do you play?" They would pose for as many pictures as possible, and the youngsters left with the unmistakable feeling of suddenly knowing who their heroes were. Whether we had 10 fans, 100 fans, or 1,000, we just signed," said Kristine Lilly. "It was important, but we enjoyed it. We never looked at it as a burden."

Mia Hamm and Michelle Akers
Photo by Tony Quinn

OLYMPIANS

There was some debate if they should go to Atlanta that July night in 1996. After all, they had a game in two days against Denmark. Shouldn't all their energy, all their focus, be reserved for the Danes? This tournament, the 1996 Olympic Games, was important for so many reasons. First, that awful taste from the 1995 World Cup loss to Norway was still fresh, that image of the Norwegian players celebrating as you watched is burnt into your brain. Being third is very un-American, isn't it? No one rejoices with the chant "We're number three, we're number three."

So re-establishing their place at the top of the women's soccer world was crucial. Their country is hosting the Olympics this year. Family and friends don't have to fly to Europe or Asia to watch them play. And maybe new fans will be made, maybe the event will draw some people who will like what they see and come back. After all, isn't that what they've been working for all these years. Maybe they should just stay in Orlando. Their coach, Tony DiCicco, understands some things, though. Fortunately, one of the things he understands is that taking part in the Olympic Opening Ceremonies—especially on your home soil—is a once-in-a-lifetime opportunity for an American athlete.

So here they are. They can hear the crowd, but can't see it. Heck, they're not even inside yet. Everyone still has to cross a parking lot and go up some long stairs. And to make the wait even more unbearable, the hosts are last in line. Without a doubt, the place is packed. What's it like in there? Never mind in there. Look around. It may be the greatest gathering of American athletes in your lifetime, maybe your parent's lifetime. Just look! U.S. Olympians are all around—sprinters, swimmers, gymnasts, basketball players—people seen on TV, celebrities all over the place. The players are starting to understand. They, too, are Olympic athletes. They're at Atlanta Fulton County Stadium waiting to enter the stadium for the Parade of Nations. The procession that started with Afghanistan and went alphabetically through Zimbabwe is nearly completed.

"You could hear them announce the United States of America, and you could hear all the fans just go nuts," said Mia Hamm. "Everyone kind of started pushing to get to the top to see what it was like. When we got to the top we just wanted to stop, just stand there and look at all these people cheering. Then you get the goosebumps and try to hold back tears. Then you just start running down the ramp, and the organizers are saying, 'Please, in an orderly fashion!' And I'm thinking, 'Are you kidding me?' You feel like you are five years old, and it's your first time at Disneyland. Your stomach is churning, and there is so much emotion it's incredible. You're waving, screaming, hugging, and crying. That's when it all kind of hits you."

It might have been the first time, but it certainly would not be the last. The players took pictures and videos of people taking pictures and videos of them. Years later, Brandi Chastain would liken it to a zoo, but she was never sure who was in the zoo and who was looking in.

Now back to Orlando, where they spent the past year living and training as part of a residency program paid for by the U.S. Soccer Federation. Kind of anti-climactic, isn't it? Still, the team has moved into the Olympic Village, with all the other soccer teams. The village is a highly protected quad of dorms on the University of Central Florida campus. There are gates and check-points and guards. Visitors are escorted the entire time they are inside the fences. The escorts are attractive UCF co-eds, who inform you that a day earlier, a Saudi Prince tried to buy them. Yes, buy them. Security is tight, but the atmosphere is loose. The head of security tells you his name is Captain Bob, and when you ask why you don't see any weapons anywhere, Captain Bob coldly replies, "You aren't supposed to."

"Everywhere we stayed, drove, or played, we had FBI, Highway Patrol, Riot Police, SWAT teams, Federal Marshalls, canine units—you name it, we had it," said Michelle Akers. "At practices we had helicopters flying overhead, metal detectors, bomb dudes. They were all incredible, and they became some of our biggest fans." Uniformed law enforcement officers had their pictures taken with the players, and the team signed posters, balls, and T-shirts for their new friends. Members of the detail assigned to the U.S. team would become fans and stay in touch with some of the players over the years. While all the security was new and exciting to the players, the best part was the ride to the stadiums. A collection of police cars would arrive at the Olympic Village and escort the team bus to the stadium, sirens blaring. Leading the route was a helicopter checking out the path ahead. "Traffic parted like the Red Sea, and all of a sudden, we were someone special," said Akers.

The USA played their first-ever Olympic match in the Citrus Bowl in Orlando on July 21, 1996. Briana Scurry started in goal. Carla Overbeck, Joy

Fawcett, and Brandi Chastain were the three defenders. Kristine Lilly, Julie Foudy, Tisha Venturini, and Shannon MacMillan made up the midfield, while Michelle Akers, Mia Hamm and Tiffeny Milbrett formed the latest version of the Triple Edge Sword. When the players took the field 90 minutes before the match to warm up, roughly 10,000 people were in the stands. It was by far the largest crowd that had come out to see the team play in the U.S. The players, still unaware of the type of social impact they were having, were delighted to see so many people in the stands. "We were thrilled," said Tisha Venturini. "Hey, if we see a couple thousand people, we get stoked." Then, they went back into the locker room.

In the locker room, every player had their own routine before games. Some listened to music, some sat quietly, some preferred nervous chatter. "Eventually, everyone ends up at the same place—the tunnel," said Michelle Akers. "It's one of my favorite places, because we are all there high-fiving, giving encouragement, and getting pumped up." The tunnel is one of the most interesting places in sports. It's where the players spend those last few minutes of that excruciatingly long wait for the game to begin, the game they have worked toward and looked forward to for so long. It's the place where they have nothing to do but think. Nothing to do but wonder what the game will bring and what they will bring to it. Can they bring their very best? And if they can, will their very best be good enough? Eventually, their time in the tunnel ends, the game begins and their questions are answered. The 11 starters lined up next to Denmark's 11 starters and walked out of the dark tunnel to the Olympic theme music and found an overwhelming sight—a crowd of 25,303.

"When we came out of the tunnel, and the music started playing, I was like, 'Oh my God! This is the Olympics,'" said Mia. "This is what I watched on TV growing up. I saw my family holding up their sign, and I saw my sister wipe her eyes. Then I started crying." The USA settled down quickly and took a 3-0 win from Denmark.

Trivia question: Who is the first American woman to score a goal in the Olympics? Mia Hamm? Nope. She was second. Tiffeny Milbrett? Wrong. She was third. Michelle Akers? Kristine Lilly? Nope. They didn't score. Tisha Venturini is your answer. Thirty-seven minutes in.

Just getting to the Olympics was a major accomplishment for Akers. With her illness now correctly diagnosed as Chronic Fatigue Immune Dysfunction Syndrome (CFIDS), she had hope. Once she could ask the correct questions, she could find the right solutions. The question was, "What do I need to do so that I can play?" The answer was, "Cut back on just about everything you have been doing your whole life. Save your energy for the important stuff." On May

11th, she gave a speech to Congress on CFIDS Awareness Day. What follows is what she said.

"My name is Michelle Akers. I am five-feet, ten-inches tall and weigh 150 pounds. I'm muscular. I'm tanned. I have wild, sun-bleached, curly hair. My teammates call me Mufasa from The Lion King. I love to laugh. On vacations, I love to hike with my dad and brother in the Cascade Mountains near Seattle, Washington. I am the starting center forward for the world-class American women's soccer team. If you saw me today, you would see a healthy, physically fit, elite athlete."

"But I'm not. I am sick. And I am hanging on by the very will and courage that helped me attain my status as an elite athlete. It all began in 1991 immediately after the first FIFA Women's World Soccer Championship in China. Upon my return to the U.S., I felt tired and lethargic, but thought nothing of it. My travel and career schedule was extremely hectic and demanding. I was on the road three weeks every month. In addition to travel, I was constantly training. I mean, who wouldn't be tired? After several months, I was becoming concerned about my increasingly diminished energy levels and visited a doctor. And on his advice, rested a month or so, then resumed my soccer and appearance schedule. I also visited a nutritionist, thinking it might be diet related. But even with a diet change, the fatigue, dizziness, migraines, night sweats, Gastro-intestinal upsets, and metabolism problems remained. Over time, they worsened. Then in 1993, I finally collapsed during a game. My collapse led to the unmistakable conclusion that I was sick, not just tired or run down. After various tests—echocardiogram, heart stress test, blood tests—I was diagnosed with Mononucleosis, then Chronic Epstein Barr Virus, and finally six months later in the spring of '94, Chronic Fatigue Immune Dysfunction Syndrome."

"From 1992 to the end of 1995, I felt I was in Hell. At my worst, I was barely able to function or complete day-to-day activities. It was an extreme effort to do laundry, prepare a meal, or attempt the exercise bike for five minutes. Many times, just doing these small chores knocked me out for days or weeks. At my best, I could play 15 or 20 minutes, or if I was really lucky, I could last 30 minutes of a 90-minute match. I could train with light-to-moderate intensity to stay in some kind of shape for the national team, and maintain a skeletal appearance schedule for my sponsor, Umbro. The repercussions were migraines and overwhelming fatigue during, and especially after, activity. They lasted for days, sometimes weeks. It was a constant trade-off. Being able to maintain *my involvement in my career and in the normal world would have to be traded with feeling the devastating effects of that activity on my body. Other symptoms included neck pain, muscle and joint stiffness, water retention, fuzzy brain, loss of balance, forgetfulness, night sweats, poor sleep, GI upset, diarrhea or constipation, high or low metabolism, weight gain or loss, emotional upheaval, sugar cravings, shortness of breath, and heart palpitations."*

"I can honestly say these few years were pure hell for me. I struggled to get through the day or hour or minute, depending on how bad I was feeling. I desperately searched for medical answers and help, but found very little. I frequently asked myself, 'What happened to that strong, dynamic, tireless Michelle Akers? Will I ever see her again? And who am I now?' I was alone. I was scared. And I was in agony."

"Some days, it was all I can do just to get through the day, let alone be an elite athlete. On those days, the only way to step on the field was to stop, close my eyes, take a deep breath, and gather every ounce of strength and will, focusing solely on surviving the hour-and-a-half of practice ahead of me. Most days, I survived the practice. Sometimes, I did better than survive and actually saw glimpses of the player I used to be. Those days were glorious. To feel good. To have energy. To be light on my feet and strong. That's what it's supposed to be like—fun and carefree. I revel in the feeling and the gift of good health."

"I've been injured quite a bit in my career. Injuries, to me, are a part of the game. Yeah, I got hurt, and, okay, I had surgery and then rehab. But who really cared. Injuries were just a pit stop and nothing but a small distraction. I suspect some of them were due to being worn down, but I was beat up in every game I ever played. The majority of these injuries were from collisions and fouls. I had torn ligaments in knees, cartilage stuff, sprained ankles, head injuries, dislocated shoulders, knocked out teeth—all part of the game and part of being a goal-scorer. Nothing to write home about... anymore. I would usually call home and tell my father, 'Uh Dad, I did my knee again and have surgery scheduled for blah, blah, blah date.' After a while, it became pretty trivial."

"This illness, this Chronic Fatigue Immune Dysfunction Syndrome, is very different. On the very bad days—the days when it is all I can do to survive—I walk off, drag myself off, the field. My legs and body feel like lead. God, they seem to weigh so much. My breathing is labored. It's all I can do to get to the locker room, change my clothes, and keep from crying in utter exhaustion and weariness. I am light-headed and shaky. My vision is blurred. My teammates ask me if I am okay. I say I'm fine. But my

eyes tell the truth. They are hollow and empty, dull and lifeless. It scares me to look in the mirror when I get like this. I shake my head knowing I overdid it again. I crossed the invisible line between functioning and being very, very sick. How long would it take to recover from this one?"

"I slowly get to my truck and concentrate on the road, willing myself to keep moving, to not pull over and rest. 'Almost there,' I tell myself, 'Just a few more minutes.' But the time I arrive home, I leave my bags in a pile by the door and collapse on the couch. I have no energy to eat, to shower, or to call someone for help. I have migraines so bad I wish I could go to sleep and never wake up. I have severe neck pain and knots, muscle weakness, uncoordination, and an upset stomach. At night I sweat so bad, I go through three T-shirts and have wet sheets and hair. I suffer through sleepless nights, and when I do sleep, I have crazy dreams. I get a lot of chest and throat colds that makes me lose my voice and cough like crazy… brain fog… no concentrations… no short-term memory. Sheer awfulness."

"I tell you these things not to gain sympathy, but so you too can experience a day with this illness, experience the pounding migraine headaches that can incapacitate me for days. I tell you these things so you can understand the insomnia that plagues me even though I am exhausted, the overwhelming fatigue that keeps me from going to a movie or dinner with friends because I don't have the energy to talk, sit up, or eat. And then there's the GI upset that has caused me to go on an extreme gluten-free, dairy-free, caffeine-free, sugar-free, and alcohol-free diet in hopes of finding relief or possibly a cure. And, of course, there's the 'fogginess' that causes me to lose concentration, forget where I am of how to get some place that I've been a thousand of times before. This illness demands attention in every detail of my life. And if I don't pay attention, it punishes me without remorse. It's a difficult experience to explain because it encompasses so much of who I am. It's awful to realize you will never be the person you were before this illness. Chronic Fatigue Immune Dysfunction Syndrome becomes who you are at times. Leaving you—the old you—a mere shadow."

"I have always believed you can accomplish anything through hard work and perseverance, through dedication and commitment. This is who I became a World Champion—an Olympic athlete. But that's the irony of the illness. The harder you work, the more it drags you down, the more it disables you. It's the first time in my life I have been beaten. I cannot defeat this illness through hard work, or through pure drive and desire. I have realized it's the first time I cannot overcome on my own terms, with my own strength."

"I am a fortunate CFIDS sufferer. Because I am an elite athlete, I have access to the best doctors, the best care in the United States and, therefore, the world. I have an incredible support system through my team and family. My teammates force me off the field when I am pushing too hard. They drive me home when I can't make it myself. My friends pray for me daily. They encourage and lift me up when I am at the end of myself. My family, friends, coaches, and employers—the U.S. Soccer Federation and Reebok—are sympathetic and flexible, in regards to my health and limitations. They have never doubted that I am sick and not just depressed, mentally unstable, or God forbid, faking it. Yes, I have lost a lot. Yes, CFIDS is a devastating illness. And no, I am not the same person I was before I was stricken with CFIDS. And I probably never will be. But this is not a message of hopelessness or defeat. It's a story about courage, growth, and challenge. This is a story about overcoming. I have gained a lot from this illness. It's nothing that can be touched or measured. But through suffering and heartache, I have gained a strength and purpose that carries me when I cannot do it myself. I have seen I cannot do it myself. I have seen and experienced God's grace and peace only because I have been in the valley. I now know it took this long visit in the depths of this illness to open myself to a more meaningful and purposeful life."

"I live by the verse in Second Corinthians which says, 'My grace is sufficient for you, for my power is made perfect in weakness. That is why, for Christ's sake, I delight in weakness, in hardship and difficulties. For when I am weak, I am strong.' Through this weakness—this illness—God's power rests in me and I am strong. His power is made perfect in me. I will overcome but not through any effort of my own. That's the final irony. The more I struggle to save myself from this illness, the more it takes my life away. The moment I just rest—rest in the strength of God's perfect grace—is the moment I begin to overcome. It's the moment I am whole again. I have learned to accept CFIDS as an opportunity to make a difference. I have turned this weakness into a strength. And even though it is still raging inside me, I refuse to be beaten by it."

"I will overcome. And I will show others how to overcome also."

In the audience, was a doctor from John's Hopkins, Dr. Peter Rowe, who contacted her the next day and set up some tests. She was put on a special gluten-free diet. Officially, it was called the Elimination Diet, but Michelle called it the "everything-that-tastes-good-free diet." She lived on gluten-free cereal, Power Bars, dried gluten-free soups, rice milk, gluten-free pancake mix, popcorn, and rice pasta. She also got special foods sent to her by friends at an Orlando health food store.

"When she got on the gluten-free diet, she seemed to improve a lot," said Carla Overbeck. "Food is such an important part of your training. It's your fuel. She would get this stuff, and we would say, 'Let me try it.' It was nasty! I asked her, 'How do you eat that stuff?' And she would say, 'It's going to make me better.' That's a true champion."

One of the tests that Michelle underwent included an IV containing a synthetic adrenaline—a substance banned by the International Olympic Committee. When she found out, she freaked. She immediately called team director Pam Perkins, trainer Patty Marshak, and team doctor Mark Adams. They decided to confess up front, and Michelle wrote a letter to the United States Olympic Committee, as did Dr. Adams and Dr. Rowe. Adams followed up with a phone call. Her Olympic drug test was in two days, and Michelle's plan was to drink gallons of water, plenty of coffee, while sweating in the hot Florida sun to try to flush the substance out of her system. On testing day, Michelle brought all her supplements, as requested. Only then did she find out that another substance—ENADA—was banned. "I was furious," she said. "I had called the USOC hotline weeks earlier and was given the okay to take them. I called again, and they said it was okay. I called yet again with a tester present, and he says it was banned. I was freaking out! Tony, Pam, everyone was freaking out."

Fifty-eight days before the Olympics were to begin, Michelle took the drug test, and, to everyone's surprise, passed. Oddly enough, three months earlier, a USA team doctor, told Michelle she wouldn't be able to play in the Olympics because of her knee. She hurt it in a pre-Olympic match against Norway in Tampa. While warming up for the rematch in Jacksonville, the knee didn't feel right so she had the doctor look at it. The doctor was new to the team and was filling in for Dr. Mark Adams. His news was devastating. "The MCL is fried. You need reconstructive surgery right away," he told her. Translation: no Olympics. Michelle left the locker room in tears and ran to the nearest pay phone to call her agent and friend Eva Ferara. Fans entering the stadium stopped to ask her for autographs, and when she tried to get back into the stadium the ticket-takers wouldn't let her in. So she jumped a fence. The next day, she went to see another doctor who told her the knee was bad but could be rehabilitated in time for the Olympics.

# REMEMBERING THE TRAIN

With the Denmark game history, the team stayed in Orlando to face Sweden before heading to the Orange Bowl in Miami for a meeting with China. Crowds grew steadily throughout the first round. There were 28,000 people that came to the Citrus Bowl to see Venturini and Milbrett score in a tight 2-1 win over Sweden, and 43,000 showed up in Miami for the USA-China match, which was part of a double-header with the Nigerian men meeting Brazil. The U.S. and China each could advance to the semifinals with a tie. Thinking they might meet again in the finals, neither team wanted to give the other too much information, and the game ended in a 0-0 draw. The USA's best chance came from 18-year-old Cindy Parlow, who hit the top of the crossbar as time was running out.

For 408 days, the U.S. players had thought about that day in Sweden when their dream of back-to-back world championships was run over by the Norwegian train. While some wiped away tears of frustration, or laid on the field covering their eyes that day, Briana Scurry fixed a stare at the Norwegian celebration. As the Norway captain, future WUSA All-Star Gro Espeseth, triumphantly raised the World Cup trophy, Scurry was furious. "I hated it," she said, still cringing at the memory. "I watched them because I wanted to burn that image into my head so I would never forget it. You have to find something that hurts you so bad that you remember it every day. That's the only way it will never happen again." The night before the 1996 Olympic semifinal match with Norway, Scurry was up until four in the morning staring again. This time, however, her eyes were fixed on the ceiling of her room in the Olympic Village, the images playing over and over in her head.

The semifinals were played at the University of Georgia's Sanford Stadium in Athens, roughly a 30-minute drive from Atlanta. The trip would, however, take much longer than 30 minutes on July 28, 1996. Cars streamed up from Atlanta for the rematch, and the small college town could be excused if they thought it was a Fall Saturday featuring a Georgia Bulldogs home football game. A quick scan of the streets, however, turned up minivans with American flags instead of red and black UGA flags. Tailgating parties featured soccer balls and Gatorade instead of beer and barbeque. The chants of USA replaced refrains of the Georgia fight song, and eardrum-damaging screeches of MEEEE-yaaaaaaaaaaaaa took the place of "How Bout Dem Dawgs!"

There were 64,196 fans in Sanford Stadium that day. The attendance figure narrowly missed breaking the record for highest attendance at a women's soccer match. The record was set at the 1991 finals when 65,000 attended the U.S.-Norway match. Except, in an effort to fill the stadium in Guangzhou, the Chinese government handed out free tickets and gave workers the day off. Tickets in Athens certainly weren't free. Fans paid anywhere from $60 to $140 to get in.

Since first-round games were part of double-headers with men's matches, it was difficult to gauge how much of the crowds at earlier games had come to see the U.S. women play. Now, there was no question. "In Athens, we knew the fans were there to see us," said Julie Foudy. "In the tunnel, we were pumped. We were high-fiving everyone—each other, volunteers, security, the FBI. It was great."

The USA didn't get the start they hoped they would. Less than seven minutes into the match, Brandi Chastain went down with a knee injury, the extent of which would not be known until halftime. Chastain went off the field on the sideline across from the bench where the U.S. medical staff worked on her. If she was subbed out, she could not come back. The coaching staff wanted to give her enough time to get back on the field. Eleven minutes later, with Chastain still off the field, Norway scored. But a year of preparation had built tremendous confidence for the U.S. players. "There was never any doubt that we would win that game," said Julie Foudy. "Even at halftime when we were down 1-0, we knew we were going to win."

Michelle Akers, who stored a spare Power Bar in her sock, was seen on the video of the China game stripping a Chinese player of the ball, taking a bite, then going about her business. Against Norway, she wasn't thinking much about the outcome of game. She was thinking if she could make it back in the second half and battle through the July Georgia heat. "She came in the locker room, ripped off her shirt and collapsed in the corner," remembered Tiffeny Milbrett. "She didn't move much." Steve Slain, the team's trainer was helping Akers. "Her eyes were rolling back in her head and she kept saying, 'I can't do it. I can't do it,'" recalled Slain. "I told her, 'You will finish. They need you.'" She did.

Perhaps the best player on the field that day was Kristine Lilly. She took control of the left side of the field and toyed with Norway's right defender. With 25 minutes gone in the second half, Norway replaced the defender, and the newcomer was whistled for a handball in the box with 10 minutes remaining in the match. Penalty kick, U.S. "I looked around to see who else wanted it, and then I looked at Tony and he pointed at me," explained Akers. "I was very aware of the importance of the kick. If I missed it, we would probably lose." Akers drilled the kick past Norway's Bente Nordby to tie the game 1-1. Norway would have more troubles before the end of regulation. Mia Hamm had been causing the Norwegian defenders problems all night. She was on the receiving end of seven fouls, the last of which resulted in the ejection of a Norway player. Norway would have to play overtime with 10 players.

Meanwhile, Shannon MacMillan was on the bench through 90 minutes of nail-biting regulation time. "Like 10 times, someone would go down hurt or would be limping, and Tony would say, 'MacMillan warm up.' And then he'd say, 'Okay sit down,'" Shannon recalled with a laugh. "First of all, it was frustrating watching my team gut it out when I wasn't out there doing my part. Then, being up and down, up and down... it was driving me nuts. I was pleading, 'Just give me a chance.' The game was so intense, and I would get up and get psyched and then sit down... up, down, up, down, up, down. It was crazy."

Five minutes and 23 seconds into the first overtime period, DiCicco gave Shannon her chance. With her first touch on the ball, down in Norway's end near the corner flag, she awkwardly hit it out of bounds. "The ball bounced off my knee," Shannon laughed. "The hardest part about coming off the bench is finding the game and getting your touch. After my first touch, I said, 'That's not going to do it!' With her second touch, however, she ended the game.

"I saw Foudy making this run with the ball, and there was an opening, and that's really all I remember," she said. "I watched the tape and said, 'Oh, so that's what happened.' I just took off, and it was the best pass I've ever received. If it was any harder, it would have gotten swallowed up. If it was any softer, I would have had to stop and it would have gotten swallowed up by the keeper." After she tucked the ball into the net, Shannon took off sprinting toward the U.S. bench as 64,000 fans roared. Then she dove and slid on her stomach as her teammates slid into her.

With MacMillan's Golden Goal, the U.S., having disposed of the team that eliminated them a year ago, now had to regroup and prepare for the Gold medal match with China, three days later. For Akers, every second would be spent trying to recover. After previous matches, Michelle would stay on the field with her teammates, celebrating and thanking fans for their support. After the Norway, game, however, Steve Slain hurried her to the locker room. Her face was pale and she had the vacant look in her eyes that her teammates and friends had come to recognize as a sign that she was past exhaustion. In the locker room, she began what had become her post-game ritual—lie on the training table while someone packed her things and wait for the two I.V.s to give her enough energy to get to the bus.

"The crowds at the first three games were awesome," said Tisha Venturini (Hoch). "But nothing could compare to the crowd at the final. The whole time we were warming up, I was in awe. I just couldn't believe it. I was so into checking out the crowd, I had to remind myself to concentrate on the game." The crowd was an amazing 76,481—the largest crowd ever to watch a women's sporting event anywhere in the world.

Any thoughts of a letdown after the Norway game, or any fears that the crowd would be too much of a distraction for the U.S., were destroyed 18 minutes into the match with a goal that illustrated the progress the USA had made since 1995. Tiffeny Milbrett stole the ball in China's end of the field and dropped an easy pass back to Akers, who knocked it to the left flank for Lilly. With plenty of time and space in which to work, Lilly took the ball down the wing and hit a perfect cross into the Norwegian box. Mia Hamm, sprinting to the penalty kick mark, met Lilly's cross just as it landed and sent a scorching drive that deflected off the goalkeeper's hand and clanged the post. MacMillan, crashing at the goal, drove the rebound home.

China tied the match with 13 minutes left in the first half. But the USA came to the locker room full of confidence. All 16 players on the roster, the three coaches, Colleen Hacker, and the entire support staff was sure they would win. There was never a doubt.

Just under 20 minutes remained in regulation time when Mia Hamm got the ball on the right sideline in front of the benches. On Mia's left, Joy Fawcett started a sprint toward the Chinese goal. Mia waited patiently for just the right moment then threaded a perfect pass into Joy's path. Meanwhile, on the far side of the field, Tiffeny Milbrett started moving toward the goal. When Fawcett got the ball, Milbrett broke into a sprint. Fawcett zipped down the wing, past a Chinese defender, drew goalkeeper Gao Hong out of her goal and slid a pass across the front of the net to Milbrett, who completed the play by sticking the ball into the middle of the goal from eight yards away. The U.S. players raced around the field in jubilant celebration, while the Chinese sank to their knees. But there were 18 minutes remaining. "The last minutes took forever," said Akers. "It was agonizing."

When the whistle finally blew, the American bench emptied. And to the delight of the chanting crowd, they visited every corner of Sanford Stadium, clapping, giving waves of appreciation, and holding up "Thank You" signs. As a strobe of flashbulbs flickered from the stands, Carla Overbeck ran to the bench and grabbed her video camera. Kristine Lilly and others snapped photos of their own. Once again, the players took photos of people taking photos of them. The FBI formed a ring around the field and faced the crowd while three-year-old Katey Fawcett was carried to her mom by team administrator Pam Perkins.

An hour later, the team was back in the tunnel waiting to return to the field to receive their medals. Hardly any of the 76,000 had left. There is a photo taken of the team on the medal platform that described the type of team unity the national team had formed. While the camera is positioned in front of the players, all 16 heads are turned to the left because that's where the alternates—Amanda Cromwell, Thori Staples, Staci Wilson, and Jen Streiffer—were standing with the coaches and support staff.

After the medal ceremony, the locker room was bedlam. But lying in the corner was Michelle Akers. "She was just lying there on the floor, completely spent," said Colleen Hacker. "I mean there was just nothing left. She was just lying there dazed—but totally content. It was like a mixture of peace and accomplishment. And then she held up her Gold medal."

The '96 Olympic Games provided the national team with tremendous exposure. Over 273,000 people attended the USA's five matches, an average of 47,000 per game. But NBC chose not to show entire games live. The general public could only see highlight clips of the matches, and the national team missed out on a potentially huge piece of exposure when coverage of the Olympic Park bombing caused the network to cancel a Today Show appearance with several of the players. Television may have missed the boat, but newspapers were providing outstanding coverage in great detail about the players. Hardened sports writers, growing weary of fighting for a few minutes of a superstar's time or using police reports as a primary source, became enamored with the national team players. They found attractive, courteous, intelligent athletes patiently providing interviews that flowed with articulate insight and wit. The list of players the media requested grew as well. Previously, most media members, unless they were doing a specific story on a player from their coverage area, knew just one name: Mia Hamm.

Briana Scurry's off-the-cuff promise to run naked through the streets of Athens was one of the media's favorite talking points. She did, by the way, make good on her promise. In the middle of the night, on a very dark and deserted Athens back street, Bri, wearing only running shoes and her Gold medal, kept her word. A few friends and a video camera were the only witnesses. "That tape is locked safely away," she said.

The Olympics also served two very important purposes. First, it took talk about a women's professional league to a new level, and secondly it convinced United States Soccer Federation officials that the upcoming 1999 World Cup did not have to be restricted to small stadiums on one coast of the United States, as was the original plan. The success and popularity of the 1991 world championship in China was difficult to understand. The government made sure the games were well attended. The official attendance for the tournament was 691,000. In comparison, Sweden '95 had been a disappointment. Total attendance barely cracked 100,000 with per-game attendance averaging 4,300. Matches in Sweden were played in small soccer stadiums spread out around the country, and the tournament, which was originally slated for Bulgaria, was not particularly well marketed. Based on the success of the '96 Olympics and the insistence of US Soccer officials and players on the national team that they could indeed fill large stadiums, plans to hold the tournament on a grand scale began.

Mia Hamm
Photo by Tony Quinn

 # ROLE MODELS

There's a 10-year-old in Wisconsin. She can sing. In a year, she'll join the Milwaukee Children's Choir. In a decade, Grace Weber and hundreds of thousands of others will enter "Oprah's Karaoke Challenge," and Grace will be one of eight people to appear on Oprah's TV show. She will sing Natural Woman. She lives in Milwaukee, actually Wauwatosa, Wisconsin, and plays soccer. She, of course, is a Mia Hamm fan.

Her sister and her dad, Ralph, were among the folks who were captivated by the 1996 U.S. Women's Olympic Soccer team a summer ago. Her dad, you see, is one of those guys who get things done. A successful local attorney, Ralph's spare time is spent in youth soccer. He watched the U.S. women in the '96 Olympics and started thinking and couldn't stop. Positive influences, role models, character development, sportsmanship, humility, teamwork, life lessons—all the words youth soccer clubs put in their mission statements but often forget on weekends when the score is tied. So he did what all those people who get things done do— "Hey, let's call Mia. How about a brunch? And a speech? Maybe a clinic? You know, if Marquette University has a home game, maybe Mia could make an appearance at the game?" Done.

"One of the primary reasons we did this," Weber explained to the *Milwaukee Sentinel,* "is because the soccer dads felt that when we were young, we had our heroes, such as Bart Starr and Hank Aaron, and we thought about how great it would be if our daughters had heroes, too. When this group (the national team) says it is a team, they mean it. How wonderful it would be for our daughters to be exposed to that."

Yep, 10 years after discovering the national team, Mia is a hero. Her worshipers are pretty much confined to the millions of young girls who play soccer around the U.S. But the 1996 Olympics increased the wattage of the spotlight. It shone brightly on her team, as well as the USA women's gymnastics, basketball teams, and softball teams, which by the way featured a catcher named

Jillian Boxx, the sister of Shannon. You will hear about her later. The spotlight, however, was narrowing on Mia.

A couple of days before the Milwaukee event, Mia called Ralph. Would it be okay, she asked, if at the appearance she talked a little about her brother? Mia was very close with Garrett, her adopted brother. He was the one who made sure she was included in all pick-up games when other boys didn't want "The Girl" on their team. He was the one she tried to keep up with, the one who made each of the moves her family made just a little easier, the one she idolized, the one her mom said was probably the best part of her childhood.

So Mia explained the best she could to Ralph what she wanted to do. Garrett has been diagnosed with Leukemia. Aplastic anemia, they call it. He needs a bone marrow transplant, and would it be okay if she told people how since he was of Thai decent and since very few donors were minorities, it was unlikely a match could be found? Could she maybe tell folks how important it is for people to register in the national bone marrow database? Could she explain that the hospital bills were piling up, and how it was getting harder and harder for the family to pay for his treatment? Would that be okay? Of course, Ralph's only answer was "Of course!"

So here comes Mia. She has her Olympic Goal Medal. She's famous now, too. People recognize her on the street. They know her name. So when she comes walking into a group of young female soccer players, all the girls can do is stare and nervously whisper, poke each other, and giggle. Mia's nervous, too. Wait. What is that she's carrying? It's a big pickle jar, the kind you see in a neighborhood tavern filled with that red juice and those pickled eggs that you have never in your life seen anyone eat. Why in the world would Mia Hamm bring a pickle jar to an appearance? Simple—she is going to politely ask for donations. She has started a fund to help her brother, you see, and maybe someday it could help others. Maybe she could at least raise awareness, and anything the crowd could spare will help her family. "During the speech, she talked about her family's efforts, and it was extremely touching," Weber recalled. "She raised several hundred dollars in that pickle jar."

When it comes to Mia, Mia doesn't really think big. Years later, she figured out that others could fit into the spotlight with her, if she insisted. But in Milwaukee that day she was in the right place at the right time in front of the right people. Weber, being one of those guys who does think big, got to thinking again. So did Chuck Post, a pediatric dentist at the Milwaukee Children's Hospital. They both came to the same conclusion: "There has to be something we can do." A funny thing about youth soccer organizations—they are filled with influential people, the type of folks who will see a pickle jar and turn it into a fundraising event. Becky Walker worked for the Milwaukee Journal-Sentinel, Tom Waite was a successful architect, and Owen Sullivan worked at M&I Bank's Data Services. They got their heads together with Ralph and Chuck and came up with an idea. How about an exhibition indoor soccer game? What if Mia and some of the national team players played against a group of local women all-stars, you know, college players. Maybe some of Mia's former UNC teammates would play, too, if they are available? What if sponsorships were sold and admission was charged, and maybe an auction? What if the local Children's Hospital got involved and signed people up for the national bone marrow registry?

Mia's teammates, past and present, jumped at the opportunity because that's what you do when your teammate needs you; that's what you do when your team is your family. So they went to Milwaukee. Flew in from the West Coast, drove in from wherever they were. With the help of some Milwaukee-area businesses, the idea started to snowball, and the first annual Garrett Game was held in February of 1997 with Mia and the national team taking on a group of collegiate all-stars. "One of the things that have been particularly remarkable is the depth of commitment by the national team players," said Weber. "They basically dropped what they are doing for this. I remember one year, Joy Fawcett traveled all day to get here, played in the game, and had to turn around and leave."

The Mia Hamm Foundation was the big winner. Weber estimated proceeds from the Garrett Game topped $300,000, significantly more than can fit into a pickle jar. The festivities also included a dinner and an auction, where collectibles and memorabilia were happily purchased at inflated prices. Grace sang at Mia's wedding, and lasting friendships were made between the Hamm family and the Milwaukee group, partly because of what they were able to accomplish together. Thanks, in part, to the funds and awareness raised, Garrett Hamm got his transplant. It wasn't able to save his life, but it did add precious time to it. Garrett died in 1997 from complications.

After the '96 Olympic final on August 1, 1996, the U.S. did not play again until February 28, 1997. Three matches in Australia kicked off the year's 18-game schedule. One of those games was extremely emotional for Mia. It took her 39 seconds to score against South Korea in Milwaukee. It was less than two months after Garrett passed away. He was 28, married with a young son. "It was an extremely difficult time for me and my family," said Mia. "When I came out for that first game in Milwaukee, the team was wearing black armbands."

WHERE'S MIA?

There's that light again. Shining brighter and brighter on Mia. How can she avoid it? The baseball hat? Yes, that's it. Pull it down lower over her eyes and maybe the spotlight will shine on someone else. Her teammates are just as deserving, maybe more deserving, she figures. Why does it have to focus on one person? She didn't ask for the attention or seek it. She easily shares credit with her teammates for everything. Why can't she share the fame and spotlight, too?

Around U.S. National Team appearances, training sessions, scrimmages, and games, or even on the street or in a restaurant when USA players are spotted, you can be sure to hear one question. Guaranteed, 100 percent, you will hear someone ask, "Where's Mia?"

Her teammates know exactly where she is. She's outside, sharpie flying across T-shirts, programs, pictures, photo cards, foreheads, dollar bills, nearly anything and everything thrust in front of her. She's going as fast as she can. She's uncomfortable, but tries to talk to as many kids as possible, "Do you play soccer?" she asked. "What's the name of your team?" She still has a line 75 kids long expecting her autograph while her teammates are waiting on the bus. What are her friends on the bus thinking? It's not exactly a task they can help her with. It's not like they can pull her into an elevator like they do when the doors can't seem to close while she is signing for another group of fans. How long should they be expected to wait? They're tired and hungry and have a schedule to keep. She's tired and hungry and has the same schedule to keep.

What can she do? She will certainly be yelled at again by another mom if she leaves before they are all signed? Do they even know how often she does this? Do they care? As long as they get what they want from Mia, everything is fine. "Mia Hamm is so nice," they'll say. "What a wonderful experience," they will tell their friends. Do they care what her day was like? Should they care? Is she allowed to be in a bad mood?

"In public places, it can get bad," explained teammate Kate Sobrero (Markgraf). "When every girl is asking for her autograph, it gets hard. Sometimes they won't want my autograph, but they'll ask me to get hers. I don't think parents realize how demanding they can be. They'll say stuff like, 'You didn't smile in that picture with my daughter. I want another one.' If she doesn't fit into who they think she should be at that moment, they let her know. That has to be very difficult. It's harder for her in private situations when she is not ready for it. She'll get put into a situation when she is not expecting it, and that has to be hard. It's not the kids, it's the parents. You'd think they'd know better, but they don't. Sometimes I just shake my head and say, 'Are you serious?'"

"She carries the weight of the sport on her shoulders, there's no question," said Julie Foudy. "And not only does she carry it, but she's carried it for how many years now? That is exhausting. But she is so gracious about the way she deals with people. There are times when she is getting mobbed and people are complaining, 'I didn't get her autograph.' She's carried herself in a way that shows the younger kids, 'Here's a superstar that doesn't put herself above anyone else.' That's a great lesson. She constantly says, 'First, I want to thank my teammates,' and it's so genuine. She sets the tone for that with the team, and that has been the foundation for the team for so long. I don't know how she does it."

What if they knew about all the things she does that aren't publicized? Would they care then? Tell them about the little girl and her mother standing in the rain as the bus pulled away. In the type of scene that tugs at your heart, the mom and little girl drove hundreds of miles and couldn't find the team after the game, arriving too late. Mia made the bus stop and made the little girl's dream come true. If people knew that, would they cut her some slack?

What do people think of her when they see her on TV playfully competing with Michael Jordan in a "Whatever You Can Do, I Can Do Better" make-believe rivalry? Talk about a pedestal. What is she supposed to think of the thousands of Mini-Mia's, the pre-teens and teenage girls who wear her jersey and screech her name? Does she hear it in her sleep? Meeeeeeeee-Yaaaaa! What about those fat guys with no shirts, the ones with "I Love Hamm" painted on their protruding bellies? Okay, that's just funny. But you can hear the exhaustion in her voice, the slight bit of panic over the phone when she drives to a small soccer field in the D.C. area to make an appearance for a youth girls soccer team, expecting maybe 20 people and seeing 150 waiting for her? What is she supposed to do? What do her teammates think? "I can't imagine what it is like to be her," said Foudy, echoing her teammates' thoughts. "I don't know how she does it?"

All she wants to do is be part of team. Can she pull her baseball hat any lower to hide her identity? Can she make it down the street or through the mall staring at the ground so as not to draw a crowd? "I've probably missed a lot," she said. "But I can tell you everything about my shoes."

But hold on. Maybe she can make it work, make it acceptable to everyone, maybe even benefit others. It worked with the pickle jar. She saw a way to use the spotlight to talk about the impact that sports, particularly soccer, had on her life and could have on the lives of millions of girls. She was beginning to realize the full impact she could make on women's soccer and the millions of girls who played the sport.

"It started right after the Olympics," she said. "People want to know what helped you to have that success—both individually and as a team—and companies started bringing me to speak to their employees. Corporations are teams. They are trying to get all these different personalities—incredibly gifted and intelligent people with their own personal goals—to succeed in a team format. It's all applicable to what we do, and that's when I started thinking, 'Gosh, this makes a difference.' Obviously, going out and speaking to kids makes a difference, but being able to cross over into the corporate world is important. They are people who can potentially be involved in a league or some sort of foundation. It's huge because it allows us to impact more and more girls."

Other players—Julie Foudy, Brandi Chastain, Kristine Lilly, Briana Scurry—were using their new-found fame in similar ways. A common theme for the players was "role models." In the '70s and '80s, when the national team players were growing up, there were no female professional team sports. "I grew up watching eight-foot men play basketball," said Foudy. "There weren't many female role models." The only women athletes they could find on TV were tennis players, golfers, gymnasts, and track and field athletes. Now that they were being seen as role models for young girls, they were determined to treat the responsibility with the seriousness it deserved. As the 1999 World Cup approached, the opportunities would be more readily available.

Scurry says her role model is her nephew, who battled Leukemia and won. That led her to work with the Make A Wish Foundation, something few of her teammates knew. "When I asked her about it, she kind of blushed and said her parents didn't even know about it," recalled Michelle Akers. "It was her own private thing. That's so rare."

Foudy she served as an analyst for ESPN for the network's coverage of the men's World Cup. She spent hours educating herself about all the nation's in the tournament and agonized over the pronunciation of players' names. After the tournament, she received rave reviews from *TV Guide*, *Sports Illustrated*, and *Time* Magazine.

"I don't think a group of people could have handled it any better than they have," said Tracey Leone, who was beginning her tenure as the head coach of the U.S. Under-19 National team. "I don't think they could have been better role models. It was a quick drive to fame. In '96 it was boom. In '99 it was BOOM. They got involved with causes that helped women's sports and helped mankind. They truly believed that they could make a difference and they have. They've embraced their opportunity."

SELL THE GAME, PART XV

So it's 1998. The Olympics have come and gone. But the Games exposed women's soccer as an exciting product with likeable players who could serve as role models for the millions of girls playing the sport in the U.S. The players even seemed willing to do what other professional athletes avoided. They signed autographs, carried on conversations with strangers, made appearances at clinics and games with smiles on their faces, and, believe it or not, they were willing—no, eager—to promote their game with little compensation.

"I think sometimes it can get fatiguing, and it can wear you down," said Leone. "But they know it is an added responsibility. They understand that it's a part of their job, so to speak. Some athletes will do the minimum. This team has spent hours and hours signing autographs. They are tired. It might have been a long trip. They might have lost. How many times do you see that? The little extra is a big extra, and it impacts people. It's an important part of their jobs, careers, and livelihoods."

Heinrichs can understand the mentality. She, after all, helped create it. "Good times, bad times. When everyone is watching, when no one is watching. When the microphone is on and when the microphone is off. Their character is pretty outstanding," she said.

"Sell the game." The phrase that was drilled into their heads for 15 years, beginning with Anson Dorrance and continuing through players and coaches each year, became very real. "Anson would always say, 'Sell the game, sell the game,'" said Julie Foudy. "I was always thinking, 'Shut up, I'm just playing soccer.' But now I get it."

The U.S. Soccer Federation and the national team were determined to make World Cup '99 a tremendous success—financially, socially, and yes, even culturally. An aggressive schedule was set that would take the team around the country in a kind of traveling women's soccer evangelism tour. From January 1998 to June 6, 1999, the team went to 15 states, Portugal twice, and took one trip each to China and Japan. Every step of the way, they gave clinics, made appearances, and talked about the upcoming World Cup in such a way that fans thought they absolutely had to see it. The grassroots movement was running full-speed ahead. Foudy constantly chirped, "Fill every seat!" to her teammates, and the team never doubted that World Cup '99 would be a success.

Every time a player got an opportunity to speak to the media or to any group of people, they talked about the World Cup. But not just in soccer terms. "We were criticized for making it more than just a soccer event," said Julie Foudy. "So we would say, 'Well, yeah, it is more than a soccer event.' That's what this team has always been about. We've been dedicated to our sport, but we also get the bigger picture. You are making a different in people's lives—children, families, girls, boys, women, men."

The team opened 1998 with a trip to China, where a total of 5,400 people watched three matches. Then it was off to Portugal where crowds were even smaller. But once back in the United States, double-digit crowds began to turn out, and by March of '99, attendance was reaching into the 20,000 mark. But when the venues for the World Cup were announced, there was no shortage of skepticism. Giants Stadium in New Jersey would host the USA's first match. Soldier Field in Chicago and Foxboro Stadium outside of Boston would also host first-round U.S. matches. The quarterfinals would be played in Jack Kent Cooke Stadium in Landover, Maryland, the semifinals in Stanford Stadium in Palo Alto, California. The final would be held on July 10th in the cavernous Rose Bowl in Pasadena, California.

Ambitious? Yep.

Answering some of the same critics five years earlier, the United States had successfully hosted the 1994 men's World Cup, filling huge stadiums with over three-and-a-half million spectators. An important lesson was learned—Americans like events, big events. Even if they weren't soccer fans, they would likely buy tickets to be a part of the event. That mentality played right into the women's hands. The long-time mantra of "Come watch us play and then decide" was never more appropriate. But it was far from an easy task.

"We really had to sell the game, and it's not like we were really making inroads," said Foudy. "We would do interviews and people would doubt us. I remember a press conference before the World All-Star Game in San Jose before the 1999 World Cup. It was in this huge ballroom. It was (World Cup Organizer) Marla (Messing), Tony (DiCicco), me, and Carla. There were all these cameras, and it was just packed. The very first question was, 'You're lying about ticket sales, you're saying you're going to fill these stadiums, but it is just going to be an embarrassment to the United States. You're going to play in half-empty stadiums.' That was the mentality we had to face the entire time, and we really believed we could change it. Carla and I smiled and said, 'All right, we'll see if you have that same question when we have a full house at the Rose Bowl on July 10th.' He was the first person I sought out after the final."

During the lead-up to USA '99, the media was getting to meet and chat with players other than Mia Hamm. There seemed to be a concerted effort on the part of U.S. Soccer and Aaron Heifetz, the team's press officer, to push the likes of Lilly, Foudy, Chastain, Scurry, and when she was healthy, Akers to the forefront. Hamm didn't hide, and U.S. Soccer didn't try to withhold her from making media appearance. She was still the most requested and most visible player on the team. But as late night talk show host David Letterman, who became enamored with the team, quipped, "You'll come for the Hamm but stay for the Brandi." The press loved what they found—strong, confident athletes who loved what they did, truly got along with each other, smiled, joked, laughed, and gave insightful, helpful answers.

The team was fully invested in making USA '99 a roaring success. Talk had been going on for two years about a professional league, and the team wanted to use the World Cup as a springboard to launch the league. It was seen at the times as the best, perhaps last, chance to get a league of their own. Needless to say, it was difficult. Not only did the women feel responsible for filling seats, they also felt as if full-time soccer employment for themselves and future generations depended on it. Oh, and by the way, they were expected to win the tournament. The big picture, however, remained clearly in focus. "When it comes down to it," said Cindy Parlow, "you look at the girls screaming and dreaming that they can be you, and you realize that this is pretty special and you're pretty lucky."

Even newspaper reports predicting an enormous crowd for the USA opening game at Giants Stadium could not convince the skeptics. Just because they say they've sold all those tickets doesn't mean people will show up, they argued. Kristine Lilly grew up a New York Giants football fan. She was excited just to play in the stadium where she watched the Giants play, and on the way to the stadium, she began to worry. "Shoot, there's traffic," she said. "I didn't know what the traffic was for. I'm from the area, and there is always traffic, but not that bad. Then I realized it was for our game. I couldn't believe it."

Brandi added, "I'm telling you, riding that bus to Giants Stadium for that first game was the most amazing thing. When we got closer to the stadium, we saw the kids with their faces painted and the banners and balloons. The next thing you know, you can't decide if you are the animal in the zoo or you are the person looking at the animal in the zoo. We were taking pictures of the fans, and they were taking pictures of us."

It was the largest crowd ever to see anything—except the Pope—at Giants Stadium. Every seat in the place was filled; there were 78,972 people there that day. "I remember walking into the stadium," said Brandi. "It was a dark tunnel and then you hit that field and it was the brightest colors and it was packed. I get chills every time I think about it."

START STRONG, GET STRONGER

H amm got the weight of the World Cup off her shoulders early in the match, hitting a gorgeous shot from 19 yards that sizzled and swerved past the Denmark keeper and sent the crowd into a high-pitched frenzy. Mia took off in a sprint to celebrate her goal, and she slid to a stop in front of the bench yelling, "I don't score those kinds of goals!" Foudy and Lilly also scored that day, and the 3-0 win gave the U.S. the solid start they needed.

The convincing, if not dominating, performance helped build momentum. Curious fans that had "come to watch and then decide," had discovered something very likeable in the national team. It is hard for the players to describe or understand the depth of the attraction. But they took to using aliases and code words when checking into hotels, fans followed their bus, sometimes on foot, and teens and pre-teens stood behind barricades just to look at them. "The fans felt they were just like us," said Kristine Lilly. And to a certain extent, they were just like their fans. They looked like someone who might live at the end of the cul-de-sac, except they played a sport better than anyone in the world.

The American public was not able to watch the team on TV during the Olympics, and NBC was hounded with complaints from the ever-vocal soccer community. The mistake was not repeated in 1999. ABC/ESPN decided to show all 36 matches of the tournament, whether the USA was playing or not. The U.S. games were given the prime slots. One million households tuned in for ABC's broadcast of the U.S.-Denmark game, featuring J.P. Dellacamera at play-by-play and 1991 alum Wendy Gebauer as the color commentator. It was the smallest TV audience the team would draw during the tournament.

The team moved on to Chicago to meet Nigeria at Soldier Field, the historic home of the Chicago Bears. Nigeria—unorthodox, athletic, and very physical— posed significant challenges. Courage was a necessary element in facing the African champions, who defeated North Korea in their first match, 2-1. The USA had to be careful of the explosive offensive weapons Nigeria possessed, and sure enough, as the Americans struggled to find a rhythm early in the match, the Nigerians shocked the 65,000 fans at Soldier Field with a goal less than three minutes into the match. That turned out to be the wake-up call the USA needed. Michelle Akers forced a Nigerian defender into scoring an own-goal 17 minutes later. By the 23rd minute, the U.S. had a 3-1 lead after Hamm and Milbrett struck. By the time the halftime whistle blew, the score was 6-1. Akers and Sobrero rested during the second half, giving Lorrie Fair, the only collegiate player on the '99 team, and Sara Whalen a chance to get their first action of the tournament. Shannon MacMillan replaced Mia Hamm 11 minutes into the second half.

As the team bus pulled away from Soldier Field, a young fan started running alongside. "That was awesome," said Tiffany Roberts. "That's one of my favorite memories. Whenever we left a stadium, there was always a bunch of people around the bus waving goodbye. In Chicago, this girl, dressed in full-out national team stuff, was waving goodbye and jumping up and down. Then she just started chasing the bus. She ran for a long time. She was great, but we were getting worried about her— 'Watch out for the pole!' Someone finally said we should give her something, and Brandi signed a pair of shoes, had the bus driver stop, and threw them to her."

The ESPN broadcast of the Nigeria match was watched in 1.85 million homes. The country was falling in love with the national team, and TV was playing a large part in the courtship. Nike, Adidas, Gatorade, and Bud Light were running a series of brilliantly crafted commercials that were focused on capturing the personalities of the players. Nike's commercials showed Tisha Venturini, Briana Scurry, Tiffeny Milbrett, Sara Whalen, and Mia Hamm in a series of spots sharing everything, including fillings at the dentist— "I'll have two fillings, too." In another, the whole group joined Venturini on a date. Adidas featured Lilly, MacMillan, China's Sun Wen, and Germany's Silke Rottenberg in commercials showing them as toddlers and adults. Bud Light featured Foudy having her reflexes checked and booting the doctor through the wall. But the most popular and most effective commercial was undoubtedly Nike's commercial starring Mia Hamm and Michael Jordan. To a song called, "Anything you can do, I can do better," Hamm and Jordan went one-on-one in every sport imaginable and ended with Hamm, dressed in judo attire, throwing Jordan to the ground.

Nearly 150,000 people had attended the first two matches, about 50,000 more than attended the entire '95 World Cup. But the crowd following was not restricted to the stadiums. The national team had always had a policy of practices being open to the public. Previously, only a handful had been interested enough to come watch. Now, thousands of people clever enough to find out where the team was training, were showing up. Fields had to be roped off and security personnel were assigned to crowd control. Girls, boys, and their parents patiently watched the often tedious 90 minutes of training and lined up for autographs. U.S. Soccer had to assign extra personnel to help facilitate the various television and print requests. Chairs with players' names attached were set up away from the crowd, and the media had roughly 30 minutes to get what they needed as players were shuttled from the interview area to the autograph line. "That whole World Cup was crazy," said Kate Sobrero. "We had 3,000 people at our practice. That's the point where you say, 'Oh, my God!'"

THE SUBCULTURE

C an you sit on the bench during important games and be supportive? Can you keep a positive attitude when, right in front of you, everything you worked for your whole life is happening without you? Can you be happy for someone who is getting the chance you dreamed about? Can you come to practice every day and play as hard as you ever have simply to make someone else better? That's what national team reserves have to do.

"A reserve shouldn't be content with their role," said Wendy Gebauer (Palladino) who was a key reserve in 1991. "That's not the case at all. It's not the mentality which got them on the team in the first place. Once your role has been defined, you have to create goals which are both attainable and realistic, so you can to continue to be motivated and confident. Practice was as close to playing in a game as it gets a lot of time. I constantly reminded myself that I loved the game all my life, and that just because I was not getting a lot of match time, I was still doing what I loved. Even as a reserve, I could still extract the same elements which I loved so much about the game from those practices. The level of competition in practice was intense. We always played to win, and every element existed which you get in a game itself. The only thing lacking was the thrill of hearing 70,000 fans cheer a great play. That's okay, however, because I could share the same thrill just with brilliant assist in practice."

"It was always very hard to just practice, practice, practice but not get much match time," continued Wendy. "It's a true test of character and motivation. After all, where we came from we were all the best players, and the true test for the reserve comes in dealing with that. The quicker they can deal with it, the better off they will be and probably will become a more important piece of the puzzle. Sure, I wanted to be in every game, getting as much playing time as possible. The question I had to ask myself once my role was clearly defined was, 'Do I want to be part of a great team, a chance few people get, or do I want to consume my life with feelings that tend to be so destructive not only for my confidence but also for the entire team?'"

During the 1999 World Cup Tony DiCicco, for the most part, was using the same lineup. There would be tweaks in the formation from time to time, but Scurry, Fawcett, Overbeck, Sobrero, Chastain, Lilly, Akers, Foudy, Hamm, Milbrett, and Parlow were the usual starting lineup. That meant Sara Whalen, Danielle Fotopoulos, Saskia Webber, Tracy Ducar, Lorrie Fair, Tisha Venturini, Shannon MacMillan, Christie Pearce, and Tiffany Roberts were the reserves.

"Not many people would think of being a reserve as a fun job," said Tiffany Roberts. "But we had a blast. We were like our own little team. We had so much fun." Never would you see one of the reserve players sitting on the bench, moping about not being on the field. They all wanted to play, obviously, but before the tournament began, DiCicco and Gregg explained to every player their role.

"We all accepted our roles," added Roberts. "We were the reserves, and that was how the team was. So we were like a little sub-culture. One of the things we did was mess with the fourth official. It was the fourth official's job to keep everyone in that little box they have marked off, and they were pretty serious about it. We were hardly ever sitting down on the bench, and we had this game we would play. When someone wasn't paying attention, we would come up behind them and push them on the field. I remember Tish being pushed out there a lot. Since Fotop (Danielle Fotopoulos) was so big, she did most of the pushing. We couldn't push her out there too much. We also had our own goal celebrations. It would be like, 'Okay, Fotop is going to dive, and we will all pile on top of her.' We had a blast in the Nigeria game. We scored seven goals— 'Okay, Saskia you have the next one.'"

Between games, the sub-culture merged back into the team seamlessly. "It wasn't like the starters hung out together and the reserves hung out together," said Roberts. "One of the best things I remember about '99 was at each hotel they set up a hospitality area for us. It was pretty awesome. It was usually a big room with couches, TVs, VCRs, games, puzzles. It was like a rec room for us where we could hang out together and watch movies and stuff. Mac, Joy, and CP liked to do puzzles, so they would be in one part of the room doing a puzzle, and we'd be watching a scary movie or something. We spent a lot of time together that way. It was great."

Another way the team spent time was shopping, which was by far the favorite pastime for all the players. Since the beginning of the program, every time the national team went anywhere—Portugal, China, and Costa Rica were among their favorites—there was shopping involved. In fact, it's not a coincidence that team hotels on virtually every trip were conveniently located within a short distance of a mall. For years, the players could wander streets and malls anonymously. Now, however, they were being noticed. "It was different because unless we were dressed in USA gear, people wouldn't notice most of us," said Roberts. "In '99, they knew who we were. More of us were getting noticed."

Once the team arrived in L.A., there was plenty of free time. Up to this point, the U.S. had been playing games every three or four days. Between the semifinals and final, the teams had a week off. While the extended rest did wonders to help rejuvenate the players, it also was an agonizingly long wait for the match for which they worked so hard. "We spent a lot of time on the main strip in Pasadena," recalled Roberts. "I drank a lot of Jamba Juice."

Players also spent a lot of their free time painting—hair, fingernails, toenails. "I got my hair dyed really light in L.A.," explained Tiffany. "The whole tournament, we had been doing a lot of crazy things. We started painting each other's fingernails red, white, and blue. Then we started painting stars and stripes on each other nails. Saskia started spray-painting her hair like a flag. Kate lost a bet with Joy. Since Joy scored against Germany, Kate had to dye her hair red."

On June 27th, the subculture got their day. The third and final game of group play, the North Korea match was an opportunity to rest some of the starters. This was the day the subculture had been anticipating. After providing constant support and encouragement, and after giving maximum effort every day in practice to push the starters, this was their chance to contribute on the field. Venturini, MacMillan, Whalen, and Roberts all started, while Akers, Foudy, Sobrero, and Milbrett got much-needed breaks.

Mia Hamm scored two goals in the USA's first two games. Coach Tony DiCicco would later question what happened next. The plan all along, you see, was to build a cushion with wins in the first two games, then rest some starters and count on the reserves to carry them through against North Korea. The plan worked, of course. Akers got the rest she needed, Kate Sobrero rested her bad ankle, Foudy sat for half the game, and Hamm was given a rest. DiCicco, knowing that Mia scored in streaks, wondered later if he interrupted her momentum. She didn't score again in the tournament, but as the tournament progressed, opposing teams paid considerable attention to the player whose number was worn by half the crowd in attendance. As was her habit, her passing and defensive work increased as her scoring chances decreased.

Before the North Korea game, MacMillan and Venturini both believed they would score. They even went so far as to discuss what type of goal celebrations they were going to perform. "I'm going to do the slide," said MacMillan, referring to the belly-flop celebration she made famous during the Olympics. "I'm going to do a back-flip," said Venturini to the astonishment to everyone within earshot. "Can you even do that?" MacMillan asked.

The first half ended goalless and time was running out for the reserves to put the game away. DiCicco inserted Milbrett for Parlow and Foudy for Hamm to start the second half. DiCicco would joke later that he put the energetic Foudy in the game just to get her away from him. "She's like one of those wind-up rabbits that never stop," he said.

MacMillan unleashed a drive that fooled the North Korean goalkeeper to give the USA the 1-0 lead in the 56th minute. Good to her word, she raced toward the U.S. bench, dove, and slid. Then it was Venturini's turn. She nailed a header to make it 2-0 and ran away from the pack of teammates, with MacMillan trailing close behind. Venturini turned and, over her shoulder, asked MacMillan if she should do the back-flip. Still skeptical of Venturini's gymnastic ability, Shannon shook her head no. But nine minutes later, Venturini dove to head in the USA's third goal. She quickly rose, sprinted toward the corner flag, did a handspring, and then went right into a back-flip, the perfection of which shocked even her closest friends. "There is a great picture," said Venturini. "It's of me doing the back-flip, and in the background is Foudy with this stunned look on her face, like, 'How did she do that?'"

With two goals in a 3-0 win, Venturini, who had lost her starting job when the lineup was reshuffled after the Olympics, was the hero. The media clamored for her after the match, but she was not available. After each match, players were randomly chosen to take a drug test, and Venturini was off somewhere deep in the stadium trying to pee in a cup. The seemingly simple task often took dehydrated players hours to complete.

Michelle Akers was in good health after the North Korea match. She did not play at all, so she was able to conserve precious energy for the quarterfinals and, hopefully, beyond. After the game, as had become the team's custom, the U.S. players toured the field thanking fans. Akers went behind one of the goals and started reaching up to high-five some of the fans. "I was running along slapping hands with fans, thinking 'This is a pretty cool way for me to interact with the fans,'" she said. "Then one guy thought it would be funny if he grabbed my hand." When the man grabbed Michelle's hand, it pulled her backwards and her feet went out from under her. As the man held on, Michelle's right shoulder twisted and dislocated. After 14 years of suffering injuries on the field—knee surgeries, foot injuries, teeth getting knocked out, being rendered unconscious from blows to the head—she suffered a potential World Cup ending injury in a game she didn't even play. "How am I going to explain this one to my dad?" she said. But she would be ready for the quarterfinals, where an impressive German team loomed.

A HUGE SCARE FROM THE GERMANS

Traffic again. The worst yet, backed up on the roads leading Jack Kent Cooke Stadium outside of Washington, D.C. So bad was the jam that, at game time, thousands of cars were still pulling into the parking lot. The First Family—President Bill Clinton, wife Hillary, and soccer fan daughter Chelsea—sat in one of the luxury boxes with Donna Shalala, the Health and Human Services Secretary who was becoming a vocal and powerful proponent of the national team. After the World Cup, Shalala and Ripley Forbes partnered with national team players on a successful anti-smoking campaign.

Just five minutes into the match, as fans were still settling in to their seats, Brandi Chastain pushed a back pass to Scurry. The two miss-communicated. Carla Overbeck and Kate Sobrero chased Chastain's errant pass in an agonizing and hopeless attempt to keep it out of their own goal. Chastain melted as she suddenly realized the potential magnitude of her error. But Overbeck didn't waste any time. She got in Chastain's ear. Using the calm, yet assertive voice on which her teammates had learned to depend, Carla said, "It's early. We can come back. But we need you. Don't disappear now. We need you!"

Tiffeny Milbrett brought the game back even in the 16th minute, pouncing a German defensive error and drilling it home. But Bettina Wiegmann, Germany's classy veteran center midfielder, sent her team to the locker room with a 2-1 lead after firing a left-footed rocket to the upper corner less than a minute from the halftime whistle.

Akers was struggling, cradling her right arm next to her stomach to ease the shooting pain in her shoulder. On one occasion, and after being knocked to the ground, she laid on her stomach kicking her feet in pain. "At halftime, we thought she would have to come out," said Lauren Gregg. "But as I approached her, she said, 'I can make it. I can make it.'" That was good enough for Gregg.

Four minutes into the second half, Chastain tied the game again. The first to arrive at a loose ball in the German box after a corner kick, Brandi redeemed herself by burying a shot into the roof of the net. With the game tied 2-2 and heading for overtime, the USA was awarded a corner kick. Shannon MacMillan, entering the game for Cindy Parlow, sprinted across the field to take the corner in the 65th minute. It was the first time she would touch the ball that game. Having paid attention from the bench to Germany's defensive alignment on corners, MacMillan set the ball, looked up, and made eye-contact with Joy Fawcett. "I saw Joy, and I tried not to give away what I was going to do," MacMillan said. Then she drilled a line drive right to Fawcett's forehead.

"I knew Shannon was going to put it to the near post," said Fawcett. "She hits it so hard you really don't have to do much with it. I just wanted to get my head on it." Fawcett snapped a header just inside the near post, and the USA had survived their toughest match so far. Next up, Brazil.

A THUNDERSTORM

It was all very difficult to explain, but every newspaper and sportscaster was trying. Julie Foudy, though, came the closest when she likened the atmosphere at the games to a cross between a sleepover and a Beatles concert. Girls had flags painted on their faces, their hair dyed red, white, and blue, their favorite player's name and number on their shirts. They screeched and screamed and lived and died with every moment of the match. And they were accompanied by their mothers and brothers. And all of a sudden, there was a father-daughter sporting event, something dads could enjoy with their daughters. If they didn't all enjoy soccer, they were either becoming fans or simply enjoying the event and atmosphere together.

To explain the frenzy surrounding the event, *USA Today* columnist Mike Lopresti wrote, "I am not big on this sport, and never will be. But one need not be a meteorologist to notice a thunderstorm." The thunderstorm hit Northern California on the Fourth of July when the Americans took on Brazil in Stanford Stadium in Palo Alto for the right to go to the Rose Bowl for the final. That it was Independence Day was just a happy coincidence. The Brazilians featured the tournament's leading scorer, Sissi, and dangerous forward Katia, both of whom would later make the Bay Area their homes while playing in the WUSA for three seasons. The USA knew they couldn't look past Brazil. Thinking about the Rose Bowl was avoided as much as possible. But it was on the players' mind.

Part of Lauren Gregg's scouting report indicated that the Brazilian goalkeeper, Maravilha, had a tendency to drop balls. Cindy Parlow heeded the advice and gave the U.S. a quick lead by being in the perfect position to nod home a header that Maravilha bobbled in the fifth minute. Brazil tried desperately to get the equalizer, but Sobrero, Overbeck, Fawcett, and Chastain were sturdy, and Briana Scurry made two magnificent saves to keep the lead. Then Akers had her moment.

When you are allowed to observe the U.S. Women's National team up close, you learn a lot. You learn there are strict rules. You learn to keep your distance.

You understand how complicated it all is. And you learn that the equipment manager is vital. You know that every player depends on him for not only properly inflated balls and clean training clothes, but countless other things, the most important of which certainly is the snack trunk.

One of the jobs equipment manager Dainis Kalnins did that was not in his job description and should have required hazard pay. He was Michelle Akers' wall. He would stay late after training with Michelle while she drilled shots, with any luck, just past him, as he stood 10 yards away forming an imaginary wall. Then he would jump in goal while she worked on penalty kicks, diligently honing her shot until it was unstoppable.

Have you ever heard Michelle Akers' shot? Yes, that's right, heard her shot. You don't have to see her hit the ball to know it's coming. First, you hear the noise of a perfectly struck soccer ball, a ball smacked in the center with force—a thundering thwack. Then the sizzle. The closer it gets, you can hear it pop as it goes by. There seems to be a perimeter of safety when Michelle shoots during training. When players chase errant shots, they look over the shoulder to see if it safe. If Michelle is next in line, they stop, take a few steps back, and wait. "When I first joined the national team, my first memory is of Michelle being on the field before everyone arrived and staying after everyone left," said Julie Foudy. "I always ask kids, 'Why do you think she has the hardest shot in the world?' It's because she works on it all the time."

On a scorching Orlando afternoon, Tracy Ducar and Briana Scurry were alternating in goal. They each went all out on every shot. They quickly got to their feet to ready themselves for the next shot, diving, jumping, scrambling to a rebound. "When Michelle shoots, you kind of forget about technique a little," explained Tracy. "It's more about self-protection. Just block it."

That's what Dainis subjected himself to daily. His willingness to put himself in daily danger combined with Michelle's gratitude is why Dainis Kalnins became the "International Man of Mystery." Few knew of Dainis's off-duty activity, but Michelle, who was accustomed to practicing alone, certainly appreciated it. With Dainis, she had a target to—again with any luck—avoid, and someone to help shag balls. And he was the guy who was in charge of keeping all the team's balls. She also had a friend who she could have coffee with early in the morning. Perfect.

A day before the semifinal, after training, her shoulder packed in ice from the separation she suffered a week ago in Boston in the high-fiving accident, Michelle looked exhausted. It was her eyes. her teammates knew the look, and they have checked for it since 1996. She would have this dull look in her eyes when her energy was almost gone. She would be fine, she told the media, which translated into, "I'll be playing, and it will almost kill me, but I'll be playing."

The next day against Brazil, she certainly was fine. She was a wrecking ball against Brazil. The artistry of Brazilian midfielders was met with pure force and the intimidation of five-feet, 10-inches of muscle and hair. Even the street-fighter tactics of the Brazilians—in the form of Brazil's star Sissi raking Michelle's face with the bottom of her cleat—was brushed away quickly and forgotten. The USA had a tenuous lead in the second half. Brazil was capable of offensive brilliance and the mood in the stadium was tense. Until, that is, the 80th minute. That's when Brazil was whistled for a foul in their box, and the U.S. was awarded a penalty kick. As long as she is on the field, Michelle is the first-choice when a PK comes. She wasted no time, grabbing the ball, and owning the moment. Michelle smashed the ball into Brazil's net.

Michelle jumped in celebration, arms and legs kicking, and then she raced to the U.S. bench. She saw Saskia Weber—with her red, white, and blue hair—and Lauren Gregg and Dr. Doug Brown. And then, finally, she saw who she was looking for. She found Dainis, jumped in his arms, and planted a kiss on top of his shaved head. Photographers caught the moment. Reporters saw it. Who is he? What's going on? Why did she kiss him?

On Monday, July 6th, *USA Today* called Dainis Kalnins the International Man of Mystery.

While the USA was eliminating Brazil, China defeated Norway by a shocking 5-0 margin. Everyone knew China was for real, but could they be peaking at precisely the right time?

A STEEL ROSE BLOOMS

A player receives the ball at the top of the penalty area. All eyes are on her, scrutinizing her from every angle. The referee, an un-athletic woman with perfectly styled hair, seemingly out of place, moves clumsily out of the way. Inept defenders converge in awkward uncoordination. They swipe helplessly at the ball as the star takes a small touch and drills a shot past the goalkeeper, who dives late, way too late, to makes the save. "Cut... Cut! Let's start again." The star player goes to the sideline, and a crowd gathers around her. Someone puts smudge on her face, someone else, with one of those little bottles you use to squirt water on flowers, sprays her in the face, others mess with her hair.

It's been a long day already. When you do these types of things, supposedly, you have to start when the sun comes up and try to finish before the sun goes down. But that's just a guess? Never seen television commercials made before. Three things for sure have been learned about the process, though. First, it's boring. Rarely, do you sit in a soccer stadium with so much activity occurring on the field and so little to watch. It takes forever to set it up, seconds to shoot it. Then, do it all over again. The second thing learned is that the end product looked absolutely nothing like what was witnessed. Third, the person with the water squirter is called the "spritzer." That's her job for the day.

Until Nike decided to take a stab at ruling the soccer world, Adidas was soccer. Adidas was doing a series of commercials for the 1999 Women's World Cup called "There from the Start," a nice way to point out that Adidas was there when the soccer stars of the 1999 World Cup were little kids starting out in the game. Do you recall the commercials? Remember an infant Kristine's Lilly's make-believe mom putting her down in front of a soccer ball, and she immediately races off out of site, dribbling the ball all the way. Or German goalkeeper Silke Rottenberg in a playpen swatting away toys, yelling "Nein!"

That's what was going on in Lockhart Stadium in Ft. Lauderdale. After Lilly, Shannon MacMillan, Rottenberg, and China's Sun Wen and Liu Ailing filmed their commercial, they went to the top of Lockhart Stadium and sat for an on-camera interview conducted by one of the producers. Of course, Rottenberg, Liu, and Sun Wen conducted their interviews in their native tongue. So the process was—question, question translated, answer, answer translated. Except if you have ever been to Lockhart Stadium in the afternoon, you'll understand that the process is more like—question, question translated, jet flying overhead, wait for jet noise to die down, question translated again, answer, answer translated. Fortunately, there were some very good translators who seemed to be giving the answers pretty much as they came from the athlete. Not like the replies that usually come from the North Korean delegation. A long answer in North Korean would be translated to "Coach says he wants to praise our great leader. He says he feels the referees favored the opponent and cheated us of the game."

In Lockhart Stadium that day, because of Sun Wen, impressions of the Chinese Women's National Soccer team, known at home as the Steel Roses, changed. The Chinese team had always seemed regimented, with an overwhelming sense of sameness. They seemed to lack the flair on which other counties put extremely high premiums. They seemed to be the anti-Brazil, which is a collection of personalities who viewed soccer as a means to express their individuality. The Brazilians laughed and danced. The Americans smiled and enjoyed each other. The Chinese, on the other hand, seemed to be all-business, a small piece in a giant governmental structure. They seemed to be a machine, and a very high-performing one at that. Sun Wen proved enlightening. She spoke with a confidence and optimism that mirrored that of U.S. athletes. She never complained about moving away from home at age 11 to a special school for promising athletes, choosing to see it as a great opportunity instead. She spoke of being intimidated and wanting to go home when she saw all the other athletes. She explained how her father urged her to give it a try. She was polite and funny, although it's hard to have comedic timing through a translator and jet engine noise.

Fans, coaches, and opposing players had marveled at the way she played the game, being so simple and so dangerous at the same time. Her vision of the field was extraordinary, and she was as deadly passing the ball as she was shooting it. "A coach taught me to play with my brain, not my feet," she said. Her feet, though, were special. She did not possess Mia Hamm-like acceleration, nor did she have a Michelle Akers-like thunderous shot, but she was the whole package, as much as anyone in the world. How, you wonder, was she able to grow into such a special player in a system—a country—that encouraged and praised the group and downplayed the individual? What kind of courage and character it must take to excel past your teammates, to drive yourself to be the best, to be outstanding when everyone else is in sitting?

Part of the reason became clear. She told a story about a coach she had when she was around the age of 14. The guy told her flat out, "You will never be a good soccer player. You should stop." She explained how there were no tears, no hysterics, and never was there the iota of a chance she would take his word for it. "No, it made me work harder," she said. She was asked if she had seen him recently. "I have seen him a lot," she said, a sly little smile appearing as if it can't be helped. And what does she say to him? "I don't need to say anything. He is no longer a coach, and I am going to the World Cup." Yes, she is. And she is going to put on quite a show.

Other than being from literally the other side of the world and from a country as opposite as can be imagined from the U.S. and developed in a manner vastly different from all other countries in the tournament, Sun Wen is the same. She wants to shop. She wants to hang out with her teammates and laugh. She wants to be the best, and she wants to win. In 1991, Sun Wen was too young to be an impact player on the Chinese National team when her country hosted the Inaugural Women's World Cup, but she watched and dreamed and worked. In the 1995 Women's World Cup, her Chinese team lost to the USA in the third-place game.

Since the start of Sun Wen's career, her parents, despite the heavily male-dominated society in which they lived, took great pride in her accomplishments, one of the forces that drove her to become the best her country ever produced. "Many fathers were not happy about letting their daughters play football, but mine was different," she once told FIFA.com. "I was, and still am, very happy about that."

Much like Mia Hamm, Sun Wen faced tremendous pressure, much of it self-imposed, to do it all for China. U.S. fans could assure themselves of a World Cup title by reciting the phrase, "Mia will win it for us." People in China, who were rising early in the morning to watch their team play, were using the same phrase with Sun Wen's name inserted.

Sun was held scoreless in China's opener, a 2-1 win over Sweden, but entered the final with a tournament-high seven goals, tied with Brazil's Sissi. After a hat-trick against Ghana, she scored two goals in 12 minutes in a 3-1 win over Australia. The U.S. players and coaches did not need to see her in action in either of those games, nor did they need an Adidas commercial as a heads up to her talent. "She is very, very good," Carla Overbeck said. "She's a very smart player. She can run at our defense and cause us problems. She's a very sophisticated player."

It seems she is a sophisticated person. She calls herself a romantic. She sings a lot, devours literature and poetry, and she writes. She's particularly proud of a poem that was published in a Chinese newspaper. However, most of her writings remain private, with the exception of a poem she published before the Sydney Olympics, the last line of which reads, "Come on girls, do not wait to follow your dreams."

Sound familiar? It should. It's the same message the U.S. players have been preaching since the program began.

Julie Foudy
Photo by Tony Quinn

OFF THE RECORD, PLEASE

Come on in. This could be good. Tomorrow, the whole thing is going to come to an end, and this is the last chance to talk to people involved.

When it was first announced, skeptics nearly laughed out loud. Playing soccer—women's soccer, at that—in some of the largest and most storied stadiums in the United States? It will be embarrassing, a massive failure for sure. And the final will be in the Rose Bowl! Are you kidding me? It's a great idea, if you are partial to echoes. It will be perfect TV for those who enjoy the sneaker-squeaking sound of an NBA regular-season game between two cellar-dwelling teams. Fans will love having their choice of seats with plenty of room in front, behind and next to them. But If you believe the players on the U.S. Women's National Team, it will be enormous, a ground-breaking, even historic, event for women's sports.

The players were the ones trying to sell out football stadiums for the 1999 Women's World Cup. They didn't have much help either. Five years earlier when the men's World Cup came to the U.S., our melting pot of immigrants certainly helped drive ticket sales. And diehard soccer fans in every nation from Romania to Brazil and Switzerland to Morocco booked flights. How many Danes do you think will jump at the chance to go to Giants Stadium to see their women's soccer team play? Could the Nigerian population of Chicago be expected to flock to Soldier Field? And the North Koreans could certainly be counted on to help fill Foxboro, right? Wrong. It was largely up to the U.S. players and their family-friendly road show that covered 15 states to create a parade of young girls and their parents to ticket windows. The players will, they said, go door to door if they have to. "Hi, I'm Brandi. Sorry to bother you during dinner, but can I interest you in tickets to the Women's World Cup? What's that? No. I'm sorry. I don't have any Thin Mints. That's the Girl Scouts, but I could find you some if you buy four tickets."

Guess what? No one had to go door to door, and the turnout was astonishing. Only the Pope drew more people to Giants Stadium than the women did when

78,972 showed up for the USA's opening game. Another 65,080 turned out in Chicago to see Nigeria put on a clinic on how not to defend. Over 50,000 showed up in Foxboro, about 17 of them North Korean fans. "Shocking!" skeptics said. "But Americans love an event. They would show up for anything big, right? It just happens to be women's soccer this year." But it was becoming more and more evident that the naysayers were running out of excuses. After all, 322,301 people had shown up to see the first five games, an average of almost 65,000 per game. The team was right, and Julie Foudy, the most vocal of the bunch, the one who came just short of Joe Namath-like guarantees that the monstrous stadiums would be filled, was the rightest. So, come on in. You must be curious. The "I-told-you-so's" are going to come flying, don't you think? Let's go in and hear what the women have to say now.

The room is not small, but the crowd makes it appear that way. Television cameras mounted on shoulders and tripods. Power packs, cables, microphones, and more cables are everywhere. There are reporters, and others pretending to be reporters, to get close to the women who have captivated the country. Some have come to talk to the players, others to listen, all in the room somewhere beneath a building that is probably listed in some historic registry of national treasures. If it's not, it should be.

Right out there, down that ramp is the Rose Bowl, a cavernous and famous sporting venue. Anyone who grew up a sports fan knows the Rose Bowl. And, as you probably know, it holds about 100,000 folks. Today, on July 9, 1999, there's about 300, which is as good as empty. But down here, everyone is crammed in to the old locker room. There was the usual jockeying for position, but it seemed friendlier, less stressful. The reporters had done this before, many times. For this event, editors and producers sent the A-list, not the usual group that covers soccer in America, a group consisting of about a dozen until now. The A-List has reached the top of their craft by being doggedly single-minded in their quest for something unique, different, or scandalous. But they seem less tenacious today. Perhaps they have learned something from the women they have covered for the last month. It's the biggest sports story of the summer, easily. And it's almost over. In fact, it will end in just over 24 hours, and the conclusion promises to be enormous. The Rose Bowl will be packed with 91,185. Another 40 million will watch it on TV. And here's the odd part—it's soccer... women's soccer.

"Sell the game," was the instruction their coaches had given them since their first days with the national team program. And they sold it to anyone who would listen, and even to some who wouldn't. "Come see us play," they told skeptics, soccer purists, and novices. The more people that saw them play, they figured, the more that would see the commitment they've made, the grace and grit with which they played. More people would fall in love with the game the way they did when their ponytails were pigtails and the color of their uniforms matched the name of their team—the Pink Panthers, the Blue Penguins, or in Julie Foudy's case, the Green Machine. By the way, "No-no-no-body messes with the Green Machine." We know that because Foudy has reminded anyone within earshot, in as close to a melody as she can come, many times through the years.

Foudy is the team captain, sharing the duties with Carla Overbeck. Foudy is also brilliant, a Stanford grad who grew concerned at the possibility of her sponsor, Reebok, using child labor in third-world countries to make soccer balls. She expressed her concerns, and Reebok told her to go see for herself. She did. She went to Pakistan, bringing significant attention to the matter. She championed Title IX and served on the President's Commission. She became close with the Clinton family and Health and Human Resource Secretary Donna Shalala, and she sat with Hillary and Chelsea at the President's State of the Union address to Congress. Her first national team coach, Anson Dorrance, predicted that someday we would be calling her Senator Foudy. Foudy is tough, too. Sporting an infectious smile, a cutting wit, sharp debating skills, and an intellect that challenged interviewers to be at their best, she could spar with the best of them. When Dorrance, an accomplished debater himself, teased her about choosing Stanford over his University of North Carolina, he told her she passed up four national championships. She quickly fired back, "I chose an education instead."

In perhaps the easiest casting job ever, Foudy was given the role as team spokesperson. She entertained reporters for months with quips and tales about her teammates. At one point, she labeled the team "Booters with Hooters," and she occasionally made Press Officer Aaron Heifetz's job more challenging. But she was born for the job, despite a tendency to go overboard ("How many times in my life have I said, 'Did I just say that out loud?'") She liked to joke about her teammates, both publicly and privately. In the official media guide, she listed her favorite actress as Brandi Chastain. She listed her hobby as "beating Brandi at golf." Her long-term goal was "beating Mia at golf," and she listed her short-term goal as "cheating to beat Mia at golf." Then there was the skit she performed privately in front of the team—fully unclothed—mimicking Brandi's pose in *Gear* Magazine.

Sports reporters, sentenced to the detached, monosyllabic responses of pro-athletes, or the self-centered, ego-driven agendas of those they covered on a daily basis, found Foudy both refreshing and interesting. "Tell us about the sacrifices you made to be an elite athlete growing up?" they asked. "I didn't make any sacrifices," she said. "I made choices." Hold on a minute, they thought. These women are intelligent. They are attractive. They look like my neighbor. They're intelligent, and they may very well be the best in the world at what they do.

So look around. The Rose Bowl is empty now, except for the guys on the mowers. But the room is packed. The game is tomorrow—the USA vs. China for the 1999 World Cup title. There is more on the line for the U.S. women than any single game in the program's 14-year history. You see, a new professional league is in the works. Their best chance at finally earning a living playing soccer will be greatly enhanced with a win tomorrow. But China is good, very good. And they are in a polar-opposite position. Media attention means little to them. In fact, two days earlier at a training session outside of L.A, the Chinese team would not leave the bus until all media—everyone actually—left the area. Close to an hour later, assured of a spy-free campus, they held their double-top-secret training session. Adding intrigue to the match up was the tenuous relations between the U.S. and Chinese governments and the fact that President Bill Clinton was coming to the Rose Bowl.

Representing their country has a different set of pressures for Chinese athletes than it does for the Americans. The Chinese players are athletic, proud, and very good. They have, however, been in a strange land for months, away from families and friends. The food and language is unrecognizable, the people unusual. A dozen years earlier, when the U.S. team ventured to China, the locals had never seen anything quite like the Americans with their colorful clothes strange looking hair, their physical stature. And while in China, the Americans were in the unenviable position of trying not to insult their hosts at banquets held in their honor by asking for rice instead of veggies with insects inside, snake soup, a side of pigeon, and a main course that still had a head. In the U.S., odd customs awaited the Chinese players at the most inopportune times, most notably being frightened and rattled by the U.S. Air Force jets that did a fly-over at the Rose Bowl just after the national anthems.

For both teams, the journey was almost over. And the U.S. players learned over time that it's the journey that matters. What will be remembered is not the final game, or really any of the games. The final score, of course, is important. They didn't reach the top of their profession by saying "Oh well," after a loss. Titles are very important, too. That's why Foudy to this day still calls her 2000 Olympic Silver medal "White Gold." After all, the end result is just that—a result. It's a product of hard work, camaraderie, tears, setbacks, and victories, both small and huge. That's what is memorable. That's why they come back and do it all again and again. That's why they smile when they tell you about travel conditions they endured in the early years. Or their favorite of all time, the snack trunk they packed for every journey. Tomorrow another journey ends. Another set of memories will be stored away until they get together again. The stories and the laughs will be shared between each other, because they are more than just a team. They have a bond that we can't fully understand. That's what they will remember when they pull out their medals to show to their grandkids. But make no mistake, tomorrow is huge. The sense of responsibility—to their country, to the army of fans which is approaching half a million, and, most importantly, to each other—is enormous.

You can't see it, can you? Where is it? The tension, the nerves. It's not there. You get the impression that as soon as they are alone in the old room, the music will blare and a dance party will break out. Why are they smiling? How do they put up with the same questions over and over? Why don't they take the bait when a reporter tries to get under their skin? Why hasn't anyone snapped back with an ugly response to an intrusive or insensitive question?

"Could I have everyone's attention please? Everyone, could I please have your attention?" It's Foudy. She's standing on a bench, and she doesn't look too happy. She's using her serious face, the one usually reserved for Child Labor or Title IX issues. "Could everyone please turn off their cameras and tape recorders? We would like this to be off-the-record." Okay, let's face it. Through her entire soccer career, rarely has Foudy had to use the term "off the record."

The old beat writers knew immediately what was happening. "Here it comes," they whispered. They knew for months that the women were too good to be true. No athletes are that polite, accommodating, or even that nice. The pressure has gotten to them. It all has come to a head, and it's about to erupt. The writers are sure of it. The pressure has taken over. "She's pissed at us. Probably because of the Booters with Hooters stuff we printed," one old reporter murmured. Others thought she would close an old wound from a packed press conference in San Jose before the World Cup to promote the event, when she was told the '99 World Cup would be a flop, an embarrassment, and that the whole idea was stupid. Certainly, Foudy is going to bring that up, don't you think? Some of the reporters seemed pleased at the idea of getting yelled at. Wouldn't that mean they were right all along? They aren't as nice as they seem. And after all, being (eventually) right is the most important thing to them.

Foudy surveys the room, doing her best to make sure her statements would indeed be off the record. Then, a tiny bit emotional, she says, "We would just like to thank all of you for all you have done."

Wait… what?

"We really appreciate everything you've done to make this event as big as it has been."

Hold on a minute! Who goes off the record to thank people? Foudy does. She just defined sincerity in front of a lot of folks who rarely see it. By going off the record, she just made sure that no one could report that she and her teammates are genuine, gracious, and willing to do the right thing when no one could blame them for making the moment all about them. After all, while the tournament is a massive public event, it's also a very personal triumph for each player. And aren't personal triumphs best celebrated alone or with friends?

Now look around. The humbled faces, the bewildered eyes, those are what believers look like. That's what it looks like when the cynical become a little more optimistic. When the half-empty, dirty, cracked glass gets cleaned and can be seen as full. For a dozen years, Foudy's work helped make her teammates and the team relevant. She fought for things like uniforms that weren't handed down from U.S. men's teams, training shirts the players didn't have to buy themselves, and salaries so the women could at least not lose money while representing their country. She met with potential sponsors. She negotiated with the soccer federation and helped create a player's association to ensure all of the above for the next generation and longer. She didn't do it alone, though. Just like always, she did it with her teammates, her friends. But don't tell anyone. It's off the record.

 # JUST DOING HER JOB

On a team full of characters, Kristine Lilly set the tone for character. The players gave nicknames to each other, like Hammer, Mustafa, Beef, Gumby, Sobs, Millie and Hollywood. For Lilly, they came up with just "Lil," a moniker so simple it's perfect. When it comes to soccer, Lilly is all business. Dependable, reliable, intense are simple descriptions of her. But her teammates know more. Like Shannon MacMillan, who could pick her brain when she made the move from forward to midfielder, or the countless young players, like Kate Sobrero (Markgraf), who found their first few experiences with the team easier because Lilly reached out to them.

"Lil is so intense that there are two ways to act around her," say Kate. "You can tip-toe around her, or you can make fun of her. That's one thing I've learned about how other people get Lil out of her shell – you just make fun of her. She doesn't get upset. She never gets offended. I think Julie (Foudy) has a way to bring things out of her."

There's little doubt that Foudy had something to do with the costume Lilly wore to a Halloween party after Sobrero's wedding. "I got married on Halloween, and we had a costume party afterwards, just because I didn't want people dressing up in costumes at the ceremony," says Kate. "Mia and Nomar (Garciapara) were the couple from Grease. TR (Tiffany Roberts) was the girl from Boogie Nights. And Kristine was Catwoman. The girl was dressed in head-to-toe black spandex. Knowing Lil, that is a real stretch for her."

On this day, however, Lilly was dressed in her business clothes. She's wearing USA uniform with number 13 on the back, the number she first wore because none of the boys she played with growing up wanted it. Later, when she got to choose, she kept No. 13.

A canyon of red, white, and blue screamed all day. Young girls and boys, their moms and dads, were riveted to a tense match that would see neither team give an inch. For China and the U.S., winning the match didn't seem as urgent as not losing it. Neither team was willing to fall behind, and a defensive battle was waged through the entire 90 minutes. Neither team could spring their offensive weapons— Hamm, Milbrett, and Lilly of the U.S. and Sun Wen or Liu Ailing of China. The media, critical for so long of the nil-nil nature of soccer, understood the elevated stakes of this one and got a grasp of the intensity with which every pass, every tackle, and every shot was made. The crowd understood the difficulty the Americans faced every time China took possession of the ball. The quick passing and constant movement of the Chinese caused the U.S. to chase and run non-stop in the sweltering mid-day heat. But no one knew the difficulty more than Akers.

Already low, her energy level was close to empty as the clock ticked down to the end of regulation. A cross from the left corner of the U.S. end sailed to the near post. Akers and Scurry went up with a Chinese player. Scurry, never willing to give an inch of real estate in front of her goal, aggressively punched at the ball, nailing Akers in the head. Michelle crumbled to the turf near Scurry's post. When the ball was safely up field, Bri checked on her teammate then quickly motioned to the training staff to come to Akers' aid. Michelle had been knocked out and would spend the rest of the game with the doctors in the locker room.

Overtime was the last thing either team wanted. It became a matter of who could last longer in the 100-degree heat, who would make the first mistake, and who could make that one last final push. Once again, the teams proved equal. China reached down to mount a late attack and earned a corner kick as the end of overtime approached. As Scurry came out to play the ball, Fan Yunjie, the same player whose attempted header in 1995 knocked out Akers, snapped a header that was ticketed for the left side-netting. Scurry looked over her right shoulder with the same helpless look on her face that she had against Germany nine days ago when Chastain's back pass scooted into the goal. "I thought, 'Oh shit. It's over,'" remembered Scurry. But then, the ball flew back away from the goal, and Scurry thought, "Oh shit! It's not over." Scurry should have known. It was Lilly's job to guard the post and make sure the ball stayed out of the net. "There was Lil, right where she always is," said Scurry.

If Kristine Lilly was nervous, she fooled several million people that day. She was one of the American players who successfully made a penalty kick in the tense shootout to determine the World Cup Champion. She ran up to the spot 12 yards away, took the ball from the referee, waited for the whistle, kicked the ball in the net, and ran back to her teammates celebrating at midfield. She was, she'll tell you, just doing her job. "Lil, quite possibly, has a huge case to argue that she is the most under-rated player in the world," said Tiffeny Milbrett. "But she doesn't worry about that stuff, and she has a right to. To be honest, I don't think she worries about anything outside of trying to do her best day-in and day-out. She is that consistent. We all go through days where we're trying 100 percent, but we're just awful. Whether or not Lil is the greatest or worst player on that field that day, you know she gave it her all. She just wants to play soccer. That means she loves what she does and she tries to do what she can every day. That is why I admire her."

One of the hardest working players in history, Lilly is a fitness machine. In fact, a word new to the English language emerged from the U.S. players. When describing their own fitness level, they might say, "I'm fit but not Lilly-fit," referring, of course, to the standard by which they measured themselves. She is also the definition of dependable. "If I had to choose to rest all the responsibility on one player's shoulders, Lilly would be one of the first I'd choose," said Julie Foudy. "She's always there in the clutch, and she's so consistent."

And she loved her work. She enjoyed her teammates more, though, and she never took for granted the opportunity she had been given. On July 10, 1999, she became the owner of her second World Cup championship medal, which presumably would be tucked away somewhere with her Olympic Gold from '96. A year later, she would win a Silver Olympic medal, and she would go on to win another Gold. None of it, you can be sure, was done with selfish motives.

After the USA nipped China in the '99 World Cup final, the amount of media in the interview area was shocking. Getting from the press box to the interview area, a process that used to be a leisurely stroll was daunting. First of all, the Rose Bowl is not a small place. Secondly, having President Clinton, the Secret Service, FBI, and whatever the Chinese call their security folks, clogging up the place didn't help. Walking into the interview area, the media members scrambled to find the players they wanted to interview.

Look to the left, there's Brandi Chastain. She scored the game-winning penalty kick and ripped her shirt off revealing her sports bra and six-pack abs. The shot would be the cover photo for countless newspapers and periodicals. Brandi, obviously, drew the biggest crowd of reporters, and she is busy explaining her moment of "temporary insanity." Briana Scurry, the goalkeeper who dramatically saved one of China's attempts, is explaining how she knew it was coming. Others stood behind the barrier separating them from the hundreds of reporters. Down the row, is Kate Sobrero, smiling and joking as always, this time about the near breakaway she had in overtime. A defender, Kate had never scored a goal for the U.S. She also explained her place in the order of penalty-kick takers. "I was the 10th kicker," she explained. "Bri was No. 11. I would have gladly been No. 11. I was petrified." Mia Hamm, the most famous of the players on the team, was in the training room suffering from dehydration. Michelle Akers, still goofy from a punch in the head, was receiving treatment for exhaustion and dehydration.

Look over to the right and there's Lilly. The reporters are three deep in front of her. You see, the reason the game went into PKs, the reason the USA didn't lose, is because of Lilly who saved the day with a header off the line. Maybe it's the barrier, the sturdy metal thing that looks like an old-fashioned bike rack, which helps the players relax in what appears to be a very intimidating situation. Questions come rapidly. Lilly is, as always, calm. She's accommodating and polite, but she doesn't go out of her way to give elaborate answers drawn on deep psychological insights. She doesn't overelaborate, just answers the questions.

Wait. What's going on? Who is that with Lilly? As you gently work through the crowd, you notice there is someone sitting on Lilly's lap. What the…? It's six-year-old Katey Fawcett. Katey's mom, you see, is Joy, who has played with Lilly forever. Today, Joy nailed a penalty kick in what might have been record time. She set the ball, backed up, and drilled it into the corner like her car was double-parked with one of her kids in it. She would explain later that she was so nervous her knees were shaking. It certainly didn't show. Chinese goalkeeper Gao Hong, the most animated Chinese player in history, simply smiled and gave a shrug like "What am I supposed to do about that?" Today, Joy is the victim of FIFA's random drug-testing policy. She was somewhere under the Rose Bowl in a room trying her best to pee in a cup while dehydrated. Lilly, one of Katey's 22 world champion babysitters, gladly took charge of the six-year-old and brought her to the interviews. So, as Lilly answered questions, Katey sat on her lap, as intent on finishing her lollipop, as the reporters were on getting the story of the header. With a red, white and blue ribbon in her hair, Katy licked away, and Lilly did her best.

"Tell us about the header late in the game? What were you thinking? Did you see it coming?" It was funny at the time, Lilly's expression. It looked like she didn't expect the question. Like who would ask about a great play at a pivotal time in a huge game? It appeared she couldn't understand why it was so important, and her answer explained why. "I was just doing my job," she said. "It was right there. It came right at my head. I would have looked pretty stupid if I didn't head it. It just didn't seem like a big deal at the time."

Next question?

THE SHOOTOUT

At the time of Lilly's save, Lauren Gregg was putting together the list of players who would be taking penalty kicks in the shootout that would decide the winner. Carla Overbeck would go first, then Joy Fawcett, then Lilly. Mia Hamm, reluctant at first, would shoot fourth. The player who would normally take the fifth kick—the shot that usually decides the outcome of shootouts—was flat on her back in the locker room with IV tubes running into her veins, asking what the score was even though a TV showing the game was in the room. "I was loony," Akers said.

So Gregg approached Brandi Chastain, who had rattled a right-footed penalty kick off the crossbar in a 2-1 loss to China four months earlier. "Brandi, do you think you can make it?" Gregg asked. "Yeah, I do," Chastain replied. "You'll have to use your left foot," said Gregg. "Okay," said Brandi. Unknown to Foudy at the time, she was Gregg's pick to take the fifth kick if Brandi didn't. "I could've been a hero. I could've been someone," Foudy laughed years later.

The national team had practiced penalty kicks from time to time throughout the tournament, but when Overbeck and Foudy talked to the team before the shootout began, they made it seem like there was no better team in the world at taking penalties. "Carla and I were telling everyone, 'We are good at this... we are ready!'" laughed Foudy. "But we really had no reason to believe that. We hadn't practiced them all that much, and Carla and I were thinking, 'What are we going to do?' But we put on a spin on it."

After China took a 1-0 lead in the shootout, Overbeck proved her point when she drilled her shot past Chinese keeper Gao Hong. The team knew Gao well. She was an extremely agile and a quick goalkeeper, as well as an entertainer who liked to get inside the heads of opposing attackers. Through a series of smiles and hand motions, Gao would communicate with the other team, trying to throw them off their game enough to gain an advantage. Word quickly spread through the pack of U.S. players waiting their turn near the midfield line. "Don't look at Gao!" China made it 2-1, and Joy Fawcett stepped up for the USA's second shot. Fawcett never looked at Gao, and barely changed facial expressions until breaking into a smile during the trot back to her ecstatic teammates after making it 2-2.

As players mingled around the field waiting for the shootout to begin, Scurry was in her own world. She sat alone on the turf, knees up, head down, preparing herself for the shootout. Kristine Lilly walked up and slapped Bri on the shoulders and told her just how good she really was. Owning cat-like reflexes, Scurry paced like a panther anxious to choose her meal. The pressure Scurry felt was all self-imposed. In shootouts, kickers are expected to score. Usually, a shootout is decided by someone missing the goal or shooting right at the keeper. DiCicco talked briefly with Scurry. "I just told her all she could be was a hero," he said. "There was no way she could be the goat." Scurry, however, wasn't about to wait for a Chinese player to make a mistake. She wanted to take the offensive. She needed just one. "I knew I just had to stop one kick, and my teammates would do the rest," said Bri. China's first shot of the shootout fooled Bri, but she nearly got to the second. As Lie Yin walked up to take China's third kick, Bri had found what she was looking for. "Just looking at her, I thought this is the one I could stop," Scurry said. "Just the way she walked up."

As Lie approached her shot, Bri sprang to her left and got both hands behind the ball, shoving it wide and sending the crowd into delirium. Scurry hopped to her feet, shot a fist into the air, and let loose a scream. Scurry had done her job, and her teammates knew it. The USA needed to capitalize on the momentum, and Lilly, counted on for a dozen years because of her consistency and reliability, jogged up to take the third kick. After calmly picking the upper-left corner, she jogged back to her teammates. It was business as usual for Lilly, and her demeanor served to illustrate the psychological strength of the U.S. team. Faced with the cruel do-or-die consequences, every U.S. shooter seemed oblivious to the crowd of 90-plus-thousand and the world-wide television audience of 40 million. They simply took care of business.

China made their next shot, and Hamm was up. Earlier, Mia approached Shannon MacMillan, who according to the U.S. goalkeepers possessed the team's hardest shot after Akers. Mia asked what number shot Shannon would take. Mia did not like taking penalties, explaining earlier in the tournament that she lacked the necessary confidence to perform in that situation. When MacMillan told her she was not one of the first five, Mia went to talk to Lauren Gregg. "Why isn't Mac shooting?" Mia wondered. "Give her mine." It was too late, however. The list of shooters had already been given to the referee. Gregg simply said, "Mia, you're taking one."

"Her sense of responsibility to the team is tremendous," said Foudy.

So there she goes, jogging from midfield to the white spot 12 yards from goal to take her turn against Gao. Look at the eyes. Look at the jaw. If you saw that look on the street, you'd go the other way. Is it determination? Probably. But it looks much more like she is just plain mad. It's a stark contrast to earlier USA kickers. Overbeck and Fawcett, approached the spot as though they had been waiting in line at the grocery store fighting boredom. They took their shots and trotted away like their children were late for school. Kristine Lilly made her shot, and it looked simple. Mia took the ball from the ref, set it carefully, and backed up, all the while staring at the ball with enough force to make it start smoking like in one of those cheap psycho-thrillers. She moved that same piece of hair out of her face, the one that's been there her entire career, and tucked it behind her ear. Then with all the force she could muster from her physically and emotionally spent body, she slammed the ball past Gao. She sprinted away from the spot like she couldn't wait to leave it behind, leaping and pumping a fist. She unloaded a scream that no one ever heard. A goal celebration it was not. She was celebrating the fact that she didn't let anyone down.

In the broadcast booth, Wendy Gebauer was silent, and she had been for the entire shootout. "I got some criticism for that," Wendy said. "But what people don't realize is that the decision had been made to let the crowd tell the story. J.P. (Dellacamera) would set up the situation by saying who was shooting and what the score was, then we would just let the crowd take it from there."

On the sideline, Tiffany Roberts and Cindy Parlow sat together. "C.P. and I were sitting Indian style and holding hands," Roberts remembered. "If one of us moved, we would be like, 'No, no, no—go back to Indian style! Put your legs back like they were! Hold my hand!" The USA's second group of shooters—Foudy, MacMillan, Venturini, Sara Whalen, and Kate Sobrero—were getting themselves prepared for their moments.

Sun Wen was China's last shooter. The magnificently talented striker was respected and admired by all the U.S. players for her skill and grace. Sun would later come to the U.S. to play in the WUSA. Scurry and Cindy Parlow were her teammates on the Atlanta Beat. After giving the ball a kiss, Sun tucked her shot neatly into the corner, setting up Brandi Chastain to be the hero or goat. Her teammates called her Hollywood for her love of the dramatic. "If you need someone in a do-or-die situation, I'll take Brandi any day," said Mia.

"As soon as the whistle blew, I just stepped up and hit it," explained Brandi. "When it went in, I just kind of lost control, I guess. I was like, 'Oh my God, this is the greatest moment of my life.' It was temporary insanity." She ripped off her jersey, waved it over her head, and sank to her knees. Her goal and ensuing celebration sent the Rose Bowl and the country into a frenzy that would last for months.

Abby Wambach was 19 years old at the time and remembered watching the game on TV. After Brandi scored, Wambach was at first surprised Chastain took her shirt off. And then, she was more shocked by Brandi's abs. That, according to Wambach, is the moment she decided to take her physical conditioning to the next level.

The image of a jubilant, muscular Chastain on her knees was plastered on every front page of every newspaper in the country. It was on the cover of *Sports Illustrated*, *Time,* and *Newsweek*, and it was shown on TV news programs over and over. It became one of those sports moments that people remember where they were when it happened.

# KATE GOES TO WASHINGTON

She was easy to overlook that summer. When she was trotted out in front of the media, it was usually because someone else couldn't make it. The press, at first, didn't know what to ask her. She just came out and smiled, answered questions best she could. But those who had spoken to her before the 1999 media event called the Women's World Cup loved it when she came out. You just knew, if you listened closely, you would chuckle. Then later, after you thought about it more, you'd laugh out loud.

Kate Sobrero was not a recognizable athlete on that team, a group which included Mia Hamm and Kristine Lilly, and Michelle Akers, Julie Foudy and Bri Scurry. Heck, she wasn't even the most recognizable player among the four players that played the least recognizable positions on the field – the defenders. To her right was Joy Fawcett, who gave a brand new, far more-detailed definition to the highly overused term "Soccer Mom." Joy had two kids, for crying out loud. After giving birth to Katey in 1994, she took all of two weeks off then returned to train with the team. Ankle sprains require more rehab time than that. By the time Kate Sobrero made her first appearance with the national team, Katey Fawcett was four. Next to Kate in the other central defender position was Carla Overbeck, the team co-captain, perhaps the greatest leader in the history of women's soccer and someone who commands respect when she walks into a room. When Carla first joined the national team, Kate was 11. Over on the left side is Brandi Chastain. Brandi's a soccer freak, can't get enough. When she's not playing, she's watching, thinking or talking about it. She's married to a soccer coach, Santa Clara's Jerry Smith, and now everyone knows her. Then there's Kate, who was perhaps better at her particular job than anyone else in the tournament.

Kate proved that you can rise to the most elite of elite levels of a sport if you do one thing extremely well. In soccer, there are players that create. There are players who finish, there are players who do the hard work, the ones who help make the creators creative and the scorers score. Then there's Kate. There are players who have God-given natural talent, like Mia and Millie and Michelle. Then there's Kate. There are players who have an uncanny ability to see things others don't, to make the game-changing pass, or the pass that leads to the game-changing pass, like Lilly or Foudy. Then there's Kate. There are players that the team can depend on to make the right play at the right time, the key tackles that destroy the opponent's scoring chances before they become scoring chances, or even that last-second poke of the toe that takes away a sure goal, the ones who put their bodies in harm's way because her team needs her to. That's Kate.

She wasn't always a defender, though. As a high school freshman, she was a four-foot, 11-inch, 85-pound forward. She says she was never the best player on any team growing up. She simply worked harder than anyone else. Her work ethic kept her on the field and coaches moved her around to a variety of position, until she landed on the back line. "I get a bigger thrill out of shutting players down," she says. "I love to get them frustrated and watch them get all mad. Defense is my thing. I also told myself I would never play dirty. The big kids were always pushing me off the ball, and I promised myself if I ever had any size, I would never play like that. I want to be a player other players respect because I play defense honestly."

The player on the team with the least experience, Kate earned her job on the back line by being that dependable destroyer, the one who gets as much satisfaction by denying a goal as others get from scoring one. She was just steady, reliable and was the perfect fit for the job that needed to be done. But ask any offensive guard on a football team, any defensive specialist on a basketball team, any .227- hitting, smooth-fielding shortstop on a baseball team, or any of those folks with the brooms on a curling team, the media tends to ignore the role players, no matter how good they are. That's the way the Summer of '99 media throng treated Kate. Most of the questions asked of her where about her teammates, "What's Mia really like ... the team can't get along as well as they tell us they do ... who is the most difficult player on the team?" But Kate just kept smiling and answering the best she could. And, amazingly, we learned later that she was extremely uneasy through the whole tournament.

"I didn't feel comfortable until 2000, to be honest," she admits. "I think I played 40 games total before the World Cup. Then I was playing with all these amazing women. Other than Cindy (Parlow), who had been on the team for a long time, I was the only new starter from the 1996 team. I was the youngest player in terms of games played. I was playing on fear. I was motivated by fear. I just didn't want to make a mistake. That was the whole point every game. It kind of took the fun out of it for me a little bit because I was so freaked out. So in terms of enjoyment on the field, '99 was not a fun year. But in terms of so many other goals and dreams I wanted to achieve, it was amazing. I was just nervous the whole time. I was driven by fear. Carla was great. So were Joy and

Brandi. All the veterans were so good with me. I wasn't at the level they were at, but they let me grow with them. At the end, defensively I was definitely at their level. Offensively is another story."

She kept her anxiety well hidden. It was the smile that masked it. That goofy grin she somehow maintained while rattling off rapid-fire sentences no reporter is quick enough to keep up with. If you are going to talk to Kate, bring a tape recorder because you are going to miss something good. Like her ability to handle the intrusive questions with the timing of a stand-up comic. Kate didn't miss a beat in replying to the question, "Are you gay?" She left the reporter bewildered when she said, "I'll have to ask my girlfriend and get back to you." If you spend your time asking Kate about others, you'll miss the whole story, and it's a good one, especially if you are entertained by slapstick.

You are going to miss the reasons why her first two national team training camps didn't go too well. "Do we have to talk about that?" Kate asks. Sorry, but we do. We have to mention it for the same reasons we mentioned how an 85-pound high school freshman became one of the best defenders in the world. We have to tell the story because it helps explain how she thinks, her competitiveness, her determination, her unwillingness to give up and, well, it explains Kate. She's embarrassed to talk about it, you see, because she's not thinking about what the story says about her. She's just focusing on the failure, not the fact that everyone has setbacks. She's not thinking about what happened after the disappointment, or that a lot of players would have quickly come up with a new, more easily attainable dream after what happened. And she's not thinking about what the story can mean to young players.

The first time she was invited to play with Mia, the first time she had the chance to play next to Carla, the first time she was welcomed to the team by Lilly and Foudy, it didn't go too well. It was a disaster, in fact. In 1995, she was a sophomore at Notre Dame, enjoying a very successful second season with the Irish, a consistent national contender. When she arrived at camp, she was recently named first-team All-American, and U.S. coach Tony DiCicco wanted to take a look at her for the '96 Olympic team. National team camps were infamous for the fitness-level required of the players. "We don't train fitness here," DiCicco would say. "We test it." Kate, you see, thought she was fit, just as dozens of others before her thought they were fit. She was, in fact, in the best shape of her life. But she had the flu. Combine that with nerves, Orlando heat and a fitness standard set by freaks like Lilly and Joy, and it was not a good combination for Kate. She passed out.

That's it, she figured. I blew it my chance. They are never going to ask me back … and I don't blame them. There are two reasons why someone will never be invited back to a national team training camp – being a selfish teammate, and whining. That's the culture – No Whining! There are, of course, other reasons, like not being good enough. But not being fit enough is not, by itself, a reason to give up on someone. The culture created by the veterans, the ones who went to China in 1991 to win the first-ever Women's World Championship, was based on worrying only about the things you can control. It boils down nicely to two things – fitness and your attitude. Kate's attitude, an extension of that 85-pounder who liked to ruin forward's days, was exactly what was needed. Fitness, she could take care of. So she went back to Notre Dame, watched the '96 team win Olympic Gold and worked on fitness.

But in Kate's case, staying fit and staying healthy are two distinctly different things. Ask others about Kate and her journey to the national team and you won't be sorry. Go ahead, ask Jen Renola, the former Notre Dame goalkeeper and one of Kate's close friends. She knows her as well as anyone. "She's a klutz," Jen says. "She's always hurting herself." Sit back and listen and you'll hear tales of Kate twisting ankles by falling off curbs, tripping over invisible obstacles in the hall, and her teammates begging her to tie her shoes because they know for sure a dangling lace pretty much ensures a visit to the trainer.

Jen will tell you this story, too, another one Kate would rather not have told. You see, Kate's late again. Notre Dame is heading out of town for a game and everyone is on the bus. Everyone but Kate. It's early in the morning, but her teammates know the hour of the day is not the reason for her tardiness. She's late because she's Kate. Renola spots her coming down the street. "Here she comes," Renola announces. Everyone's attention – the players, the coaches, the support staff, the bus driver – turns to see Kate pedaling furiously on her bike, carrying her bag and a pillow.

Renola gets that sick feeling again. Untied shoelaces are dangerous. But Kate on a bike? Kate on a bike in a hurry? Kate on a bike in a hurry with a bag and a pillow? "Come on, you can make it," Renola pleads. "You're almost here." Nope. She can't quite pull it off. There are different theories about what actually happened next. It might have been a hand-brake mishap. You know, when you pull the front brake instead of the back. Or it could have been a pillow case to the spokes that did her in. Whatever it was, what the people on the bus saw was Kate go flying over the handlebars, bag, snacks and pillow soaring through the air, followed by Kate and her goofy smile landing on the pavement. She's up! She might be okay. Nope. Stitches to the chin. It will be just another notation on her medical chart, which is quickly growing in length and detail.

She stayed healthy enough to earn two more All-America honors, garnering as much attention as anyone playing her position could get. Now it's 1998. The national team is training for the 1999 World Cup, and Kate's attitude and fitness earn her another chance. This time she's ready. She knows what to expect and she's going for it. She's not the fittest player in camp – something that cannot be accomplished by anyone at any camp that includes Kristine Lilly – but she is solid. She's confident, too. And she's healthy, a miracle in itself.

Really? The first day? You're kidding, right? It's one of those moments where two teammates go after the same ball. There's confusion, hesitation. "I got it … you take it … It's mine … it's yours." In the carnage, goalkeeper Tracy Ducar's knee won the fight with Kate's jaw. "I probably should have taken that as a sign," Kate says with a laugh. "I should have just quit when I had the chance." She was sidelined for two months, but received a third invitation in April of 1998. She was impressive enough to be invited to residency training camp in January of 1999. Suddenly, she was faced with the real possibility of playing in the 1999 World Cup. But five days before residency began, Kate went for a run. She stepped on a piece of wood and turned her ankle. "I got to camp, and I couldn't play," she remembers. "But I could do the fitness drills. We did 120s, and I passed! I was like 'YES!' It was such a huge relief. I think if I hadn't passed that fitness test, I wouldn't be here today. The rest of the week I could just play. It's was a huge mental thing."

As the 1999 World Cup began, playing on fear worked. She played well in the USA's first two World Cup matches, wins over Denmark and Nigeria, but she hurt her ankle the next day. "It doesn't surprise me that I got hurt, especially in practice," she said at the time. "It seems every time I get hurt, it's in practice. I think my luck is changing, though. A year ago, I would've broken my ankle. This time I just sprained it." That's when her face time with the media doubled. "Would she be able to play?" they asked. "Who will replace her if she can't," they wondered. "Oh and how do you say her last name? It's not like one of those Mexican hats is it?" Like most of her injuries, the ankle problem didn't last long. It had been trained to heal by years of stepping off curbs. She sat out the North Korea game in Boston, and returned for the quarterfinal match against Germany. She just did her job, did it well and fell back out of the spotlight.

Picture this, though: Late in the second overtime period, score tied 0-0, players are dragging, emotionally and physically wasted in that 108-degree heat and intense circumstances. A U.S. player breaks past the midfield line and races toward China's goal. Wait! Who is that? It's Kate! She might get a breakaway! She might score the first goal of her career. Look, her shoelaces are tied, she might get there first! What a story this is going to be, what a dramatic and unthinkable ending. A swift Chinese defender got there first, though, and Kate made a beeline back to her position.

No, Kate wasn't involved in the ending. She probably injured a couple teammates with flying elbows or an inadvertent head-butt in the melee after Brandi Chastain beat Gao Hong and won it for the U.S. But Kate was entertaining any reporter who came to her after the game in the large media room under the

Rose Bowl. The ones who came to talk to Kate gave up trying to get close to Brandi, or were from the *Detroit Free-Press*, her loyal hometown paper. The goofy smile was as big as it had ever been, the sentences came faster than usual, an example of what adrenaline can do to someone. "Was that you who almost got a breakaway," she was asked. "Yeah, was that crazy or what? I couldn't believe. I was like, now what do I do?"

The next morning, the celebration tour began. The Today Show, Letterman, Leno, MTV, the whole list of famous places famous people go as soon as they become famous. Add one more place to the list: The White House. President Bill Clinton was not stupid. Having significant women problems of his own, the President caught wind of the tidal wave of Americana parading itself through the U.S. that summer. Bill, Hillary and daughter Chelsea attended the U.S.-Germany quarterfinal match in Jack Kent Cooke Stadium in D.C., and watched the U.S. pull out a dramatic come-from-behind victory that day. He was either caught up by the same things the rest of the country was, or recognized it was a great political move to attach himself to the team – or both. Whatever the reason, he went to the Rose Bowl for the final, telling the team after the game, "I wish I played on your team."

Six days later, Kate would find herself at the White House. The team was being honored on the South Lawn. Look behind Bill's head, second row, behind Tiffeny Milbrett and Sara Whalen, next to Danielle Fotopoulos and her video camera, there's Kate. It's a day *Sports illustrated* called "sweltering." In his speech, Clinton said it was over 90 degrees so he cut his speech in half. Vice-President Al Gore was there, too. It may have been the day he formed his theories on global warming.

Kate called it "hot!" In fact, she has a bone to pick with whoever picked the outfits the women wore to the White House. The black skirts were fine, but the thick lavender shirts? Apparently, when you go to the White House, you tend to wait a while. Makes sense, doesn't it? The President is probably a busy guy. So the team waited and waited for the ceremony to begin. They waited outside in the heat, which was a problem for Kate. "We had these purple blouses on, and I'd like to talk to whoever picked purple," she said. "You can sweat through those things and they become see-through at that point. I do, unfortunately, sweat like a boy, so I was drenched."

But Kate had an idea. She grabbed Sara Whalen and went into the ladies' room inside the White House. "We were trying to dry out our shirts," she said. "So we were standing there in our skirts and bras and waving our shirts up and down trying to dry them. Then it dawned on me -- we are in the White House! There are cameras everywhere! We're standing there in our bras! So we just looked up, waved and said, "Hi President Clinton.""

That's Kate.

Brandi Chastain
Photo by Tony Quinn

PART III

AREN'T YOU THE ONE WHO... ?

They keep looking over here. By now it's clear they recognize someone. There are three of them. One guy holds a pole in place while he not-so-secretly glances over at the table in the shade. Another guy connects another pole. It drops on the cement, clangs, rolls, and rattles. They begin again. The third guy is arranging the canopy-thing that will go on top of the poles, that is, if they ever get in place. Can't really blame them, though. It's probably not often their day is interrupted by three extremely fit, attractive women—two blondes and a brunette—and one unfit, unattractive guy, lounging around their work site.

Wait, is he coming over here? Really? Is it his break time already? Yep, here he comes. His buddies are trailing behind, letting pole-holder guy take the lead. What's he thinking? "Three of them, three of us... let's go boys." This should be good. What happens next explains it all, everything being talked about at the table in the shade, everything they have accomplished, everything that caught the country by surprise in the summer of 1999.

That was four years ago now. Four years since Americans filled football stadiums to cheer and squeal for the U.S. Women's national soccer team. Four years since they were on the cover of *USA Today, Sports Illustrated,* and *Time* Magazine. Four years since they did Letterman, the Today Show, the White House. It's been 17 years since they started representing their country in obscurity, travelling to places like Bulgaria, Italy, China, Blaine, Sweden, Chapel Hill, Germany, Norway, Brazil, Costa Rica, Hartford, Greece, Portugal, Australia, Japan, Sanford, Florida, and Carson, California. That's where they are now: Carson. They are training for their fourth Women's World Cup, having completed their second Olympics a year ago. A lot has changed, but little is different. There are new players, but the veterans are still leading the way. There is a new coach, April Heinrichs, but she's a familiar face, an old teammate from '91.

That's the topic for the day—the old and the new. Will the culture they created, nurtured, and insisted upon survive? Do the young players understand? Do they get it? "I worry about that sometimes," said Kristine Lilly, who has represented her country on the soccer field more times—a lot more—than any other man or women. "I hope so." Lilly, as much as anyone, owns the culture. She is responsible for much of it. "Don't worry about what you can't control, and one thing you definitely control is your fitness." That's been Lilly's guide since she was 16, back when she was invited to go to China for the first-ever Women's World Championship, a tournament to which she brought her Teddy bear, only to have it hung in a stairwell by a teammate. The leader of that lynch mob happens to be her national team coach now.

The old are wiser now. They play the game with the enthusiasm of 18 year olds but with the experience gained in their 30-plus years. They've been around the world, maybe two or three times, and have the pictures to prove it. They've seen a lot, experienced a whole lot, and can speak about it with the type of insight and understanding most professional athletes lack or take for granted. Looking back is fun for them. They don't talk about the play that led to an important goal or personal moments of glory. And any discussion of a medal ceremony is generally confined to how badly they sang the national anthem. They don't talk about fame or how it has affected their lives, positively or negatively. They just say it's an honor and a responsibility to have people look up to you. They let you know that when they were young there were very few female athletes to look up to, far fewer female team sport athletes. They have spent the bulk of their lives turning negatives into positives, using the word "choices" instead of "sacrifices," taking responsibility for their own happiness and not waiting around for others to make them happy. And it's about to happen right here in Carson, right on the Home Depot Center concourse, a graduate-level class in how to take lemons and turn them into a peach-mango slushy.

Here they come, the three of them putting on their best swagger. The three women have quietly begun to notice. The leader pauses to look over his shoulder, making sure his support system is in place. He actually knows little about support systems. The women are the experts. The culture they created includes a sentence that must be lived by "Play for Each Other." What exactly does that mean, you might ask? Play for each other? Play to win is easy to explain. Give 110 percent? Everyone knows that. But how do you play for someone else, let alone everyone else on your team? The same question was posed to a group of 14 to 17-year-old female soccer players—What does it mean to play for each other? "Be a good teammate," was the closest to the truth. Ask this: "How many of you have ever had a really bad day on the soccer field?" Hands go flying up as fast as memories come flooding back of tripping over the ball, ill-timed handballs, and empty nets missed by wide margins. Playing for each other means when a teammate is having a nightmare, you play harder to help her out because you know that when you are having an awful day, your teammate will be there to do the same for you. That's a support system. That's how these women live, and it's what drove them to be at their very best every time they stepped on the field. Because someone may need their help. This poor guy has two semi-reluctant wing men, and he's about to intrude on three married women. It's a potential nightmare, and his wing men may not be able to wake him up in time. Still, here he comes.

"You are soccer players, right?" he asks. Not bad for an opening line.

"Yep, we are training for the World Cup here," answers one of the women.

Then he looks at one of the players. It's quickly evident that she was his target all along. "You're the one who took her shirt off, aren't you?"

Yikes. Going right after it, aren't you buddy? The question should not have been that surprising. Brandi Chastain has been asked it repeatedly since she drilled the game-winning penalty kick four years ago. Her celebration—ripping off her shirt and waving it over her head as she fell to her knees—was replayed thousands of times on television, recorded on covers of countless major newspapers and magazines, and discussed over and over. Her black Nike sports bra became famous. An autographed version was even auctioned. Ironically, she is dressed right now the same as she was at the end of that game in the Rose Bowl, except her Nike shoes are replaced with flip-flops, and tan lines are where her socks and shin guards go. The sunglasses are a nice touch. She's working on her tan, while Julie Foudy chooses the shade, and Kristine Lilly attempts to tan one leg at a time, diligently trying to even out the area her socks cover every day in training.

If ever there was a time for a snippy, dismissive reply to a question, this is a prime candidate. Really, who walks up to someone and asks that? Wouldn't, "Hey, aren't you the one who scored the winning goal in the World Cup," have been a better starting point? But it could have been worse. Two years earlier in Melbourne, Australia, at the 2000 Olympics, in the lobby of the Melbourne Hilton 30 or so minutes before U.S. players were available to the media, an Italian journalist, apparently very well-known in his country, where, as you surely know, soccer is much more than a sport, approached a member of the U.S. media. Italy also produced one of the first bona-fide stars of the women's game—Elisabeth Vignotto, whose all-time goal-scoring record fell to Michelle Akers, which was passed by Mia Hamm, which was passed by Abby Wambach. The Italians played a sophisticated game that taught the Americans some valuable early lessons about the international game, lessons the U.S. used to rise to the top of the world. While Italian women's soccer was sophisticated, they received more ridicule than support from their society. Soccer was not something women did, period. Cooking, cleaning, raising children, and other womanly activities were how they were to spend their time. Not chasing a ball or "trying to be men." That fully explained the question he asked.

"Your American team," the Italian journalist began, "you have a player that strips, yes?" Not quite as adept at turning negatives into positives, the American writer strongly preferred sarcasm. "I'm not sure," was the reply. "They all make pretty good money now, so I don't think they are working second jobs." Confused, he stared as if he was miss-translating in his head. "However, I have seen a few of them with more one-dollar bills than I would consider normal. If I had to guess, If I had to pick one player, I would say it's probably..." he walked away to pursue his story. His was another in a long line of questions and situations that took attention away from the important aspects of this team, the things that can be learned, or just the things that can be enjoyed, like exciting soccer played by humble athletes. Brandi knew that. She also knew that it may have been poor judgment to pose for *Gear* Magazine wearing nothing but a smile and holding a very well-placed (or poorly placed depending on your perspective) soccer ball. She was proud of her body, she would say. And she worked her ass off to get it, clearly an exaggeration because her ass was right there, right in plain sight, in *Gear* Magazine.

Before the 1999 World Cup, the Australian Women's National Team, in an effort to raise awareness of their team and to raise money to help them continue to leave jobs to train, posed nude for a calendar. And there were very few strategically placed soccer balls. Poor decision. That was the prevailing opinion of female athletes at the time. They weren't opposed to the nudity, but it had an opposite effect on what they were trying to accomplish. They were, it was said, not viewed as serious athletes. Others saw no harm. Some of Brandi's teammates disagreed with her choice to pose in a state of undress, but they supported her right to do it, even if they thought it reflected badly on her team and its players. She did it, she said, for herself, and it really didn't matter what other people thought. She did, however, admit that her choice of publications could have been better.

Okay, this guy is pretty bold. Lilly and Foudy, having turned to see the visitors, turn back both unfazed and unconcerned about his question. Been there, heard that, is their attitude. Foudy says softly, "She gets that all the time." After a sort pause, she says, "Watch."

"Yep. That was me," Brandi says with a tone that leads you to believe her next words will be "thanks for noticing." We are watching a master at work here. "Were you there that day?" she asks, and just that quickly she has nearly turned it completely around. She turned shirt removal to soccer in five words. After all, the 1999 final was in Pasadena, the Rose Bowl isn't far from here, and since there were almost 100,000 people in attendance that day, there's a chance this guy could have been there. Within a few minutes, Brandi knows that he was not in the Rose Bowl that day. She knows his name. She knows he is a soccer fan. Soon they will be talking about the guy's favorite soccer team. Brandi throws names at him that only a true soccer junkie knows, the type of things you only learn by watching TV channels that show not only the English Premier League, Serie A in Italy, La Liga in Spain, and the German Bundesliga, but also the Uruguayan Second Division, Turkish league matches, and highlights from Scotland.

"She's really good at that," says Lilly. "I don't know how she does it." Foudy is not surprised, either. In the 1999 U.S. National team media guide, players were asked a series of basic questions. One was to list their favorite actress. Foudy answered "Brandi Chastain." They also know that no one can sell the game like Brandi. They played in front of many empty stands in small stadiums, barely more than family and friends in attendance. Press passes at big events numbered in the teens. Television coverage was non-existent. Even the younger players on the team with them today admit not knowing the U.S. had a women's national team when they started playing.

It all came together, though, in 1999. The perfect storm of a slow summer pro-sports calendar and a family-friendly, feel-good story about a women's sports team that treated each other like professionals, like sisters and acted like real people, the kind you see next door, not stepping out of a limo at a nightclub. And it ended with Brandi, twirling her shirt in the air.

Just like that, Brandi was famous. She was in demand, not just for autographs or appearances, but for sound bites and opinions and a whole lot of things she was not qualified to talk about. "It's the weirdest, most bizarre experience you can imagine," Brandi explained. "One night you go bed, and when you wake up the next morning, people think your opinion matters more than it ever has, that you are smarter than you've ever been. Whatever you do, everyone else should do. I found that very unnerving at times because you become incredibly aware of everything you do. You don't want to upset anyone, or say the wrong thing. You want to be respectful of everyone. But at the same time, it's an incredible feeling, because that's the platform you want for soccer. Now, everyone is going to listen because they asked you. I was like, 'Okay, now you're going to hear it.' That's the paradox. On one hand, you are kind of shell-shocked by it and very careful, but on the other hand, you have this great opportunity."

The media and general population saw a different paradox. They saw professional athletes who knew how to behave. In 1999, pro-football player Rae Carruth was charged with murdering his pregnant wife, baseball legend Daryl Strawberry was arrested for drugs, and the U.S. Olympic Organizing Committee was hit with a bribery scandal. That's just part of the climate the U.S. women entered in 1999. "It's unbelievable how many people say to us, 'I can't believe you care so much,'" said Foudy. "I always think, 'Of course we do.' We are just normal people, and it's funny that they would think we are something else. Why is the persona of the professional athlete so bad? Why are we so refreshing? That's so sad. People think that just because you are a professional athlete, you are automatically a jerk. Or stupid, self-centered.

The visitors are still here, enthralled by Brandi, who by now knows that the guy has never seen a women's soccer match. But he is willing to give it a try. He might even buy a ticket for the game a few days away. Why does Brandi bother? Why give these guys the time of day? They are spending an hour with this interview, time they could have to themselves. After all, they have another training session later today. Why do they do it? Because that's what they do. They sell the game. To Brandi, every conversation is an opportunity. Everyone she meets is a potential fan.

"It happens to her every day," said Kate Sobrero (Markgraf). "She always handles it very well. Brandi can sometimes take what can be a negative thing, or something that is annoying, and turn it into a positive. She'll turn it from the shirt thing to women's soccer. She'll turn it from 'She's the one who took her shirt off,' to 'Yeah, but she won the game.' Granted they remember Brandi as the girl who took her shirt off, but they also remember the reason why. That's awesome."

No one except Mia Hamm sold the game like these three women, each in their own way. Foudy could walk unfazed into board rooms and convince corporations to invest. That was not Lilly's style, however. She was subtle, explaining in simple terms what her team, her teammates, and representing her country meant to all of them. But the job was not over, and it never would be. The 1999 World Cup was a cultural revolution, and the best revolutions, after all, are constant. Who would continue after they retired? The young players in camp with them didn't have to struggle with part-time jobs. They never had to fly to Europe in a cargo plane to save money. When they went to China now, the flight is not a 52-hour ordeal, like the one the 1991 World Champions endured to get home. Do the youngsters understand what it took to get to this point? Do they know the amount of work it took so they can make a nice living playing soccer? Do they care?

Brandi is finished now. The guys are slowly getting back to work. She turns back to our group and joins in the conversation. After all, the comments from our conversation will be printed for people to read, and there is still work to do, stadiums to fill, fans to be made. That's when you understand. For Brandi and her teammates, the job will never end. And that's because it's not a job. It's a passion.

"What we did transcended generations," Kate said. "I think that's why it is so special, because a lot of different generations witnessed it together. Everybody has a story about where they were. The best thing about that is having them all come up to us later and tell us their stories."

"THERE ARE BIGGER THINGS HAPPENING HERE"

The immediate aftermath of the victory was just as they had always dreamed—thousands of fans cheering, players hugging and crying, a huge private celebration in a very public place. However, what the players did for the ensuing months was nothing they ever expected. "This is history in the making. There are bigger things happening here than just us winning a game," said striker Mia Hamm in an interview after the game.

After spending the night partying with family and friends (most of them, anyway; Mia slept until late the next day), the team took off on a coast-to-coast celebration tour. Brandi did the rounds of morning talk shows, despite not having slept in over 24 hours. When the team arrived in New York on Monday after an all-night flight from the West Coast, they found a group of girls, dressed in USA uniforms, that had slept in the airport to greet them. They went to Disney and paraded with Mickey, Minnie, and Goofy. They made appearances non-stop, did interviews, and discovered what being a sudden-celebrity was like.

After 1999, the players were thinking more seriously about the legacy they wanted to leave. Foudy and some of the other veterans were always aware of the bigger picture, but now the entire team realized the impact they were making. "It probably started in '96, but '99 put it over the top," said Kristine Lilly. "Some of the things we did or would able to do, we were like, 'Are you kidding me!' It did something that women's sports hadn't done. They respected us, not only as players but as people."

U.S. women's soccer didn't start on top of the mountain, and they were proud of the climb. The previous 14 years, the years of challenging travel and food and playing in front of tiny crowds, prepared the players for the fame. Making an impact became very important. "We have a greater commitment to the community we grew up in, the people we see every day, their brothers, sisters, fathers, mothers, people in the business world," explained Chastain.

"Julie reminds us that we are trying to impact society in the big picture. Why is it that we have held male sports in such high esteem and valued those athletes for so long and simply deny half of our population? Why is it that women spend the most money on the products you advertise, yet you spend only a quarter the amount of money talking to them? I think one of the things Julie has helped make people aware of is a passion about making a difference. One of the things we all realize is that if you are not a part of the solution, you are part of the problem. If you can't stand up and do something, you are in the way. That's the kind of leadership that you don't usually get out of sports. And that's how Julie is."

Foudy was forced to increase her leadership when Carla Overbeck endured a series of setbacks in 2000, including knee surgery to correct a problem that was worse than what Carla or her doctors first thought. The biggest change, however, was the coach. Tony DiCicco decided to resign after the 1999 World Cup. On a conference call with the team to tell them about his decision to resign, DiCicco told the team of his desire to be with his family more. April Heinrichs, who had put together a solid resume at Princeton, the University of Maryland, and the University of Virginia and as DiCicco's assistant, had been also coaching the Under-16 girls national team. Federation president Bob Contiguglia chose Heinrichs over Lauren Gregg, the team's top assistant since before China '91, whom DiCicco had endorsed.

Heinrichs started her tenure with a camp in Florida, which concluded with a match against Norway. Three years later, she would admit that she made some mistakes in that first camp—communication mistakes. Some of the players from the 1999 championship team were left out of the first camp and replaced by what was seen as the next wave of national team players. Siri Mullinix emerged as the player who would challenge Briana Scurry for the starting goalkeeper spot. Danielle Slaton and Aly Wagner, teammates at Santa Clara, looked ready to compete for playing time. Nikki Serlenga, another standout at Santa Clara, fit in as a quality defensive midfielder.

The euphoria over winning the 1999 World Cup had not yet subsided when the team had to begin focusing on the 2000 Olympics. The Sydney Games kicked off just 14 months after Brandi Chastain's Cup-winning penalty kick, and the USA had three huge question marks. First, it was not clear whether Overbeck would be able to play. Her knee injury was a lingering concern. She diligently worked to strengthen the knee in hopes of being able to help the team to its second Gold medal in four years.

Another concern was Scurry. The post-World Cup demand for the '99 team was more than anyone expected. They were invited to appear on TV talk shows and to make appearances at a wide variety of events. "The Save" put

Bri's picture on publications across the country, and all of a sudden, she was famous. "We were sensations overnight, literally. I went from being a complete unknown being recognized on the street everywhere I went," she said, adding that 50-year-old men would come up to her on the street to tell her that they cried when the team won the World Cup. Initially, Bri thought she would have her normal post-tournament rest period, during which she would go home for a week or so and then begin training again. But with opportunities of a lifetime being presented to her on a daily basis, she took advantage of her sudden fame. "Over the next three months, I was in New York seven times," she said. "But I wasn't going to the gym as often as I had been, and I was eating random food at random times."

In February of 2000, Bri and the team were in Las Vegas to receive their ESPY Award for the best sports team of the decade. She stepped on a scale in the hotel and was horrified. She had gained 30 pounds in seven months. "The extra weight helped cause some injuries," she said. "I pulled a quad muscle. Then I got shin splints that turned into a stress fracture." While Scurry was sidelined with the stress fracture, Siri Mullinix won the starting job, and when Scurry came back, Mullinix was still playing very well and kept the job. Waiting for a shot was a University of Washington sophomore named Hope Solo. Everyone knew she was the future, but Solo didn't make her first international appearance until five months before the Olympics kicked off. It was an 8-0 shutout over Iceland in Davidson, North Carolina.

The third major concern was Akers. Her career leading into the '99 World Cup had included a dozen or so knee surgeries (she says she lost track) and a handful of concussions. After the World Cup, she had her knee operated on again. She also had shoulder surgery. All that on top of her chronic illness made playing soccer very difficult, but she pushed on. She rehabbed her knee and shoulder and stuck to the diet that helped keep her energy up and bouts of Chronic Fatigue down. She thought she could make it through the 2000 Olympics and then retire. She played for the USA once more. On February 9, 2000, she started in a 2-1 to Norway in Boca Raton, Florida and then unceremoniously faded away.

Michelle Akers
Photo by Tony Quinn

THE WARRIOR AND THE SEA

The crowd, about 300 folks who came on a Friday night to listen to her speak, is curious. Like everyone she meets, they are taken by her physical presence, the regal stature and the way she carries herself that screams "athlete." Over the years, she has become a good public speaker, setting aside one-liners and popular themes to just talk. Her story is captivating, and she delivers it from her heart. This time, though, it's a little different. As she talks about the 1996 Olympics and her teammates, her eyes well up and her voice uncharacteristically cracks. The microphone drops to her side. She bows her head, steps back, and apologizes to the crowd. The crowd, however, erupts into supportive applause.

Michelle Akers is in Reformation Hall at St. Mark's Church in Burlington, North Carolina. It turns out the church's Pastor, Bob Disher, is a big sports fan, able to work into his sermons countless references to long-distance running, baseball, football, and especially Duke University basketball, references to which you learn to see coming several pews away. He'll use sports as reference points. Every sport, that is, except soccer. He knows nothing about soccer and makes that clear the night before Michelle's appearance during a meal his wife Susan carefully prepared within the restrictions of Michelle's diet.

Bob was very helpful in the process of writing Michelle's second book, *Standing Fast, Battles of a Champion*. The book described her struggle to the 1996 Gold Medal, an incredible story that involves injuries, a debilitating illness, doctors, misdiagnoses, diets, more doctors, another diet, more diagnosis, and a lot of soccer told through Michelle's words and personal journals. Most of her story revolved around her faith in God, and Bob was the expert. At dinner, Bob grilled her about being an elite athlete. He is fascinated by the inner-workings of Michelle, her determination, and, of course, her faith in God. She quickly earned a status in the Disher hierarchy just below Grant Hill. The only thing that could have possibly raised Michelle's status is if she played power forward for the Blue Devils. That summer in 1999 as the world watched women's soccer, Bob was a soccer fan. He didn't miss a game as Michelle and the USA beat Denmark, Nigeria, North Korea, Germany, and Brazil to reach the final. Knowing her story, he worried about Michelle as she suffered through each match. He was concerned as her energy, a precious commodity she guarded extremely carefully, quickly drained. He prayed for her daily. And when it came to the final, he was as nervous as any life-long soccer fanatic.

When he came out for Saturday night service at St. Mark's on July 10, 1999, Bob addressed the congregation. "This is serious," he said. "Don't anyone tell me who won the game. I taped it."

On that July night, when Bob watched the ending of the USA-China thriller, he wouldn't see Michelle on the field. He wouldn't be able to find her in the celebrations, in the interviews, or in any post-game photos. Michelle had lived the clichés—she literally gave it everything she had. She really did leave it all on the field, and she pushed herself to the actual limit. After 90 minutes in 100-degree heat, after waiving off the stretcher and staggering to the bench in a daze, she sat on the ground with cold towels on her head and slowly faded in an out of consciousness while she told DiCicco, "I can play, Tone." DiCicco, who would obviously be thrilled if she continued, looked at Dr. Doug Brown. DiCicco then gently said, "You're done Mish."

The story of Michelle's illness really starts six years earlier. Late in 1993, in a match at the Olympic Sports Festival in San Antonio, Michelle collapsed on the soccer field, something she hadn't done before. Of course, her collapse sounded alarms throughout the national team, and Michelle was forced to face the reasons. She had been suffering from migraines and fatigue. She had been struggling to do routine things, tasks that had always come easy. She said it sometimes seemed she was looking at the world through a tunnel. And there was this fog. Her collapse was her worst nightmare because it caused others to get involved. In any description of Michelle Akers, two of the first words used are usually strong, which was apparent by looking at her, and independent, which was obvious after you had any kind of interaction with her. She knew who she was and what she wanted. She would do it and succeed, and she really didn't need any help. That mentality, that temperament, formed the relentless competitor, the determined, goal-achieving star that earned her the label of FIFA Co-Player of the Century, along with China's Sun Wen.

The diagnosis she finally received—the correct one after years of misdiagnoses—was of an illness that caused her to change nearly everything that had gotten her to where she was in life. It was not something she could battle one-on-one like a defender between her and the goal, not something she could fix through pure will, stubbornness, and hard work, like one of the countless injuries had overcome. And it wasn't something that could be broken, like the spirit of so many soccer opponents over the years that had just simply chosen to give up rather than sacrifice another piece of their body for a soccer ball. But she tried. Feeling tired? Go work out. Not feeling 100 percent? Who cares? Work through it! Let's play! Come on. This was nothing. After all, a week before the 1991 World Championship opener, she slid into a sprinkler head and ripped her knee open. She scored 10 goals in six games anyway. When was she ever 100 percent? But her chosen method of cure was exactly wrong for this new thing. The more she worked, the more she fought, the worse she got.

At first they called it mono. When it didn't go away, it was obvious they were wrong. Then they called it the Epstein Barr virus, which Michelle understood to be a more serious, more debilitating form of mono. When it didn't go away, it was obvious they were wrong again. And Michelle became frustrated and scared. Finally, the doctors hit on the right diagnosis—Chronic Fatigue Immune Dysfunction Syndrome, an illness of which little was known at the time. What was known was that it was very dangerous for Michelle to be working as hard as she had been. Really she should stop. That's what the available information said. But she happened upon an expert living in Charlotte, North Carolina—Dr. Paul Cheney. Dr. Cheney and two of Michelle's most trusted allies, Dr. Mark Adams and Dr. Doug Brown, both U.S. National team doctors, learned how to help Michelle. And without those three, Michelle Akers might not have ever played in the 1996 Olympics or the 1995 or 1999 World Cups.

First, though, she had to learn to accept help from others. And that was hard for her. "I have always been a low-maintenance person, no special attention or needs," she wrote in her journal. "Now I see all these special considerations, excuses and rules to live by. I am high-maintenance. I'm fragile."

She found, however, that her teammates wanted to help. They had been trying to help. But she didn't want to be a burden. She just figured they had their own things to do to get ready, so why bring hers into it. Turns out, they admired what she was doing and learned lessons from it. Michelle chose to eat disgusting food that she couldn't stand to smell—the dreaded Elimination Diet. She chose to train and sleep, nothing else.

Why? That's a really good question. Why did she put herself through it all? The answer is nowhere to be found in the usual clichés, the easy answers we read about all the time because they are, well, easy. It wasn't for the love the game. It wasn't for the joy of competition, or any of the others. Only Michelle can answer why, but you can be relatively sure that it was a test. It was administered by Michelle and God. Her faith pushed her because that was God's plan for her. She did the rest with the help of those around her. Numerous setbacks didn't deter her from her path. But every now and then, she needed a reminder, like when team psychologist Colleen Hacker told her, "God can't guide your steps unless you are taking some." And in the early history of women's soccer, when Michelle Akers took steps, the world went with her. She was there from the start—the first training camp, the first game, the first trip abroad.

In 1995, at the second Women's World Cup, after working years to get ready, she lasted six minutes before being knocked unconscious. Doesn't seem fair, does it? Doesn't hard work pay off? Isn't effort rewarded? What about clean-living? Was her reward six minutes of soccer, 24 straight hours of sleep, and three games of sitting and watching, which by the way is something she is really bad at? Publicly, she was able to maintain dignity and even a sense of humor. When she was interviewed on ESPN by her longtime friend and college roommate Amy Allmann, Amy asked her what she remembered about the play that sidelined her. "Nothing, Amy," she laughed. "I was unconscious, remember?" When they watched the replay together, Michelle said, "Ow! That must have hurt." But she hid her red eyes behind sunglasses and tried to be the supportive teammate. She perfected the composed exterior while expecting to erupt at any moment.

Michelle, however, never expected anything she didn't earn herself. And she expected the earning part of it be very difficult. So she went back to work, setting her sights on 1996, the first-ever Olympic Soccer Tournament for women. She got her Gold medal in '96, and you felt a certain amount of vindication for her. It was much more than all that, though. The meaning, it's now evident, was not something easily explained. And that's what makes Michelle Akers so interesting, so complex, and so mysterious.

Pushing yourself to exhaustion. It's such a common phrase, one used by people who sit at desks and athletes who think they are working hard, but don't really know what hard work is. They have never experienced the truest sense of the word exhaustion. Would you do it? Would you push yourself, literally, to exhaustion every single day? Would you do it if you knew that when that day is done, you would struggle mightily just to get home? Or knowing that once you got home, you might not make it past the kitchen floor because it felt so cool lying there? Or knowing that you would be waking up several times during the night and have to change the shirt you sweated through—again? Would you insist on playing a game in 100-degree heat knowing that IVs would be required for you to have enough energy to get dressed? What would the reward have to be for you to go through all that and more? A Gold medal, maybe? Fame? Glory? How about the pure satisfaction of accomplishment? Or just for the test?

Why do people climb a mountain? Contrary to popular folklore, it's not because "It was there." Michelle climbed mountains with her dad. It was their idea of fun. They ran 5ks and marathons. Why do people do those things? Because they're tests—they're competitions. The mountain and the finish line are opponents. You can either win or lose, and winning and losing were very important to Michelle. Once after a youth soccer game, Michelle's father Bob asked his daughter, "Did you have fun?" Michelle thought, "What a stupid question? He obviously doesn't understand sports. You play to win. If you don't win, you failed."

Anson Dorrance described her by explaining that "All great players have a button they can reach down and press that takes them to another level. Michelle hit that button constantly." What did Tony DiCicco call her? Right, a warrior. Warriors are in it to win. But don't warriors go to battle so they can make a triumphant return to adoring crowds? Don't they sometimes relish in the spotlight? Some do, probably. Some don't. Michelle never had the triumphant return, no final bow. There was a brief appearance on the awards stage after the final where she received gentle hugs from her teammates, who seemed afraid that a firm embrace would send her into more pain. Then there was an introduction and a wave to the crowd at the opening game of the new professional league in Washington, D.C. two years later.

Oddly enough, in 1982, in Cooperstown, New York, a speech by Vin Scully, the legendary L.A. Dodgers announcer, explained it. Scully received the Ford Fricke award for journalism that day at the Baseball Hall of Fame. In that unmistakable tone and in the captivating style only Scully could use, he told a story about a Native American chief who wanted to test the manhood of his tribesmen by making them run up the side of a mountain to see how far they could go. "Early on the appointed morning, four braves left camp at sunrise," Scully began. "Later that afternoon, one of the braves came back with a twig of spruce. Later still, another came with a bough of pine. And it was late in the afternoon when a third brave arrived with an alpine shrub. But it wasn't until late at night by a full moon that the fourth brave arrived back in camp. 'How high did you climb? What did you bring?' asked the chief."

"The brave said, 'Where I ran, there was no spruce, no pine to shield me from the sun. There were no flowers to cheer my path. There were only sharp rocks and snow and barren land. My feet are torn, I come back late. I am empty-handed and I'm exhausted.'"

"And then a wondrous look came in his eye, and he said, 'But I saw the sea!'"

In 1999, when the final penalty kick was made and China was defeated, and her teammates were on the field hugging and crying with confetti flying around the Rose Bowl and 90,185 people cheering wildly and millions of people across the country, Bob and Susan Disher included, jumping up and down in front of TV sets, Michelle was in the locker room, shoulder throbbing, head pounding, I.V.s in her arm. She played 90 dominant minutes, during which she intimidated, even frightened, the Chinese players around her. She got I.V.s and drank coffee at halftime to get her energy up. She got punched in the head by her own goalkeeper and was knocked out. Where she had gone where was nothing to shield her from the sun, no glory, no flowers to cheer her path. The path was paved with illness, injury, and sacrifice. Like the Native American warrior, she was exhausted but not empty-handed. She had won. She passed her own test on her own terms, and on July 10, 1999, Michelle Akers finally saw the sea.

WHITE GOLD

In the 1995 World Cup when Akers suffered a concussion just six minutes into the first match, she was replaced by Tiffeny Milbrett. At that time, Milbrett showed the qualities that led observers to believe she would someday be an unstoppable offensive force. That time came in 2000. Milbrett scored 15 goals in 2000, trailing only Cindy Parlow's 19 as the team leader. In Olympic preparation games, Milbrett scored against Canada four times and added goals against Russia as well as future Olympic opponents Brazil and Norway. She saved her best performances for the 2000 Games, however. The U.S. was grouped with China, Norway, and Nigeria for the first round of the Sydney Olympics. Only two of those four teams would advance to the semifinals of the eight-team Olympic tournament, meaning that either Norway, China, or the USA—universally viewed as the best three teams in the world at the time—would be heading home at the end of the first round.

In the USA's opening match against Norway in Melbourne, Australia, Milbrett got the team off to a 1-0 lead and then hit both posts and the crossbar in the course of the match. Mia Hamm added a goal to give the USA a very convincing 2-0 win over the Norwegians. The U.S. then tied China 1-1, before eliminating Nigeria 3-1 on goals by Brandi Chastain, Kristine Lilly, and Shannon MacMillan. Meanwhile, Norway defeated China, sending the Chinese home early and ruining a chance at a rematch of the 1999 thriller between the U.S. and China. The U.S. advanced to meet Brazil in the semifinals, where Milbrett's goal sent the U.S. to the Gold-medal match to once again face Norway, who had defeated Germany in the semis.

In the opening match of the 2000 Olympics, the USA had thoroughly dominated a surprisingly lethargic Norwegian team. In particular, Milbrett ran rampant over the seemingly slow Norwegian defenders. In the final, it took just five minutes for Milbrett to give the Americans the lead, a devastating blow to the confidence of their opponents. But Gro Espeseth and Raghnild

Gulbrandsen, a future member of the WUSA's Boston Breakers, scored second-half goals to give Norway the late lead.

Growing up in Hillsboro, Oregon, in a single-parent home, Milbrett was a sideline spectator for her mom's soccer games. Elsie Parham played in an adult recreation league, one of the few for women at the time. From that point on, little Tiff was dying to be part of a soccer team, and later when Tiffeny joined as many teams as she could, her mother had just one rule—no quitting. If you commit to a team, you stick with it. "With heart," her mom told her, "you'll find a way."

Down 2-1 with literally seconds remaining in the match, the USA seemed destined to be receiving Silver medals, or what Julie Foudy prefers to call them—white Gold. But Mia Hamm chased a long pass into the right corner. In reality, few players could reach the ball before it trickled out of bounds, and even fewer could launch a playable cross once they got to it. But Hamm could. And she did. From there, Milbrett, with heart, found a way. At five-foot-two and the smallest player on the field, Milbrett leapt to reach Hamm's cross. Straining for what was possibly her personal-best vertical jump and stretching her neck as long as it would go, Milbrett nodded the ball over Norwegian goalkeeper Bente Nordby for the unlikely equalizer. The USA bench exploded, and the small band of friends and family were sent into a tizzy. The complete scope of the drama became evident after Norway kicked off to resume play. As soon as Norway touched the ball on the kickoff, the referee blew the whistle ending regulation, meaning Milbrett's goal was scored in the last second of play.

Espeseth, Norway's captain who would later star in the WUSA as Milbrett's teammate on the New York Power, would say after the game, "When Tiffeny scored, I said to myself, 'Why do they always have to win?'" But the Norwegian's regrouped and ended the game on a sudden-death Golden goal by Dagny Mellgren in the first overtime period. Through exhaustion and tears of disappointment, USA took to the podium and received White Gold.

THE WUSA CREATES NEW STARS

All of a sudden, players on the U.S. bench at the Melbourne Cricket Grounds, the cavernous 100,000-seat stadium that hosted the USA's three first-round matches, started jumping up and down, high-fiving each other, and pointing. No goal had been scored, the referee had not awarded a penalty, nor had anyone just delivered candy to the bench. What in the world are they so excited about? The scoreboard! Look at the scoreboard! Next to a head-shot of Tiffeny Milbrett, was her number, and the words "New York Power."

It was real. The professional soccer league the women had worked long and hard to form, was set to kick off in 2001. Seeing it up in lights on the scoreboard was a vindication and reminder of what they had accomplished. At the time, the Women's United Soccer Association consisted of eight teams. Each team had four players. The 20 members of the 1999 World Cup team and four others—2000 Olympians Nikki Serlenga and Michelle French, as well as LaKeysia Beene and Mandy Clemens—were allocated to the eight teams. The league, a long-time dream of the national team, was slowly taking shape.

The first-ever women's professional soccer match in the United States was played at RFK Stadium in Washington, D.C. on April 14, 2001. There were 34,000 fans that showed up to see the Washington Freedom, featuring Mia Hamm, defeat the Bay Area CyberRays, featuring Brandi Chastain, 1-0, on a 79th minute penalty-kick goal by Brazilian striker Pretinha. The CyberRays, led by Chastain, LaKeysia Beene, Tisha Venturini, Australian Julie Murray, and a pair of Brazilians—Katia and Sissi—won the championship that year. Murray slotted the winning penalty kick of the tie-breaking shootout past the Atlanta Beat's Briana Scurry.

With the advent of the WUSA, the national team had something it had lacked for its entire history—a large pool of players competing on a daily basis against the world's elite. And getting paid for it. Former college stars added depth to league rosters that included international stars like China's Sun Wen, Gao Hong, and Liu Ailing, Canada's Charmaine Hooper, England's Kelly

Smith, Japan's Homare Sawa, Germany's Maren Meinert and Bettina Wiegmann, Norway's Hege Riise, Dagny Mellgren, Bente Nordby, and Gro Espeseth, and Brazil's Sissi, Katia, and Pretinha.

The result was that the national team played just 10 matches in 2001, only two in the United States. Two games, the last two matches of the Nike U.S. Women's Cup, were cancelled. On September 9, 2001 in Chicago, the U.S. posted a 4-1 win over Germany in the first match of the tournament. The team then traveled to Columbus, Ohio, for a game with Japan. The U.S., China, Germany, and Japan arrived in Columbus on September 10th, and the Americans and Chinese checked into the Hyatt Hotel in downtown Columbus. They awoke the next morning to news that terrorists had attacked the World Trade Center and the Pentagon. By noon, the games were canceled and teams began to search for ways to get their players home. Some of the national team players were able to catch flights a day or two later, but many, including West coast residents Joy Fawcett and Shannon MacMillan, drove home. Shannon, Joy, Katey and Carli Fawcett, along with Kim Pickup who was serving as team nanny during the tournament, rented a van and headed west.

The shortened Nike U.S. Women's Cup concluded the national team's schedule for 2001. The following year, the team played a 19-game slate, winning 15, tying two (Germany and Sweden), and losing twice to Norway. But up in Canada, the Under-19 national team, coached by Tracey Bates Leone, was playing in the first-ever world championship for U-19 women. The USA 19s played an aggressive 19-game schedule leading up to the world championship tournament. The youngsters lost just twice: 4-3 to the German Under-21 national team and 3-2 to the WUSA's San Diego Spirit. They outscored their opponents 89-16, led by the dynamic front line of Lindsay Tarpley, Heather O'Reilly, and University of Texas freshman Kelly Wilson. The trio combined for 52 goals in the run-up to the world championships, with Tarpley, the team captain, leading the way with 21 in 17 games, and O'Reilly with 17 in 12 games.

In Victoria, British Columbia, the USA ran through its three first-round matches, trouncing England (5-1), Australia (4-0), and Chinese Taipei (6-0). Wilson scored four times in the three games, while Tarpley tallied three times, and O'Reilly added two goals. In the quarterfinals, the Junior Triple Edged Sword accounted for all six goals (Wilson 3, Tarpley 2, O'Reilly 1) in a dominating performance against Denmark. Germany fell 4-1 in the semifinals as Wilson recorded her fourth multi-goal game of the tournament. Tarpley and Jill Oakes scored the other two. The USA and Canada met in the final in front of 47,000 fans in Edmonton. Tarpley provided the heroics with a goal late in sudden-death overtime.

On March 3rd in Ferreiras, Portugal, the USA won its 200th game, and by the end of 2002, the team's all-time record had jumped to 213-46-27. With the team in Portugal was 17-year-old O'Reilly. She made her national team debut on March 1st, against Sweden in a 1-1 draw. O'Reilly had her sights set on making the team for the 2003 World Cup, scheduled to be played in China.

"I was in and out of a lot of camps at that time," Heather recalled. "April was high on me at that time. I never really knew for sure, but I thought I had a decent chance of making the team. A lot of it was coming down to how I was performing at the time." O'Reilly was performing well. She played in all four matches of the Algarve Cup in Portugal, coming on as a substitute each time, and she scored her first international goal against Italy on October 6th at the Nike U.S. Women's Cup in Cary, North Carolina at SAS Soccer Park, the home of the Carolina Courage and just down the road from the University of North Carolina, where O'Reilly, Tarpley, and Under-19 teammate Lori Chalupny would attend college.

In the WUSA, the Carolina Courage—led by Germany's Birgit Prinz, Norway's Hege Riise, and the USA's Danielle Fotopoulos, Tiffany Roberts, Danielle Slaton, Carla Overbeck, and 2000 Olympics backup goalkeeper Kristin Luckenbill—won the league championship, dubbed the Founders Cup, by defeating the Washington Freedom.

Roberts (Sahaydak) made her international debut as a 16-year-old. She played in a World Cup before she entered college, playing in five of six matches at the 1995 World Cup as an 18-year-old, and won an Olympic Gold medal when she was 19. At the University of North Carolina, she won a pair of national championships. At age 22, she was a member of the 1999 World Cup champions, and at 24, she was a professional soccer player. But in 2000, she was left off the USA's Olympic team roster. There was no time to feel sorry for herself, though. She went to work, improving the technical aspects of her game that had been overshadowed by her relentless defending and superb fitness. In 2003, she not only earned a spot on the World Cup roster, but she captained the Carolina Courage to the WUSA championship.

Remember, this is the same person who as a third-grader drew a picture of herself on the Olympic podium sporting three Gold medals. One day in 2003, she was asked about all her early success and reminded that by age 26, she had accomplished everything she set out to do. She was asked "What do you do when you have accomplished all your goals?" She just smiled and said, "I guess I have to set some more goals."

HOSTS AGAIN

In early 2003, China was hit by an outbreak of the deadly SARS (Severe Acute Respiratory Syndrome) virus, and the soccer community began to murmur that the World Cup, scheduled to be played in China from September 23rd to October 11th, would have to be moved to a different host country. On May 3rd, FIFA and the World Health Organization decided that playing the tournament in China presented too much of a health risk. On May 6th, Julie Foudy was told by a reporter that FIFA was moving the event to the United States.

"Shut up," Foudy said.

"No really," said the reporter. "They are going to announce it tomorrow."

"How do you know?" said Foudy, getting more and more excited. Foudy, now satisfied with the legitimacy of the information, let out a head-turning "Yeah" and chest-bumped the reporter, knocking him backward a few feet.

Sweden was the only other country to bid for the tournament, but the USA's success in organizing and staging the '99 Cup, combined with availability of large stadiums, was the obvious and best solution. FIFA hoped to be able to keep the same tournament timeframe and the USSF was able to accommodate the request. The start date was pushed back just seven days. With just four months' preparation time, the USA put on a tournament in Boston, Philadelphia, Washington, D.C., Columbus, Ohio, Portland, Oregon, and Los Angeles that attracted 365,527 fans over 32 matches, an average of 21,502 per game.

Perhaps hosting another World Cup would help refuel interest in the WUSA. The league's product on the field was very good, attendance was acceptable but not overwhelming. Management, however, was, let's say, lacking. Evidence that the ship might not run all that smoothly came with the first press release issued from the league office. The release, honest to God, was titled "Insert Catchy Headline Here." The league, however, was serving a very important purpose.

Before the 1991 world championship, the national team's player pool was developed in college. Training camps were few and far between, and the players who were selected to go to China were the ones who diligently organized their own training regimens away from formal camps and matches. For the 1995 World Cup, the U.S. Soccer Federation provided more funding for programs, international tours, and training camps. Prior to the 1996 Olympics, the player pool was sent to a USSF-funded residency program. The team was housed in Orlando, Florida, and spent months training together in preparation for their Gold-medal run. Preparation for the 1999 World Cup was done in the same residency environment, again in Orlando. Because of the quick turnaround between the '99 World Cup and the 2000 Olympics, a shorter residency program was offered. Preparation for the 2003 World Cup was done almost exclusively through the high-level competition in the WUSA.

Among the players who successfully used the WUSA to win a spot on the national team was Shannon Boxx. Her remarkable emergence proved without a doubt the need for a professional women's league in the United States. A Notre Dame graduate, Boxx, was picked up by the San Diego Spirit in the WUSA's first season. She teamed with Foudy in the Spirit midfield, playing a defensive role. She played in front of Joy Fawcett and behind forward Shannon MacMillan. She immediately won the respect of all three. Soon the rest of the league learned her value. But an invitation to train with the national team eluded her. Prior to the 2003 league season, she was traded to the New York Power, where she was recognized as one of the most dominant midfielders in the league. Still, when rosters were announced for national team training camps, her name was always seemed to be missing. With two weeks to go before the World Cup opened in Washington, D.C., Shannon's chances of making the roster were non-existent. Then, the national team held a training camp in conjunction with the 2003 Founders Cup in San Diego, where the Washington Freedom and Atlanta Beat were playing for the league's third title. Boxx was invited to the camp.

"If it wasn't for the WUSA, I never would have gotten a chance," said Shannon, who went on to make nearly 200 appearances over a dozen years for her country. "After college I went to Germany and played on a semi-pro team in Saarbrucken for a year, and when I came home I thought I was done with soccer. There just weren't that many opportunities to play at a high level after college. Then the league came along and it was great. The level of play was so high. Every game was a great challenge, and even though I didn't have any caps, April was able to see me play against the highest level players and that gave her confidence that I could do it."

The USA had two warmup matches remaining before the World Cup began: September 1st against Costa Rica and September 7th against Mexico. Against Costa Rica, Boxx started and became the first player in the history of the women's national team to score a goal in her first international appearance. Six days later against Mexico, she scored again, increasing her career stats to two games played and two goals scored. Ironically, Boxx went through the entire WUSA season without scoring a goal, although she may have led the league in hitting goalposts and crossbars. In the position she was playing for the USA, she wasn't expected to score. However, her goals, combined with her smothering defensive play, made it impossible for Heinrichs to keep her off the World Cup team.

As the women on the national team joined U.S. Soccer in a frenzied effort to promote and stage the World Cup on just four months' notice, the WUSA, which had 375 employees, 160 of which were players, had come to terms with its failed business practices. Three days before the World Cup was set to kick off in Washington, D.C.—in front of 34,000 fans at RFK Stadium who came to see the USA play Sweden—the WUSA suspended operations. It was a crushing blow to all the players in the league, but it stung the veterans most. Their dream of a fully professional league came to a stunning halt just as their focus needed to be on winning another world title.

"I wish we did not have this distraction," said U.S. captain and WUSA founding player Julie Foudy. "But the reality of the situation is that our team is not genetically pre-disposed to giving up. You never know. The odds are stacked against us, but I think there is a distinct possibility that we can keep it alive. The great thing is this league represents more than soccer to us. There is an element to this that is unique. There is something special about not just young girls, but young boys watching women play and learning to respect that they are professional athletes. It is a tragic loss for a lot of kids out there."

"Our women are eternal optimists," Heinrichs said. "We are all very disappointed with the league's collapse, but we're also optimistic. We have 30 days where everybody is sticking microphones and cameras in front of us. These women are well spoken, and if there are investors out there, I think this group can inspire them. I think that we will be discussing it and answering questions by the media. I think there will be a few days that we will have to deal with the black cloud and then we will have to put it behind us. I have great faith in these women and know they will be able to handle it during the World Cup."

"I am extremely proud to be a part of the WUSA," Mia Hamm added. "We are not giving up by any means. The economic times are not as favorable now as they were in '99, but hopefully we can push forward and rally from it."

On September 21st, the U.S. put aside their disappointment, ignored the distractions, and defeated a very good Swedish team 3-1 to get their tournament started on the highest possible note. Kristine Lilly took a nifty pass from Mia Hamm and put home a left-footed blast to give the U.S. a first-half lead. Then Cindy Parlow headed in a Hamm corner kick to make it 2-1 nine minutes before halftime. After Sweden cut the lead to 2-1, Shannon Boxx scored her third goal in as many international matches. "I'm very surprised," she said. "I'm not known to be a goal scorer. I've been one to set up players and let them score goals. I'm the assist person. But you know, I'm glad that it's coming right now. It's coming at a perfect time. If I'm going to score goals, great. Today's goal was just a relief."

"Coaches sometimes profess that new players should defer to veterans, but all that does is hold them back," said Foudy, who was nearly trampled by Boxx as the rookie went after the header for her goal. "Shannon is not deferring to anyone. She was like, 'Get outta my way!' That's wonderful. She has three caps and three goals. We're telling her to go 100 for 100."

The bad news about the USA's opening victory was that Brandi Chastain broke a bone in her foot and was lost for the tournament. Catherine "Cat" Reddick stepped in and filled Brandi's role next to Joy Fawcett in the center of the defense. At 20 years old, Cat was the youngest player on the team. When the World Cup was over, she would head back to school at the University of North Carolina, joining Tarpley and O'Reilly to help the Tar Heels to an undefeated season and another national championship. For now, though, she was enjoying the ride. The perpetual smile that graced her face, her southern charm, and her dream of being a television commentator made her a favorite of the media.

To those in Alabama, Cat would explain, North Carolina was considered the north. She came from a football family, her dad having played at the University of Georgia. "When I told my dad I wanted to play soccer, he said okay. Then he got a book on soccer coaching for dummies, got out his clipboard and his Georgia Bulldogs megaphone, and coached my team," said Cat.

The USA's next match was in Philadelphia against Nigeria. As is the case whenever the USA meets Nigeria, the Americans were expecting a physical battle, and they got it. But Nigeria's aggressive style backfired, and the United States came away with a 5-0 win. Mia Hamm scored twice and added an assist to bring her two-game total to two goals and three assists. Nigeria committed 24 fouls, and gave up two penalty kick goals—one to Hamm and one to Foudy. Cindy Parlow scored her second goal of the tournament, and Abby Wambach got her first-ever World Cup goal.

The WUSA was also a launching pad for Kylie Bivens. A star with the Atlanta Beat—which featured Briana Scurry, Cindy Parlow, Nikki Serlenga, Canada's Charmaine Hooper, Japan's Homare Sawa, and China's Sun Wen—Bivens, like Boxx and Hucles, earned a spot on the World Cup team through consistently solid play in the league. She was in the starting lineup for the USA's win over Nigeria and played 90 minutes of solid soccer. Her World Cup debut was a whole lot smoother than her international debut nine months earlier. On January 23, 2003, in Norway at the Four-Nations Tournament, the U.S. was playing Norway, and Bivens, a Santa Clara grad, was on the bench. U.S. coach

April Heinrichs called her name to enter the match, a move that took Bivens completely by surprise. "We were playing Norway, and I was thinking, 'Why would April play me against Norway?'" she recalled. "I was thinking that it was my first game, and that I probably wouldn't get in, but I wanted to get a sense of what I was supposed to do and where I was supposed to be."

When Heinrichs called Bivens' name, the U.S. defender/midfielder got excited and ran to the scorer's bench and ripped off her warm-up jacket. "The fourth official said, 'What number are you?'" Bivens remembered. When the U.S. comes out before a game to loosen up, they wear a set of warm-up jerseys, which are identical to their game jerseys, except they don't have numbers on the back. Bivens never changed into her game jersey. "Immediately, I said 'Oh my God!' I had to sprint in my studs across cement about 200 yards to the locker room to get my jersey. It was so embarrassing. The whole team made fun of me, but I guess that kind of brought me closer to them, because once they find something to make fun of you about, they just harp on it. But I still got in the game."

Bivens got another start in the USA's next World Cup match. But the 3-0 win over North Korea in front of a sold-out Crew Stadium in Columbus, Ohio, was Cat Reddick's day. Abby Wambach gave the U.S. a 1-0 lead 17 minutes into the match, then Reddick, a defender, scored twice in the second half to become the unlikely hero. "My expectations for this World Cup where to play as hard as I could and do whatever I was needed to do," said Reddick who had prepared herself to serve as a reserve in the tournament. "To score two goals like that is beyond my wildest dreams. It turned out we didn't need those two goals, because Abby finished off the penalty in the first half. But it was a lot of fun to score them. I saw my parents the next day, and they were so proud of me, so excited for me. My mom shed a couple tears. It still makes me smile because I still can't believe I did it. I can't believe I scored two goals in the World Cup."

After the game, the media clamored for Reddick, but she was nowhere to be found. Like Venturini in 1999, the star of the North Korea match was whisked away to drug-testing.

The USA won their group and moved to Foxboro, Massachusetts, outside of Boston to take on Norway in the quarterfinals. Always considered among the favorites to win a World Cup, the Norwegians defeated France to open the first round and then fell to Brazil by a surprisingly large 4-1 margin. As is their pattern, though, they regrouped and trounced South Korea 7-1 to set up the quarterfinal match with their American rivals.

Abby Wambach
Photo by Tony Quinn

THE PETITE ONE

They had a table toward the back of the restaurant, a little Italian place in the Federal Hill area of Providence, Rhode Island, the kind of place where the owner and his wife cook and get insulted if you don't eat a lot—in other words, too much. There's little chance the group at the table in the back will be eating light. You see, the Wambachs are here. They are minus little sister Abby. She's back at the team hotel. She has a game tomorrow in Foxboro, a short drive from Providence.

Abby Wambach, the USA's 23-year-old striker, is the youngest of seven kids in the Wambach family. She has two older sisters and four older brothers. At five-foot-11, she owns balls in the air, and her strength and ability to take physical punishment have caused comparisons to Michelle Akers. Size, you see, runs in the family. "Have you seen her brothers?" Julie Foudy said. "They are like twice the size of her. Abby's the petite one in the family."

That could be the only time the word petite was used to describe Abby Wambach, who admits that nothing that could happen to her on a soccer field could be worse than what her brothers handed out to her on a regular basis. They played tackle football, fired hockey pucks at her, and never did they give her a break because she was a girl.

Her sister Laura, who played college soccer at Xavier University, says her little sister was never afraid of the big kids and competed full-out, even as a 10-year-old. When the family went to McDonald's, she says, Abby would take a bite out of each of her French Fries so her big brothers would steal them

When talking about the history of soccer in the United States, there are certain cities that have to be mentioned, and they aren't necessarily the ones you would expect. Sure, New York, Chicago, Boston, and Philadelphia played major roles, but so did places like Milwaukee, Portland, St. Louis, and—yes—Rochester, New York, Abby Wambach's hometown. In the 1940s, Rochester became the new home of many Eastern Europeans who left war-torn Europe in search of jobs. Companies like Eastman Kodak, Xerox, and the Genesee

Brewing Company were the attractions. With the Eastern Europeans came, of course, soccer. In the 60s came professional soccer with the Rochester Lancers. In the '70s and '80s came the North American Soccer League, and Rochester played host to legends like Franz Beckenbauer, Johan Cruyff, and Pele.

The U.S. Women's National Team was in Rochester on September 18, 1998. In fact, Mia Hamm scored international goal number 100 that night. It came in a 4-0 win over Russia and made her just the fourth woman to score 100 goals. Italy's Elisabeth Vignotto and Carolina Morace and USA's Michelle Akers were the others. Ironically, the player who eventually scored more international goals than any of them, the 1997 High School Player of the Year at Our Lady of Mercy, was not there. Wambach was a freshman at the University of Florida. Seventeen days before Mia scored her 100th goal, the Gators were in Orlando, Florida, at, of all places, the University of Central Florida, where a year earlier Hamm and the U.S. team spent the first half of their Olympic journey. Florida posted a 3-0 win over UCF, and Wambach scored her first collegiate goal. She tallied 19 times as a freshman in 1998 and helped the Gators to the NCAA title with future national team players Danielle Fotopoulos and Heather Mitts.

Even though she scored 19 goals, helped her team to a national championship, and was named NCAA Freshman of the Year, Abby was not the featured attraction for the Gators. Fotopoulos lead the country in scoring with 32 goals, and Mitts was on her way to more than 100 international appearances for the U.S., as well as a modeling career and the title of ESPN's 2004 "Hottest Female Athlete."

But Abby was the featured player in Foxboro. She produced the only goal of the match, and the USA headed to Portland for the semifinals. Ironically, the loss not only knocked Norway, the defending Olympic champion, out of the World Cup, but it knocked them out of the next Olympics as well. Because of the quick turnaround between the World Cup and the Olympics—10 months from the World Cup final to the Olympic opener—the World Cup served as the qualifying stage for women's Olympic soccer. Only the top three finishing European teams would go to the 10-team Olympic Games. One of those teams would be the host, Greece. Sweden and Germany, who both advanced to the World Cup final, were the other two.

Germany, who ripped through the first round with wins over Canada (4-1), Japan (3-0), and Argentina (6-1), demolished Russia in the quarterfinals 7-1 and anxiously awaited the Americans in Portland, Oregon. The task facing the USA was daunting. Many of the German players still stung from the dramatic 3-2 loss to the USA in 1999, and many observers listed them as the tournament favorites. Leading the way for Germany was Birgit Prinz, and the USA was very familiar with her. As a member of the Carolina Courage, Prinz quickly became the most dangerous offensive player in the WUSA upon her arrival in 2002. After one match against the Courage, New York Power defender Christie Pearce (Rampone) called Prinz "technical, fast and strong—pretty much your worst nightmare."

"We've already done what we set out to do, and I think we can feel pretty relaxed," Prinz said before the match. "The pressure is on the USA now. They are the hosts and favorites, and they're expected to win the title. We've got nothing to lose."

Germany scored early. Kristin Gerefrekes nodded in a header off a corner kick in the 15th minute, and Germany entered the second half with a 1-0 lead. As the game wore on, the USA mounted attack after attack that was turned aside by an organized and steady German defense and goalkeeper Silke Rottenberg, who was playing the game of her life. Rottenberg smothered two chances by Hamm and made a diving stop on a Kristine Lilly blast. But more impressively, she handled every American cross flawlessly. The USA took 15 shots and launched 10 corner kicks but could not muster a goal. Then, with the U.S. becoming increasingly desperate, Germany caught them on two counter-attacks in stoppage time. Maren Meinert scored in the 91st minute, and Prinz added the final blow in the 93rd.

The loss was crushing to the USA, especially to the veterans. What would be the last World Cup for many of them was over before the final. The chance to relive the glory of 1999, the opportunity to again kick-start their professional league, the chance to lift the World Cup on their home soil was all lost to a superior German team. It was hard to take. The tears and disappointment lasted a day. Then, as they have done throughout their careers, they found the bright side. The USA had established a habit of collecting Olympic Gold medals. The World Cup loss was the perfect motivation. They looked ahead.

FAREWELL PARTY FOR
THE OLD LADIES

The USA went to Greece with an 18-player roster. Briana Scurry and Kristin Luckenbill were the goalkeepers. Joy Fawcett, Brandi Chastain, Kate Markgraf, Christie Rampone, Cat Reddick, and Heather Mitts were the defenders. Foudy, Lilly, Boxx, Aly Wagner, Tarpley, and Angela Hucles were the midfielders, while Hamm, Abby Wambach, Cindy Parlow, and O'Reilly were the forwards. Tiffany Roberts and Shannon MacMillan were named alternates. They would be called into action in the event of an injury or a suspension. Upon their arrival in Athens, the veterans were instantly reminded of why the Olympics are so special. "You see people everywhere walking around in their national team gear. Some of the rookies had no idea it was this big," said Foudy. "They asked me if the Olympic experience got old. I told them it never gets old, first time or third time around."

Abby Wambach added, "It's overwhelming. It felt good to finally be here and feel what it's like. We had so many different things and visions in our minds, but nothing compares to the reality of being here. It's thrilling to see so many different athletes and feel how much hard work everyone has put in to get here."

The Americans opened the tournament by disposing of Greece, the hosts who were not expected to win a game. A win over Brazil had the USA where they wanted to be after two matches, but a disappointing draw against Australia caused some concern in the media that Hamm, Foudy, Lilly, Fawcett, and Chastain were past their prime, and that ending their careers with a Gold medal was far-fetched. But a win over Japan in the quarterfinals sent the USA into the semifinals for a rematch against Germany, which was determined to stack an Olympic championship on top of their World Cup title and signal their arrival as the world's most dominant team.

Growing up in New Jersey, O'Reilly was one of the thousands of young girls who had a Mia Hamm poster on her bedroom wall. She was also part of the throng that screamed "Meee-yaaa" at national team matches. Now in an Olympic quarterfinal match, O'Reilly found herself playing alongside Hamm. Not only did she have the burden of playing with the greatest female player in history, she was doing so in an environment where winning was crucial and losing would be heartbreaking. "They don't have to say it," Heather said of the veterans heading into retirement. "It's on our minds all the time."

The Americans had taken a 1-0 lead on a 33rd minute goal by Lilly and carried the lead into injury time— three minutes into injury time to be exact. Then a shot by Germany's Isabell Bachor deflected off the hip of Fawcett and past Scurry for the tying goal. Overtime would be needed to decide this one. And as the team gathered during the break, Foudy took over— "We are NOT going to lose this game," she insisted as her teammates hung onto every word, becoming more and more confident of the outcome.

Three minutes into overtime, O'Reilly penetrated into the Germany box and knocked a soft left-footer over on-rushing Silke Rottenberg, the German goalkeeper who stymied the Americans 10 months earlier in Portland. O'Reilly's shot curled slowly toward the net and bounced off the post. "I was pretty upset about it," she said. "But you just have to forget about things like that." O'Reilly would get another chance later, and the way the moment played out should have been a sign to everyone that destiny and drama were playing a large part in the 2004 Olympics.

Nine minutes into overtime, Hamm knifed through the German defense, chopping, slashing, and changing directions like Carin Gabarra once did. Mia, of course, drew a crowd of German defenders, but she somehow found a small gap, an area the players call "a seam," between the collection of feet. Then as if one very loud fan was screaming in her ear, she heard "MEEEEE-YAAAAAA" coming from her left. It wasn't the first time Heather O'Reilly screeched Hamm's name, but it was the most forceful and the most demanding. Hamm had to hurry, though. O'Reilly's acceleration was well known among her teammates, and Heather exploded into the open space. Mia's pass arrived at the same time.

"What these women have done has been so remarkable," Heather said after the game. "This is it for some of them. As young players, we wouldn't be happy sending them out with anything but a Gold. This is just one more step toward that. Mia was amazing when setting up my goal. I was just in the right place at the right time. With a pass of that class, you don't need to blast the ball. It's more a question of guiding it home. The hard part was the run to get there."

But Mia made sure everyone knew what O'Reilly did. "Heather's greatest attribute is that she always wants to make an impact," she explained. "The goal she scored was nowhere near as easy as it may have looked. She took it really well, and that speaks volumes for her character."

All that was standing between the U.S. and the Gold medal was Brazil, a very, very good Brazil team that destroyed Mexico 5-0 in the semifinals behind the awe-inspiring play of a pair of youngsters Marta and Cristiane. Meanwhile, the Americans needed a 59th minute goal from Wambach in the semis to get past Japan 2-1. Brazil and the U.S. met in the group stage of the tournament, with the U.S. taking a 2-0 win on second-half goals by Hamm and Wambach.

It was Tarpley's turn to signal her arrival into the big time. Thirty-nine minutes into the match, with the USA giving everything they had to contain, control, and slow down the high-flying Brazilian attack, Tarpley received the ball in the center of the field 30 yards out. She took a touch and unloaded a missile that Brazilian keeper Andreia had no chance to reach. Once again, though, the Americans could not hold the lead. Pretinha, the former Washington Freedom and San Jose CyberRays striker, tied it up in the 73rd minute.

Wambach emerged as an international force in the 2003 World Cup. In the '04 Olympics, she added to her reputation by scoring three goals in the USA's first five games. Her fourth Olympic goal ended the tournament. Twenty-two minutes into overtime, eight minutes before a shootout would have decided the Gold medal, Kristine Lilly launched a cross from the left corner that Wambach buried with a smashing header. "Being part of this team with so many legends is extraordinary," she said. "They've done so much for our sport and we have a responsibility to them. By winning these Olympics, maybe we can give back to them what they've given all of us."

Much as was the case in 1999, exhaustion gave way to euphoria as the Americans stormed the field in celebration. The Olympic Games officially closed with Mia Hamm serving as the flag bearer in the parade of nations, but the enduring memory is of Hamm, Foudy, Fawcett, and Lilly on the medal stand, Gold medals hung proudly around their necks, tearfully singing, or rather screaming, the national anthem.

THE LEGACY OF "IT"

The word "legacy" was mentioned a lot as some of the veterans moved toward retirement. "When the veterans retire, their legacy should be their demeanor—the way they handle every situation," explained Kate Markgraf. "I've seen them handle the good, the bad, social, private. In every situation, a human being encounters on the soccer field or in a boardroom or wherever, they handle it with grace, humility, and dignity. Every single time. Sometimes they might not say it right, but their actions are perfect. Most of the time, they say the right thing and do the right thing. But it's intrinsic to them. It's not like they turn it on and off. They didn't say, 'Okay, now were are celebrities, we should act this way.' They always act the same way. They were acting that way in 1998 when I first came on the team and none of them were celebrities."

The veterans were more concerned with the legacy of the team than their personal legacy. Over the years, there was a simple explanation for someone who didn't quite make the team, someone with all the necessary talent, but not the extra something required to compete and succeed at the standard established by the U.S. Women's National Team. The key word was "It." Did they "Get It?" It referred to an understanding of, among other things, history and accomplishments and attitude and team chemistry. "There have been very few players over the 20-year history that don't get it or don't earn it that are here for very long," said April Heinrichs. "They always fall by the wayside. The ones that are just on the outskirts of getting it are pulled in by other players. Not the coaching staff, but by other players."

Tracey Leone added, "Now that U.S. Soccer has more youth teams, we are able to teach them 'it' at 14 years old. We can prepare the youth national teams to climb this ladder, and we can tell them that it is way more than just about the ball."

By all accounts, Heather O'Reilly always got it. From time to time, however, she needed a reminder. "I've heard stories about Haiti and Bulgaria," said Heather who is closer in age to Joy Fawcett's oldest daughter than she is to Joy

Fawcett. "When we go to China, we bring along a huge snack trunk. Once, the oatmeal was gone by the last day, and I said something about not having enough oatmeal. The veterans were like, 'Easy. We used to not have anything like this.' Even four or five years ago, their trips to China were not so great."

O'Reilly earned the respect of the coaches as well as the veterans on the team to reach her potential and wear the label of "the future" along with Tarpley. They were two of the players fortunate enough to see their names posted on a sheet on the wall that listed the players who would represent the USA in the 2007 World Cup.

"That day is just filled with so many emotions," O'Reilly said of the day the roster was posted. "There are people you lived with for three months that didn't make the team. It's tough. But a couple days later, you take a deep breath and say, 'Okay, now I can just chill out and play.' You don't have to worry about making the roster anymore. You can't let down your play or your competitive spirit at all, but mentally you just get to feel a little bit more secure."

"Abby gets it," said Julie Foudy confidently. Wambach, it seems, is one of those people who observe and learn. At age five, she learned a lesson that would stick with her forever. One of her older brothers approached Los Angeles Dodgers legend Sandy Koufax for an autograph. Koufax, who Wambach said was sick that day, snapped at Abby's brother and brushed him aside. "That really made a big impression on me," she said 20 years later. "I always said that if I were ever able to be a role model, I would definitely take the extra time to make sure that all the kids were happy. It doesn't take that much time to say 'Hello,' or, when I'm signing autographs after a game to actually make a connection, whether it's eye contact or an actual conversation with them. I set a goal for myself to try and make an impact with the fans."

With the national team, she learned from watching the commitment, the drive, the passion, and the humility her U.S. teammates exhibited. She watched and learned about the media. That, too, was a responsibility, and she excelled at it, taking over from Foudy as spokesperson for the team, someone who is allowed to speak for the team, but not for the players themselves, a fine line on which Foudy and Abby both danced expertly. And her WUSA experience gave her the opportunity to observe Mia Hamm. "She does things, and I watch," said Wambach, who had been watching the U.S. star for quite a while. In 1999, as the Americans marched through the FIFA Women's World Cup to the title, Wambach was in her second year of college at the University of Florida.

"I had posters up on my wall, and I watched the '99 World Cup," she said. "But I didn't necessarily want to be Mia. I just wanted to be able to play with her."

Wambach got her chance when Washington acquired her rights in 2002. "She's interesting because we haven't actually sat down and talked about what

I need to do to become a better person," she said. "That's all stuff I've learned through playing with her, through just talking with her, short conversations about what we need to do. Because I respect her so much, part of me wanted to stop before breaking any of her records, but I've got this World Cup title that I've never won, and I have to keep scoring goals to get there."

After winning the 2004 Olympic Gold, Heinrichs ushered Mia Hamm, Julie Foudy, Joy Fawcett, and Brandi Chastain into retirement, telling a silent locker room before their last game that "some of you someday will be able to tell your children and grandchildren that you played with these women."

Heinrichs also moved on. In 2005, she became a consultant for U.S. Soccer and began serving as women's technical director. She was replaced as head coach by Greg Ryan, a former U.S. professional player, long-time college coach, and an assistant under Heinrichs. The USA played just nine games in 2005, winning eight and tying one. Ryan, a former defender, preferred a more counter-attacking style of play than any of his predecessors. The system, without a doubt, benefitted Abby Wambach, who in 2006 scored 17 times in 22 games. Ryan's tenure, however, came to an end after the 2007 World Cup.

The USA went to China for the 2007 World Cup with lofty expectations. But in the opening match, the USA saw a 1-0 second-half lead evaporate when North Korea scored twice in a two-minute span. The Americans needed a 69th minute goal by Heather O'Reilly to escape with a tie. Three days later, Abby Wambach scored twice, her second and third goals of the tournament, to defeat Sweden, 2-0. Hope Solo recorded her first World Cup shutout. North Korea defeated Nigeria in their second match, creating an interesting final day of group play with the USA playing Nigeria and North Korea facing Sweden. A combination of a U.S. win and a North Korea win or tie and the Americans would win their group.

Lori Chalupny scored the only goal of the USA's win over Nigeria, while Sweden defeated the North Koreans 2-1. The U.S. advanced to the quarterfinals to play England, who advanced partly because of a pair of draws, first against Japan behind two goals by Seton Hall and WUSA star Kelly Smith, and then holding Germany 0-0. Wambach, Boxx, and Lilly scored in a 12-minute span of the second half to give the U.S. a 3-0 win over England and a date with Brazil in the semifinals.

Since the opening day tie with North Korea, the U.S. had rattled off three wins, scoring six times. Abby Wambach scored three of those goals. And since Kim Yong-Ee beat her in the 60th minute of the first match, Hope Solo went 300 minutes without allowing a goal.

Hope Solo
Photo by Tony Quinn

PART IV

THERE'S HOPE IN GOAL

The most toxic place in America. That's what the Hanford Nuclear Plant in Richlands, Washington, was called. The Hanford site was used as part of the Manhattan Project, which developed the Atomic Bomb during World War II. In fact, the bomb the United States dropped on Nagasaki, Japan in 1945, code name "Fat Man," was made at the Hanford site. After WWII, Hanford stayed busy as the Cold War with the Soviet Union kept the need for nuclear weapons going. The sports teams at Richland High School are named "The Bombers" and their logo is, believe it or not, a mushroom cloud. Richland is now famous for something other than its weapons-making history. Richland, you see, is the hometown of Hope Solo.

As Solo detailed in her book *Solo, A Memoir of Hope*,[1] she was conceived in prison. Her father had a mysterious past, including two social security numbers and an embezzlement conviction. He was arrested in front of her for kidnapping her and her brother simply because he loved them. Hope discovered he had another family somewhere in Michigan. The other wife, oddly enough, had the same name as her mother, Judy Lynn. He disappeared on a regular basis, leading Hope to believe that he could've been in the witness protection program. And he reappeared at the strangest times, like that fall afternoon in Seattle after a five-year absence, 200 miles from Richland, when just before one of her youth games, he came walking out of the woods where he lived in a make-shift shelter.

But she knew her dad would do anything for his "Baby Hope." And that might very well be all she needed. So what carried her through all that and helped her become widely considered the best goalkeeper in the world? Great question, and it probably has a thousand answers.

Controversy followed Solo around. But she always had sports, a place where she could consistently be successful, where she could prove herself, where her family could watch her with pride. In high school, the chants of "Nuke 'em, nuke 'em, nuke 'em till they glow," echoed in the gym at her basketball games. She played forward on her soccer team and scoring goals came easy. As she moved up the ladder to more competitive teams and into a larger pool of skillful players, she ended up in goal.

Whoever first said that it is a small world had to have been involved in soccer. In 1984, a year after Hope Solo was born outside of Seattle, Michelle Akers left town to attend the University of Central Florida. She didn't know it at the time, but a Seattle-area rival, Amy Allmann, a goalkeeper with whom she had many youth soccer battles, was recruited to UCF as well. Amy arrived on campus and went to her dorm, peeking in to get a glimpse of her new roommate. "Oh great," she said. "I have to room with her." For Akers, the feeling was mutual. The two became close friends, though.

It was Amy Allmann who was the backup goalkeeper to Mary Harvey at the 1991 World Cup. She was the National Goalkeeper of the Year at UCF in 1987. Allmann was part of ESPN's broadcast team in Sweden in 1995 where she watched Akers get knocked out and sprain her MCL. She was part of the broadcast team that covered the 1999 Women's World Cup, as well as the 2000 Olympics in Australia. In 1996, after spending three years as the first head coach at the University of New Mexico, Amy, now Amy Griffin, joined head coach Lesle Gallimore at the University of Washington. Gallimore's college career at the University of Cal-Berkeley overlapped with Carin Jennings.

Griffin began working with the Washington State Olympic Development Program, and in 1995. One player beginning to excel in the ODP environment was a 14-year-old named Hope Solo. Solo would eventually forget her desire to go to college far, far away from Richlands and attend the University of Washington to play for Gallimore and Griffin. She spurned offers from established national powers like Santa Clara, Portland, Virginia, and the University of North Carolina to help put UW on the women's soccer map. Gallimore and Griffin became important figures in Hope's life. They were her advisors, protectors, and motivators.

And to further prove how small the soccer world really is, 10 years after Hope graduated from UW, Katey Fawcett, the daughter of Joy, who literally grew up with the U.S. National team, joined the Huskies to play for Gallimore and Griffin.

One seemingly insignificant statement from Gallimore turned out to be very significant to Hope. As reported in her autobiography, a fascinating book co-authored by Ann Killion, titled *Solo, a Memoir of Hope,* Solo scheduled a recruiting visit to the University of Virginia, which was coached by April Heinrichs, who would soon become the national team coach. Gallimore told Hope that she was good enough that no national team coach was going to pick her based on where she went to college. With that, Solo picked the University of Washington and helped the Huskies into the elite group of Division I college soccer.

And Gallimore was right, just as she had been when she told Solo that she could see Hope on the Gold Medal platform someday. The path from college freshman to best goalkeeper in the world was not smooth, though.

First came her youth national team duty, where Solo earned positive reviews playing for the Under-16, Under-19, and Under-20 national teams. She was good enough to be seen as the goalkeeper of the future. Fans got their first glimpse of that future in April of 2000 when Hope, as a college sophomore, was in goal for an 8-0 USA win over Iceland, but in her first three years with the U.S., she played just seven games serving as a backup to Siri Mullinix, who would earn the starting job in the 2000 Olympics. Meanwhile, back in Pullman, Washington, Hope was piling up the wins and the awards. Four times she was named to the all-conference team, and in 2000, 2001, and 2002, she earned All-American status. After travelling to the 2004 Olympics in Greece as an alternate behind Briana Scurry and Kristin Luckenbill, she became the USA's first-choice keeper in 2005. What followed was a 55-game unbeaten streak that stretched through July 2008.

But what happened when the USA played Brazil in the World Cup semifinals in Hangzhou, China on September, 27, 2007, unfortunately, drew attention from her performance in goal.

That game was dreadful. Fans of the national team were introduced to some new feelings—inadequacy, frustration, and worse yet, hopelessness. Prior to the semifinal against Brazil on September 27th, USA coach Greg Ryan made what was seen by more than a few as an odd decision. He chose to sit Solo and play Scurry in goal. Scurry, 36 years old but still seen as world-class, had not played a game for the USA in 46 days when she came on as a substitute for Solo in a 6-1 win over New Zealand. Ryan had given Solo all the work leading up to the World Cup. Through the first four matches of the World Cup, Solo had given up just two goals, both coming in a 2-2 draw with North Korea in the opener. From there, she had shutouts over Sweden, Nigeria, and in the quarterfinals against England. But on Ryan's mind was a 2-0 shutout Scurry posted on June 23rd over the Brazilians, her last start. Ryan reasoned that Scurry was better suited for Brazil's style. Hope disagreed. It showed.

The USA's World Cup semifinal match against Brazil began with Shannon Boxx receiving a yellow card just 14 minutes into the game, and an own goal by Leslie Osborne put Brazil up 1-0. Just before halftime, Boxx received her second yellow, and the USA was forced to play the rest of way with 10 players. By that time, however, Brazil already had a 2-0 lead. Caught in the awful position of trying to push forward for a goal when you are already shorthanded defensively, the U.S. was torn apart the rest of the way. The more they tried to push forward to cut Brazil's lead, the more they were punished. Under Ryan, the USA had come to count heavily on Abby Wambach, and she usually responded. But on this day, with just 10 players and clearly out of sync, the U.S. attack fell short time after time. At the other end, Scurry often appeared alone against Brazil's dangerous combination of a natural attacking instinct, growing confidence and a chance to humiliate the USA. The Brazilians danced their way to a 4-0 victory.

A post-game encounter with a reporter, a steaming mad Solo, and some poorly chosen words was a terrible combination. It created a firestorm. Solo made her feelings known, saying Ryan was wrong. She felt sure she could have saved the goals, and that the U.S. was living in the past by playing Scurry in goal. It was interpreted as Solo being disrespectful to her coach and teammate. She was dismissed from the team amidst pile of bad press for the national team, both pro- and anti-Hope. But the Americans rebounded and won the third-place match 4-1 over Norway behind two goals from Wambach and one each from Lori Chalupny and Heather O'Reilly. Scurry was in goal.

ENTER PIA

Germany defeated Brazil in the final, becoming the first nation to win back-to-back Women's World Cups. The excellence of nations like Germany and Brazil, combined with the emergence of quality sides like Japan, England, who tied Germany in group play, North Korea, who drew with the U.S., and Australia, who tied Norway, had made international competitions less predictable. Now it seemed the recognized powers of women's soccer could lose at any time. The U.S., at a minimum, needed to keep up. More importantly, though, it needed to get back to the top. To do that, U.S. Soccer fired Ryan and hired former Swedish International Pia Sundhage, owner of credentials that appeared to be exactly what the USA needed. She had 71 international goals for Sweden. She spent eight years coaching Swedish club teams, she was an assistant for the Philadelphia Charge, and she was head coach of the Boston Breakers, both of the WUSA. In 2007, she was the assistant coach for China. And she played the guitar. In her first meeting with the team, she showed up with her guitar and sang Bob Dylan's "The Times They are a Changing." Abby Wambach would joke later that Pia's meetings were more like musicals.

A unique personality, Sundhage was different from the U.S. coaches who came before her, an interesting combination of intensity and joy. Watching her work in training sessions and on the sidelines during games, it was obvious she enjoyed everything she was doing. "She eats, sleeps, and breathes soccer," said Heather O'Reilly.

In the U.S., Sundhage became one of those personalities who are recognized by one name. She was just Pia to team members, fans and media. The media took to her quickly, partially because it's safe to safe that before being introduced to Sundhage they rarely had their questions answered with a song, which the new coach did frequently.

Pia's history with international women's soccer dates back further than the USA's, 10 years longer, in fact. She made her international debut in 1975 as a 15-year-old and played through the 1996 Olympics. Her 71 career goals were the most all-time for Sweden until Hanna Ljungberg scored her 72nd in 2009. She pretty much saw it all, and from several different angles—a pioneering player, a club coach in two different countries, and a coach or assistant coach for three different countries. She went from being a player laughed at by those who thought women shouldn't play soccer to having her image on a postage stamp in Sweden.

And, perhaps most importantly, players responded to her. "She is very, very passionate about the game, and that carries over to the team," said O'Reilly. "She has confidence in her players and that spills over. She wants players to play freely and have fun."

In 2008, the team went 33-2-1. New players were brought in seamlessly. Amy Rodriguez added a dimension of speed and quickness to the USA attack, complimenting Wambach's size and power. After appearing in just five games prior to 2008, Rodriguez, who balanced time between the University of Southern California and U.S. Youth National Team, played in 26 international games for the U.S., contributing six goals and seven assists in Pia's first full season.

The USA entered the 2008 Olympic qualifying tournament featuring a mix of the past, present, and future. Two players remained from 1999—Kate (Sobrero) Markgraf and Christie (Pearce) Rampone. Other veterans included Wambach, O'Reilly, Boxx, and Angela Hucles. Two members of the broadcast team for the 2016 World Cup were on the roster—Aly Wagner and Heather Mitts, a University of Florida teammate of Abby Wambach, who had returned to the team after recovering from knee surgery. Tobin Heath and Rachel Buehler were playing in their first major tournament for the U.S.

Also named to her first major tournament was 25-year-old Natasha Kai. Sporting over 60 tattoos, Kai grew up in Kahuku, Hawaii, a town of 2,600 people near Honolulu on the island of Oahu. Kai starred for the University of Hawaii and turned heads as the leading scorer on the 2004 U.S. Under-21 team. She got her first taste with the full U.S. team in 2006 and scored in her first two appearances, wins over Denmark and France. In 2008, she scored a team-high 15 goals. Four of those goals helped the U.S. through the Olympic qualifying rounds.

OH NO!

After successfully qualifying for the '08 Olympics, the USA won 10 straight games heading into an exhibition match with Brazil in San Diego on June 16th. The two teams played three days earlier in Colorado with the U.S. winning 1-0 on a goal by Amy Rodriguez. The rematch in San Diego would serve as the USA's going-away party before the Olympics.

There was no party. The game was just 31 minutes old when Abby Wambach sprinted after a ball in Brazil's half of the field. When Wambach, five-feet-11 inches of strength, determination, and power, set her mind on getting to a particular ball, she was going to get there. But this time, someone else was on a similar mission. Andreia Rosa, a 24-year-old, two-year veteran for Brazil and future physical education teacher, crashed into Wambach just as Abby was striking the ball with her left foot. It was nothing new to see Wambach go down, or go down hard. The most dangerous goal-scorer in the world at the time, she was often at the mercy of desperate and over-matched defenders, frantically trying to do anything to stop her. Seeing Abby Wambach on the ground was a common site.

What was uncommon, however, was seeing her lay awkwardly, legs stationary. It was certainly extremely rare seeing her immediately motion for the trainers to come to her aid. First the trainers came, then the team doctors, then the stretcher, and then a brace was put on her left leg. Just a precaution, fans hoped. Abby winced in pain as she was lifted to the stretcher and strapped down. She left in an ambulance. Soon, what the USA feared was confirmed.

Three months. That's how long she was expected to be on the sideline. That's how long you have to sit out when you break your tibia and fibula, and that's what the doctors tell you when you have a titanium rod surgical Inserted into your leg. The Olympics started in 45 days.

Now what? Just eight months ago, you were eliminated from the World Cup. You can still see Brazil dancing and celebrating after knocking off you and your teammates 4-0 in that strange, ugly game in China. Another Olympic

Gold medal seemed like a good remedy for those bad memories, right? Well, no matter how you try, you cannot fit three months of healing and rehabbing into 45 days. That has to be devastating, right? How long does it take to get over it? For Abby Wambach, the public one at least, she started getting over it on the stretcher leaving the field. It seemed to begin with a thumbs-up to the crowd as she was wheeled away.

"Obviously, it's devastating," Abby said a few days later in a press release. "But above everything else, I'm only one player, and you can never win a championship with just one player. I have the utmost confidence in this team bringing home the Gold. I'm excited to watch them and cheer them on during this challenge they've been presented with. I love them all so much and appreciate so many people involved with this game and the team. I put my heart and soul into this game every day, but sometimes accidents happen. I've gotten so many calls already, and I just want to say how much I appreciate that."

"There's no question of whether or not I'll come back from this—it's more when I'll come back," she told media on a conference call. "Will it take a lot of hard work and dedication, pain, and suffering? Probably. Do I think about the type of role model that I can be to someone who is going through the same thing? Absolutely. We aren't on the planet alone and whether people like to admit it or not, all we can do is learn from each other in the course of a lifetime. I sometimes struggle because I don't find myself inspiring, because it's just me, in my own skin. If people feel like that, then let's use this as another experience to give them a gauge in how to react in tough situations, give them a platform as a possibility. What I want the younger generation to feel and see from this, first and foremost, is that I'm coming back."

Natasha Kai scored that day, and the U.S. beat Brazil 1-0. After the game, however, she was not talking about her goal. Her "heart sank" when she saw Abby go down, she told the Associated Press. "We need her. She's a big piece of a great team." How great of a team were they without what was considered their most important piece? That's the question now. What was it Wambach called it? A challenge. And she said she had the "utmost confidence" in them. Were those just words to say when you have to say something? Or, did she truly believe the whole was greater than any of its parts? Good questions that only time would be able to answer.

One thing was for sure, though. The team was going to have to find a way to score goals. Not just goals, but big goals at big moments. They needed someone to step up in a big way. How about Carli Lloyd? Think maybe she could do it?

The 2-0 loss to Norway in the USA's first Olympic game fueled the fears that without Wambach, the U.S. would be out of medal contention. Similar to 1995 when the USA tied China in the World Cup opener without Akers, the team seemed to be a little lost without Wambach—its go-to player, the player who had always been counted on to provide whatever was needed to win a game, especially an important game. In the 2008 Olympics, Carli Lloyd gave a glimpse that she had an uncanny ability to score big goals, some of them coming at the most dramatic moments.

In 2002, Carli Lloyd represented the USA at the prestigious Nordic Cup, the top international competition for Under-21 national teams. She helped the USA to Nordic Cup title that year, while playing for Rutgers University and earning all the accolades that accompany elite athletes—all conference, All-America, conference player of the year. The U.S. Under-21 national team was a breeding ground for the senior national team, and Lloyd seemed to have paid the dues and put in her time. Now, it seemed, she would take the logical next step to the senior team. Didn't happen. The coach of the U.S. Under-21 team in 2003, Chris Petrucelli, sat Lloyd down one day at a training camp in New Jersey and told her she was talented, but there were holes in her game that needed work. He was not going to take her to the Nordic Cup.

Huh? Wait. What goes through a player's mind at a time like that? Blaming the coach is the easy part. What does he know? He just doesn't understand how I play. With Petrucelli, though, that excuse would be tough to prove. Among his players while he was the head coach at Notre Dame was World Cup and Olympic veterans like Kate Sobrero, Shannon Boxx, Jenny Streiffer, Holly Manthei of the U.S., as well as Monica Gonzalez and Monica Gerardo of Mexico, and Anne Makinen of Finland. Or maybe the player begins to think they are simply not good enough. Lloyd had a nice career, but maybe it was time to give up that dream she had of being a professional soccer player. Exercise science and sports science, her degree concentration at Rutgers, might just be her future now. Or maybe it was all of that.

Lloyd was becoming increasingly sure of one thing, though. If she could not make the Under-21 team, making the senior team was out of the question. She planned to just finish her college career at Rutgers and move on with a life after soccer. What she had not yet considered was that she could, in fact, make the Under-21 team, and eventually, the senior team. All she needed was some help, and yes, a little bit of luck. The help came in the form of James Galanis, an Australian coach in New Jersey who had coached Carli's brother. Carli's dad approached him one day and said, "My daughter needs you."

What Galanis discovered was an immensely talented player who had never had to work hard for success. Her club teams were always loaded with talent and rarely challenged. She never had to work hard to be good. As a result, her work habits were suspect, and she simply was not fit enough to play at the highest level. Galanis convinced Lloyd to work with him for three days, and then decide if she wanted to continue. After three days, she was sold. She had the help she needed. The luck came when an Under-21 national team player was injured and needed to be replaced on the Nordic Cup roster. Petrucelli invited Lloyd back in. Having rediscovered her passion for soccer and having been introduced to fitness by Galanis, she started every game at the Nordic Cup that year.

A year later, Lloyd played for the Under-21 team again. This time, her coach was Jill Ellis. She scored in every 2005 Nordic Cup game, and later that year, she played her first two games for the full national team, a team that was evolving and seeing new personalities emerge.

Before 2008, Carli Lloyd had made 43 appearances for the USA, 26 of them as a starter. Her first appearance was July 10, 2005 when she came on as a sub for Aly Wagner in a 7-0 win over Ukraine. As an attack-minded midfielder, Lloyd was at her best using her creativity—running at defenders with the ball and unloading shots with either foot. She wasn't always able to play that role, though. She shared time in the center of the USA's midfield with Lindsay Tarpley, Leslie Osborne, Shannon Boxx, and Wagner. Carli scored once in 2006 and nine times in 2007. By the time 2008 rolled around, she had won a starting job and contributed seven goals in 25 games prior to the Olympics.

It had been a month since she scored a goal when the 27th minute of the USA's second game in the 2008 Olympics came about. She gave the U.S. the lift they so badly needed when she scored the game-winner against Japan. Three days later, Lloyd would help spearhead an American attack that jumped all over New Zealand, beginning with a Heather O'Reilly goal in the first minute, and followed by Rodriguez, Tarpley, and Hucles. The quarterfinal match against Canada was next. Hucles gave the U.S. the lead in the 12th minute. Christine Sinclair, who finished her college career with 110 goals for the University of Portland and had 158 international goals and counting, tied it up 15 minutes before halftime. Kai won it, however, 11 minutes into overtime, and the U.S. was onto the semifinals and a rematch against Japan.

After falling behind to Japan in the 16th minute on a goal by Shinobu Ohno, the U.S. tied it up when Hucles scored in the 41st minute. Lori Chalupny gave the Americans the lead a minute before halftime. O'Reilly made it 3-1 in the 70th minute, and Hucles scored again 10 minutes later. Japan made it 4-2 with a goal three minutes into extra time.

 # ANGELA'S CONTRIBUTION

It was Angela Hucles who came on as a sub that day in San Diego when that ambulance came for Wambach. She now had four goals in the last three Olympic games.

An All-American at the University of Virginia, she played for first Lauren Gregg, then April Heinrichs for the Cavaliers. Angela scored an impressive 59 goals in her college career. Perhaps more impressive was her 19 game-winning goals. When her college career ended in the third round of the 1999 NCAA tournament, however, her soccer options were severely limited. As a striker, she could not break into the national team lineup. Then, in 2001, the Women's United Soccer Association came around.

"I graduated college and worked in the real world for three or four months," explained Angela. "It was my first real job. I worked for a heating and cooling company as a sales and management trainee. I was actually carrying around PVC pipe and going to construction sites. My hours were seven to seven, and I worked one day each weekend, too. Coming from college without much work experience, it was exciting at the time. But once I got to the league, I was able to do something I really loved. Some of the other girls who came straight from college into the league might not have realized exactly what they had."

Angela certainly understood the opportunity she had in the WUSA. She accepted a position switch that put her in a midfield role with the Boston Breakers, where she teamed with Kristine Lilly, Kate Sobrero, and Germany's Maren Meinert and Bettina Wiegmann. Her coach was Tony DiCicco. She earned invites to national team training camps and made her first appearance in April of 2002 in a match against Finland, a 3-0 win in front of 11,000 people in San Jose. She came on as a second-half substitute for Julie Foudy. While trying to win a spot on the team that would play in the 2003 World Cup, Angela went through the range of emotions that accompany any new player attempting to compete against the players she admired and emulated for years.

"There is always a fine line between having a certain respect for the veterans and being in awe of them," she said. "I think the reason why players like myself have been able to stick around is because I respected them without being in awe of them. I respect them for helping me get to where I am. But if I am in awe of them, that's when they blow by me and stick the ball in the back of the net. You can admire what they've done. But they'll have more respect for you if you are pushing them and challenging them and giving them advice if you see something that can help them. That's when they say, 'Okay, that's why she is here.'"

"I let myself be intimidated when I first came to a camp," she continued. "I didn't lower my standards, but I didn't play up to my standards either. You have to perform and not be second to anyone on the field. It happens to players when they are invited into the pool. When something happens, the quicker you get over it, the better off you are. You give them the respect they deserve because they are amazing players, but at the same time, you are competing for a spot. You want to be the best player you can for the team."

Angela did her part to help better the team. She even went a bit further. Each time the national team gathers for a training camp, players are asked to come up with a list goals for the camp. The players are instructed that one of the goals should be personal, one should be team-oriented, and one has to be a morale-booster, focusing on team-building. For a camp held in September of 2002, Angela wrote down that she would polish the boots of her teammates as her team-building goal.

"I was trying to do something a little more creative," she explained. "One of my teammates in college had shined everyone's boots for one of the games, so I borrowed her idea. I was actually going to do a couple, like a person each day, but then I decided why not do the whole team. It's important to be aware of the importance of team chemistry and make sure everyone's fitting in, everyone feels comfortable and feeling like they're a part of the team. It's something that you can bring wherever you go. It helps win and lose matches, win and lose seasons."

USA-BRAZIL... AGAIN

Brazil entered the Gold Medal match with but one blemish on its record, a 0-0 draw with Germany in their first match. They would face the Germans again in the semifinal. This time, however, the Brazilians crushed the World Cup champions 4-1, erasing a 1-0 deficit with goals by Formiga, two by Christiane, and one from Marta. By now, Marta was widely recognized as the world's best player. At 22 years old, she was on her way to winning her third straight FIFA Player of the Year award.

The U.S. fielded a veteran backline of Christie Rampone, Kate Markgraf, Heather Mitts, and Lori Chalupny, with Shannon Boxx in front of them and a rapidly improving Hope Solo in goal. The USA was successful in keeping Marta and her running mate Christiane from scoring in the Gold Medal match. The chances Marta had—when she deftly split defenders or dribbled through a pack—each ended with her frustrated, looking to the sky and asking why. However, the Americans could not score either. A tense, tight match needed overtime to determine a winner. Six minutes into the first overtime period, Lloyd pounced on a loose ball 25 yards from the Brazilian goal, broke into the box, and fired a left-footed shot under the diving body of Brazil's goalkeeper Barbara.

The rest of the way, Marta and Brazil threw everything they had at the U.S., but Solo and the backline turned each threat away. Lloyd almost took some of the drama out of the ending when she hit the post as the minutes ticked away. The USA had won its second-straight Olympic Gold Medal and third overall.

Coming off the bench that day, replacing Lindsay Tarpley in the 71st minute, was 21-year-old Lauren Cheney, who at age three needed open heart surgery because of a heart defect. Lauren was the player added to the Olympic roster the day before the team left for China. She replaced Abby Wambach. "There are obviously tons of emotions going through me right now," Cheney told the media at the time of Wambach's injury, "I have the deepest sorrow for Abby, but I am excited to be part of the 18 going to the Olympics."

While Wambach was in the hospital, she called Cheney. "Don't feel bad about being selected in this type of way," Wambach said during a conference call a few days after the injury, explaining her conversation with Cheney. "What's important is that the team goes in feeling that they can win. At the end of the day, that's what makes you stand at the top podium."

After the Olympics, Cheney returned to UCLA for her senior year. Her coach was Jill Ellis. Four years after graduating from UCLA, Cheney married former NBA player Jrue Holiday, who she met at UCLA. Lauren (Cheney) Holiday went on to make 133 appearances for the U.S. and was one of the most important players of her era.

ABBY'S BACK

On May 25, 2009, Abby Wambach returned to the lineup. It had been 11 months since she had that rod surgically implanted in her leg. In her first game back, a 4-0 win over Canada in Toronto, she went the full 90 minutes, a major achievement on the road back.

That brings us back to Rochester. Eleven years ago, in a game against Russia, Abby's hometown was the site of Mia Hamm's 100th goal. On July 19, 2009, Wambach ran on to a pass from Lauren Cheney and scored her 100th goal in a 1-0 win over Canada in Rochester. She became just the fifth player in U.S. Women's soccer history to score 100 goals. Michelle Akers was the first, Mia Hamm was the second, then came Kristine Lilly, and Tiffeny Milbrett was the fourth. Wambach did it in fewer games than all of them.

"Evidently Rochester is the place to come if you want to score your 100th goal," she told reporters after the game. "After this year I've had—the heartbreak of not going to the Olympics—all of that pain is worth it. There's nothing more you can ask for than play in front of your home crowd and come through with a milestone like I did today. I couldn't dream of a more picture perfect ending. I would give any Olympic Gold to do that. My teammates really made it happen for me today. I don't believe in coincidences any longer. It was meant to happen that way."

The USA only played eight games in 2009, and Wambach played in in the last four, scoring twice. The team won seven games and tied one. The following year, however, the team would play 18 games and see the emergence of a 21-year-old striker from San Dimas, California. In 2010, Alex Morgan was a senior at Cal-Berkeley, the school that produced national team stars, Joy Fawcett and Mary Harvey. Morgan would score 14 goals her senior year, giving her 45 for her career, 10 shy of Fawcett's mark which was second all-time at Cal. Morgan had already established herself as a player who seemed to thrive on scoring dramatic goals. The last goal of her freshman season at Cal sent an NCAA second-round game against Stanford into overtime. At the 2008 Under-20 World Cup, she scored the winning goal in the final against North Korea. Timely goals seemed to be a habit for Morgan, and there would certainly be more for her.

The next event for the USA was the 2011 World Cup in Germany. The qualifying tournament, to be held in Mexico, would begin on October 28th in Cancun. Qualifying had always been a foregone conclusion for the Americans. But the tournament in 2010 taught the Americans a lesson they will most likely remember for a long time. Never take qualifying for granted. Two teams from the North American, Central American, and Caribbean regions (CONCACAF) would automatically move on to Germany for the 2011 World Cup. The USA would surely be one of those teams, right? Even without Hope Solo, who was still recovering from shoulder surgery. Nicole Barnhart, a seven-year veteran of the team who had made just 24 appearances was in goal. Mexico and Canada would fight it out for the other spot—that was the rational line of thought, anyway. The third-place team would need to win a special home-and-home playoff against a European team.

The U.S. opened the tournament as it always did with a more-than-convincing win, this time over Haiti. Rachel Buehler, a center back, got one early, Wambach scored three goals in the first 62 minutes, and Amy Rodriguez got on the board in a 5-0 win. Next up was Guatemala. Three more goals from Rodriguez, two from Wambach, two from Megan Rapinoe, and one each from Carli Lloyd and Alex Morgan in a 9-0 victory. Then came Costa Rica and no surprises. Wambach, Morgan, Lauren Cheney, and Yael Averbuch scored for the U.S. in the 4-0 win, and for the third straight game of the tournament, the U.S. had not allowed a goal.

The USA moved onto the semifinals to play Mexico. Canada and Costa Rica played in the other semi. The U.S. could not be blamed to think that this qualifying tournament was like all the rest. They had never lost a qualifying game, and that seemed unlikely to change this year. Except Mexico had the best day in the history of their program. On November 5th in Cancun in front of 8,300 people, Mexico's Maribel Dominguez scored just three minutes into the game. But Carli Lloyd tied it up in the 25th minute, and everything seemed fine again.

All of which leads us back to the University of Washington, Hope Solo's alma mater. It's also the place where Veronica Perez went to college. Eight of the 24 goals she scored for the Huskies were game-winners. Perez, born in Hayward, California, was an ODP regional player and a member of the U.S. Under-23 National Team. But she held dual-citizenship with the U.S. and Mexico and played for Mexico in 2011 World Cup. She went on to play for Mexico 78 times and scored nine goals. But her 26th minute goal on November 5th, one minute after Carli Lloyd tied it up, was by far her most memorable. Previously, the U.S. and Mexico had played 25 times, including two times eight months earlier. The

USA won 24 times, and they tied once. They outscored Mexico 108-9. But on this day, Perez's goal stood up, and Mexico came away with a 2-1 win.

The U.S. had three days to ponder their fate before meeting Costa Rica in the third-place match on November 8th. Costa Rica had lost 4-0 to Canada in the semifinals. The winner would go into the special playoff with the sixth-best European team. The loser would be out of the World Cup, a chilling thought for U.S. players. The USA responded as expected. Cheney got it rolling just 17 minutes into the game. Wambach made it 2-0 before halftime and added a 50th-minute goal for the 3-0 verdict.

Europe's qualifying tournament was completed in September. Germany as the host nation qualified automatically for the World Cup and did not participate. Eight other teams played two-leg series at neutral sites to determine the four other nations that would join Germany and represent the continent. Aggregate scores from the two meetings would determine the winners. Norway disposed of Ukraine 3-0. England eliminated Switzerland 5-2, and Sweden knocked out Denmark 4-3.

In the other series, France and Italy played to a goalless draw in the first leg in Ukraine. In the second and deciding match, Italy took a 1-0 lead in the 34th minute and kept the lead at halftime. But France tied it in the 54th and took the 2-1 lead four minutes later. With Italy pushing to get back in the game, France was awarded a penalty kick two minutes into extra time. Italy made it 3-2 with a PK of their own in the 93rd minute. France advanced and Italy joined Switzerland, Ukraine, and Denmark in another playoff round called the repechage playoff—Denmark vs. Switzerland, Ukraine vs. Italy, and with the winners meeting. Italy beat Ukraine 3-0, while Switzerland got rid of Denmark 3-1. Then the Italians showed significant firepower against Switzerland, winning 5-2. All seven goals were scored in the second half. Now, the USA would face Italy in a two-game series just to get to the World Cup. The first match was in Padova, Italy on November 20th, just a dozen days after the CONCACAF third-place game against Costa Rica. Italy was working with a month's rest and preparation.

Forty-five years before the special playoff match, Anna Maria Picarelli's grandparents came to the United States and settled in Downey, California. Their children, Anna's father and uncle, got in the restaurant business, and Anna became a goalkeeper. She went to Pepperdine University and played 72 games there. Her 32 shutouts are the most in Green Wave history, and prior to her senior season, in January 2006, she earned a call-up to the U.S. Under-23 National Team camp. Jill Ellis, the U23 coach, saw her as too small at 5-foot-4.

Picarelli, who had dual-citizenship because of her grandparents, was in goal for Italy on November 20th in Padova against the U.S. She stopped nine shots on goal as her teammates struggled to score at the other end. As the game wore on and the United States becoming more and more determined to get the win away from home, Picarelli stayed strong. But four minutes before the end of regulation, Alex Morgan replaced Amy Rodriguez. That's all the USA needed. Morgan scored another huge goal in the 94th minute. It was Morgan's fourth goal for the national team, and the U.S. escaped Padova with a crucial win.

The U.S. was one game away from the World Cup. That game would be played in Chicago in one week. Again, the game was tense. But thanks to Amy Rodriguez pouncing on a rebound of a Megan Rapinoe shot five minutes before halftime, it was far less dramatic. "Obviously, we took a little different road in qualifying," said Abby Wambach. "But we never gave up and never stop believing in ourselves."

Now, there are six months to get ready for the 2011 World Cup in Germany. How do you prepare? First, you take a month off, and then you get to work. Schedule some trips so you can test yourself against the best possible opponents and see your player pool against quality competition away from home. You start in January with a trip to China. You will play three games in five days —against Sweden, Canada, and China.

Abby Wambach needed to prepare differently. Struggling with injuries, she started four of the 11 games prior to the World Cup. She came off the bench in four others but missed the three games during the January trip to China. She had one goal in the 11 games, but others stepped up. In those 11 games, nine different players, led by Carli Lloyd's five and Amy Rodriguez's four, accounted for the USA's 22 goals. The team won nine of the 11 games. Sweden beat them 2-1 in January as part of the China trip and, in April, England posted a 2-1 win in London. Twenty-three days before their first 2011 World Cup match, the U.S. ended their preparation by hosting Mexico in New Jersey. Lauren Cheney scored the game's only goal, and the team headed to Germany having won nine of their last 11 games.

Alex Morgan
Photo by Andy Mead

DRAMA

I f you like drama, stick around. The 2011 World Cup was full of it. Not just drama, though. Patriotism, pride and a whole lot of emotion were also key components of the story.

Let's start in Dresden, Germany, where the USA faced North Korea in the World Cup opener. Lauren Cheney scored, and Rachel Buehler added one for insurance, and with that, the USA got the all-important first-game win. Still to face Colombia and Sweden in group play, the USA could not afford any hiccups, and getting past the North Koreans was a positive first step. The next day, the team flew to Frankfort and bussed to Heidelberg where they would face Colombia, 1-0 losers to Sweden in their opener, on July 2nd. Their practice in Heidelberg was, however, not an ordinary training session. It was not unusual for spectators to be at national team practices. Practicing at an American military base in front of servicemen and women and their families was, however, something new. "I felt so proud to be wearing a USA jersey that day," Hope Solo wrote in her book, *Solo, a Memoir of Hope*.

With the U.S. military families filling the streets of Heidelberg, not to mention the stands at the USA's next game against Colombia, the Americans came out attacking. In the 12th minute, a poor touch by a Colombian defender set the ball in the path of Heather O'Reilly, who took a glance at the goalkeeper and drilled a 35-yard line drive to the upper corner. O'Reilly, looking a bit stunned at the tremendous quality of her strike, simply raised her arms in celebration as she was surrounded by her teammates. Then, in perhaps the greatest goal celebration of all time, the team stood in a line and saluted the red, white, and blue clad American military families in the crowd and watching on TV. Megan Rapinoe scored five minutes into the second half, and not to be outdone in the goal-celebration category, she ran to the corner, picked up a microphone which was used to pick up field noise, and sang "Born in the USA". Carli Lloyd scored seven minutes after Rapinoe's signing debut to account for the 3-0 score line.

Feeling good and playing well, the USA moved on to Wolfsburg to play Sweden, the native country of U.S. coach Pia Sundhage. Sweden had defeated 1-0 Colombia in their first game and North Korea by the same score in their second game. Both games were won with strong defending and second-half goals. The advancement scenarios were simple. The winner of the USA-Sweden match would win Group C and move to the quarterfinals to play the second-place team in Group D, either Norway or Australia. The loser would play the first-place team in Group D, almost certainly Brazil. A tie would produce the same matchups for Sweden and the U.S. Avoiding Brazil was the obvious preference of both the Americans and the Swedes. In their last meeting, six months earlier in China, the Swedes defeated the U.S., 2-1.

The USA seemed to have history and logic on its side. The loss to Sweden in China was the first time in seven years and only the fourth time since 1987 that the USA lost to the Swedes, and the U.S. had never lost a World Cup game in group play. And Abby Wambach had not scored yet. She entered the game with 118 international goals in just 159 games, which figures to be a goal every 1.3 games. Surely, she would start scoring soon. She did, but not until the 67th minute. By that time Sweden had a 2-0 lead, scoring on a penalty kick just 16 minutes into the game and adding another 10 minutes before halftime. So having lost for the first time ever in World Cup group play, the USA advanced to the quarterfinals to face Brazil on July 10th, the 12th anniversary of the USA's last World Cup championship.

And here's where things got really dramatic. It got started early, too. Just a minute and 12 seconds into the game, in fact. A low hard cross by Shannon Boxx was misplayed by Brazilian defender Daiane, who was in the lineup in place of veteran Renato Costa, and scored an own-goal. The U.S. held the lead into halftime, but the likelihood of the game ending 1-0 was slim at best. Of the 13 goals the teams had scored before the quarterfinals (seven by Brazil and six by the USA), 10 had been scored in the second half. The first half was tame compared to what happened later.

In the 62nd minute, things got strange and then got stranger. Covered closely by Rachel Buehler, Marta, the World Player of the Year for the past five years and perhaps the craftiest women's player ever, received a ball in the U.S. penalty area. Marta popped the ball over the head of Buehler. As Buehler and Marta pivoted and scrambled for the ball, they both lunged to try to get a piece of it, the Brazilian trying to put it on goal, Buehler trying to put it anywhere else. Marta nicked the ball into the waiting arms of Hope Solo, but the referee, Jacqui Melksham of Australia, awarded Brazil a penalty kick and Buehler a red card. Replays showed the call to be, at best, sketchy.

Momentum is a funny thing. In reality, it is just a state of mind, or maybe an emotion, or a mental edge. Adrenaline must factor in there somewhere. And regardless of how hard we try, we can't accurately explain it. One thing for certain, though, momentum shifted constantly in this game. What started as Buehler and Solo denying Marta of a goal, shifted into Brazil being awarded a PK and a better-than-average chance to tie the game with the USA having a player, a defender at that, ejected, reducing the players on the field for the U.S. to only 10.

But wait, there's more. As Cristiane stepped up to take the penalty kick, Solo, who had never allowed Brazil to score on her in the four games she played against them, jumped up and down and stretched her wingspan to make her appear much bigger than 5-foot-9. Cristiane, the 26-year-old left-footer and owner of 59 international goals, had successfully converted a penalty kick earlier in the tournament. It was one of two goals she scored in a 3-0 win over Equatorial Guinea. With a chance to provide a huge momentum shift and tie the game against a U.S. team that had just been reduced to 10 players, Cristiane shot to her right, Solo's left. Hope read Cristiane perfectly, getting both hands on the ball to push it away with the type of authority that embarrasses the shooter. Solo leapt to her feet and celebrated, joined quickly by Lloyd and Boxx. Brazil had just missed their best chance to turn the game in their favor. Now, still down a goal, they were faced with a rejuvenated American side and a goalkeeper who suddenly made the goal look very, very small.

Hold on. What now? Melksham decided that Solo moved too soon—or that Christie Rampone entered the penalty area before the ball was kicked. No one was really sure. What was known is that either of the two calls were rarely made. Solo was livid and earned a yellow card for dissent. All the arguing and confusion couldn't change the fact that the kick would be re-taken. Marta grabbed the ball and walked it over to Cristiane, offering her a chance to redeem herself. Cristiane, confidence shattered, refused and told Marta to take it. Solo dove right, Marta went the other way, and momentum shifted once again.

Shannon Boxx gathered the team together to re-focus. Five minutes after Buehler's foul, the game resumed, tied 1-1. Boxx dropped back to fill the hole left by Buehler's exit, and Wambach dropped into midfield leaving Rodriguez alone up front. In the 72nd minute, Alex Morgan entered the game, replacing Rodriguez. Morgan came in with instructions from coach Pia Sundhage. Boxx was to move back into midfield and Wambach back up front. Instead of sitting back and hoping to go to the penalty kick shootout, which would have been the popular, if not logical, approach, Sundhage decided on an attacking formation of three defenders, four midfielders, and two forwards. Sundhage later told *The Washington Post* that from a tactical standpoint, it was the best decision of her soccer life. The tactic worked through the end of regulation as the USA took the game to Brazil. Overtime, however, would be required to find a winner.

Meanwhile, the 25,800 fans in attendance, had turned against Brazil in general and Marta in particular, whistling and booing every time she touched the ball. But it didn't bother Marta. Two minutes into overtime, she gave her team a 2-1 lead with a clever, looping, flick from the near post that left Solo helpless. The ball touched the base of the far post and went in. It appeared the final momentum shift went Brazil's way. At this point, with still at least 18 minutes of overtime still to play, it would be silly to think there was more drama to come. Silly us.

Brazil pulled out all the stalling tactics they could find. They were infuriatingly slow on restarts, never in a hurry to take thrown-ins, corner kicks, or goal kicks. Their most popular tactic, one adopted from the men's game, was feigning injury every time they hit the ground. If ball was not in play and the clock was still ticking, they figured, the USA could not score. The American players, most noticeably, Abby Wambach, made sure to remind the referee that time needed to be added to make up for Brazil's shenanigans. In the 114th minute, Erika, a 23-year-old defender, had a minor collision in Brazil's penalty area after a U.S. corner kick. After the ball was safely up field, Erika collapsed in front of Brazil's goal in exaggerated anguish. The game was stopped as the medical staff came onto the field to tend to her. Wambach showed up on the scene and made the international gesture for the stretcher and then walked to the referee and pointed to her wrist, another international gesture meaning, "you had better add more time for this mess." Erika was carried off over the end line while Brazil temporarily played with 10 players. But before the stretcher could reach the corner flag, she jumped off and ran to the sideline among a flurry of boos and whistles from the pro-American crowd. When she entered the game, she was met with a yellow card from the referee. She had wasted two-and-a-half minutes of precious time for the U.S. It would prove to be about 30 seconds more than the USA needed.

There are several aspects of all U.S. women's national teams with which other countries have not been able to contend. One is fitness. The USA is generally the most physically fit team in any tournament. Secondly, American women hate injustice, especially if the perceived injustice is done to their friends. Don't bet against a group of American women determined to right a wrong. The third is more abstract. It's an attitude, a common trait among every woman who has ascended to that level. They are not going to whine about calls that didn't go their way. They are not going to let someone else determine whether they are successful. And they certainly are not going to give up until they there are no other options remaining. Every second counts.

The referee added three minutes to the end of the second overtime period, meaning the game would end as close as possible to the 123-minute mark. The clocked showed 121:04 when Ali Krieger stole a Cristiane pass near the USA's penalty area. She found Carli Lloyd who dribbled to midfield and put the ball in the path of Megan Rapinoe on the left flank. Rapinoe took one long touch and sent a perfect cross to the far post. And there was Abby's head. At 121:20, Wambach read the cross perfectly as Andreia, the Brazilian goalkeeper, flew past her and sent a header just inside the post. It was the latest goal ever scored in a World Cup game. After nearly an hour of playing shorthanded, after suffering what appeared to be odd decisions by the officiating crew, the USA had tied the game, sending it to penalty kicks.

"That is a perfect example of what this country is about, what the history of this team has always been," Wambach told the media after the game. "We never give up."

There were 47,000 people in Yankee Stadium watching on the big screen and countless others in bars, airports, military bases, and homes glued to their TVs as the USA and Brazil went into PKs. But the U.S. players, seemingly oblivious to it all, looking like they were in a training session as they took their penalty kicks. Boxx shot first, but Andreia, ironically, moved too soon as she made the save. Boxx nailed her second attempt. Lloyd, the second U.S. shooter, made hers easily. Meanwhile, Solo had faced penalty kicks from Brazil's first two shooters earlier that day. "I was confident they would go the same way they did during the game," Hope told ESPN. "They didn't." Cristiane and Marta both converted their attempts, and it was tied 2-2 after two shooters. Wambach drilled her shot, and Daiane was next up for Brazil with a chance to make it 3-3.

Daiane was already having a bad day, and it was about to get worse. In the second minute, which was about two-and-a-half hours ago, she scored an own goal to give the USA the 1-0 lead. When Daiane, a defender, approached the ball for her PK, she appeared less than confident. Solo, as she had done with the previous two kickers, made her wait. In comparison, Andreia, Brazil's keeper, was on her line waiting for the U.S. kickers, allowing the Americans to work on their own timeline. Solo, on the other hand, was in charge of the proceedings. She was forcing the Brazilians to look at her and perhaps get in their heads, while the Americans just focused on the ball. Daiane struck the ball well, but Solo extended herself fully to her right and steered the ball away with one hand. Solo quickly jumped to her feet to celebrate as the crowd, almost entirely pro-American by now, roared. Rapinoe was next for the USA, and she drilled it easily past Andreia. Franciella made her shot for Brazil, and Ali Krieger had a chance to win it.

Ali Krieger could certainly appreciate the situation she was in as she stepped up to take the USA's fifth penalty kick. After all, how many people have the chance to win an epic struggle and keep alive the dreams of your entire team? Especially, this team on this day, the team that played a player down for the better part of an hour, suffered apparent injustices at the hands of a referee, and used practically every tick of the clock just to get to this moment. Just six short years ago, the scenario would have seemed extremely far-fetched

In 2005, in her junior year at Penn State, the Virginia native and former two-time All-American, suffered a broken leg two days before the NCAA Tournament. The injury required surgery. A few months later after a plane ride over Christmas break, she started becoming short of breath, so she went to the doctor. She found out she had developed a pulmonary embolism, a blockage of one of the pulmonary arteries in her lung. Krieger, it turns out, was fortunate she went to the doctor, very fortunate. If she had gone to sleep that night, the doctor told her, she might not have woken up. She also learned that she had suffered six mini-strokes. And at 21 years old she was all of sudden wondering if she would live. Krieger learned to treasure every moment on the field and off. She learned to enjoy the journey.

Of all the non-German players in the World Cup, Krieger was the most likely to feel at home. She had, after all, spent the past four seasons playing professionally in Germany for FFC Frankfort, about five hours from the penalty kick spot in Dresden. She was fluent in German, so she knew she could be the heldin (heroine) if she made one shot from 10 meters. After recovering from not only the embolism, she paid extra attention to her fitness. Playing three 90-minute games and one 123-minute-and-counting thriller did not leave her leg-weary in the least. She confidently walked to the spot and hit the side-netting in the lower-left corner; she raced to her teammates, cherishing the moment and setting off a rambunctious celebration on the field and all over the U.S.

Meanwhile, France was quietly becoming a nation that required attention. They finished second to tournament favorite Germany in group play, defeating Nigeria 1-0, dominating Canada 4-0, and losing to the Germans 4-2. They got by England in the quarterfinals by winning a penalty kick shootout 4-3 after finishing overtime 1-1. Six different players accounted for their eight goals so far. After the emotionally draining, drama-filled quarterfinal with Brazil, the USA had two simple goals for the semifinal match with France. First, win. Second, do it in regulation time. They would have to do it without Buehler, though. Becky Sauerbrunn replaced the center back while she sat out her suspension from the red card against Brazil.

Lauren Cheney gave the USA a boost toward accomplishing both goals, scoring in the ninth minute off a low cross from O'Reilly. In the 55th minute, though, Sonia Bompastor, tied it up, and the USA was in a fight again. But in a three-minute span starting in the 79th, the USA put the game away. Wambach drilled a header in the 79th, and Morgan, who came on for Rodriguez in the 56th minute, scored her first goal of the tournament.

GANBARE

It's important to know that Tokyo Power and Electric (TEPCO) sponsored a professional women's soccer team in Japan, and that Karina Maruyama was one of the stars of the team. We should also know that her teammate on the Japanese National Team, Aya Sameshima, worked for TEPCO at its Fukushima Nuclear Power Plant. It was Maruyama who came off the bench to score the game-winner in a huge upset over Germany in the 108th minute, sending Japan to the semifinals. Japan, considered too small and too old to be a serious contender for the World Cup title, went on to defeat Sweden 3-1 in the semifinals. Suddenly, the Japanese were in the World Cup final against the USA.

The Japanese players, to a certain extent, believed some of the critics. Mana Iwabuchi admitted that each time they won in the early stages of the tournament was somewhat of a surprise to the players. But when they defeated host Germany in the quarterfinal, they realized what they were accomplishing.

Seventy-five days before the World Cup kicked off, on March 11, 2011, Tohoku, Japan, a town in the Northeast corner of the island of Honshu, was rocked by a massive earthquake. The quake was the most powerful ever recorded in Japan. It caused a tsunami that produced waves in excess of 130 feet. At least 15,000 people died, an estimated 13,000 by drowning, another 6,000 were injured, and 2,500 were reported missing. The quake and tsunami caused severe damage to the TEPCO nuclear plant, triggering meltdowns at three of the plant's six reactors. The meltdowns were classified as Level 7, the most severe on the 0-7 scale. After the meltdowns, a 20-mile area of the region was evacuated. An estimated 4.4 million households were left without power and 1.5 million without water. Homare Sawa said she was frightened when the quake hit. Growing up in Japan, she was used to earthquakes, but this one was different. It lasted much longer.

Japan's run to the World Cup final certainly did not go unnoticed at home, where soccer fields were turned into evacuation centers. A welcome diversion from the tragedy gripping the country and a sudden unexpected source of national pride, the matches were viewed by millions around the country.

The team was known as "Nadeshiko," a term that became popular during World War II and refers to a frilly pink carnation but came to be used to refer to the ideal Japanese woman. Around Japan, especially in the region hardest hit by the earthquake and tsunami, banners supporting the team were hung, many featuring the word "Ganbare." A word of encouragement to someone working hard, ganbare loosely translates to "Hang in There."

The team was doing their best to ganbare. Players were, obviously, concerned with friends, family, acquaintances, and strangers affected by the disaster, and they were concerned with their country as a whole. Aya Miyama's family lived where the earthquake hit. Maruyama and Sameshima had friends risking their lives to try to control the radiation leaks. They also knew, however, that their performance was bringing encouragement to those back home. Newspapers were printing special editions featuring Japan's run to the final, and people, including those who barely knew Japan had a team, were gathering to watch the games early in the mornings.

The USA was confident heading into the final. They had fought through a very difficult and emotional game with Brazil, disposed of a strong French side, and were finally in a World Cup final for the first time in 11 years. And they had not lost to Japan in 25 previous meetings. But as emotional as it was for the Americans, there was a whole other level of emotion in the Japanese locker room. Karina Maruyama cried before the Germany game. Her coach, Norio Sasaki, showed the team a video of the effects of the disaster at home, the devastation caused by the earthquake and ensuing Tsunami, and the people struggling to survive the aftermath. She wasn't the only one in tears that day.

The images were devastating for the players to watch. It was hard for them to believe they were looking at their country. But Sawa said the players realized how fortunate they were to be playing soccer when so many people were affected by the earthquake, and they realized the situation they were in. The video, she said, urged them to move forward as a team and give their country some hope.

Remarkably, Sawa's first World Cup appearance for Japan was in 1995, and the 2011 World Cup was her fifth. A familiar opponent to the USA, the 33-year-old veteran debuted for Japan at age 15. She was a member of the Atlanta Beat in the old WUSA and quickly made her mark on the league. In 2009, she played for the Washington Freedom in the WPS with Abby Wambach. A crafty and creative midfielder with a tireless work rate and a classy demeanor, Sawa was adored by fans and teammates and frustrating to opponents. She entered the 2011 final with four goals, including a hat trick against Mexico and the game-winner in the semifinal win over Sweden.

AN EPIC FINAL

The day of the final, July 7, 2011, was the third Monday in July, which in Japan is designated at Marine Day. It's a day when the country celebrates the blessings of the sea. Japanese people could be forgiven if they struggled to find any blessings from the ocean in the wake of a giant tsunami.

The Back Nine Grill in Pittsford, New York, outside of Rochester was packed. The bar owner's family was there, and that alone accounted for around 30 of the estimated 250 people staring at the televisions and suffering through every touch. The owner, you see, was more than a casual soccer fan. His little sister, Abby, was playing. Matt Wambach is one Abby's four older brothers. She also had two older sisters. The Wambach family was not the only group gathering to watch the final, though. Bars around the country were hosting Watch Parties, a relatively new phenomenon in the U.S., where Red, White, and Blue clad families turned out to eat, drink, and be American. Girls ranging in age from seven to 57 wore USA jerseys with "Wambach", "Morgan", "Lloyd" or "Solo" on the back. Times Square in New York City was packed with people watching on the big screen, and members of the military stationed in Germany who were not able to be among the 48,000 to see the game in person were glued to their TVs. Also, the 170th Infantry Brigade Combat team in Afghanistan had a gathering of their own.

Pia Sundhage made one change to the lineup. Amy Rodriguez, who had started each of the first five games at forward with Abby Wambach, would be on the bench. Lauren Cheney would be asked to play a midfield role higher up the field behind Wambach. Shannon Boxx and Carli Lloyd would join Cheney in central midfield roles, while Rapinoe and O'Reilly were given wide midfield assignments. Amy LePielbet, Rampone, Buehler, and Krieger comprised the back four, and Hope Solo was in goal.

The decision to move Cheney into a more attacking role almost paid off immediately. In eight minutes, she broke in behind the Japanese defense on the left side of the penalty area. Her shot narrowly missed the near post. On the play, however, Cheney badly twisted her ankle. She gamely made it through the first half, but would be replaced at halftime by 22-year-old Alex Morgan, with the score still tied 0-0. Almost immediately, Morgan became dangerous. Showing her speed and strength, she ran at and behind Japanese defenders and created tense moments in the Japanese box. Then, Megan Rapinoe gathered a loose ball at the top of her own penalty area, took a touch, and looked up field. She spotted Morgan and launched a 40-yard pass over the head of a Japanese defender, who suddenly found herself in a race she couldn't win. Morgan ran the ball down with the defender on her right shoulder, touched the ball to her favored left foot, and found the far corner to give the USA a 1-0 lead with 20 minutes left in regulation.

But ganbare. In the 81ˢᵗ minute, Sawa's cross into the USA penalty area bounced between Buehler and Maruyama, both on the ground. Buehler swung her leg to clear the ball, and it went to Krieger, whose clearance attempt went straight to a lurking Miyama five yards in front of Solo, and the game was tied. Japan's celebration was short and restrained. Miyama grabbed the ball out of the goal and ran to midfield, trying to restart the game as quickly as possible. The message Japan was sending was simple—they weren't done yet.

The last 10 minutes of regulation was tense, end-to-end action with a quality not expected from two teams playing their sixth game in 19 days. Japan was slipping runners into the USA penalty area while the U.S. launched balls into Japan's box searching for Wambach's head. But neither team could get on the end of anything and overtime was needed—again.

Two headers on goal by Wambach in the first minute of overtime could not find the net, but the large majority of the first 10 minutes was played in Japan's half. With less than three minutes remaining in the first 15-minute overtime period, the USA increased the pressure on Japan, pressing and swarming the ball trying to gain an advantage. Rapinoe and Morgan, controlling the left flank, both launched crosses searching for Wambach, but Japan headed each away. Then, with the clock reading 103.02, Morgan picked up a loose ball near the sideline and deftly beat her defender to the end line. With only inches between the ball and the end line, Morgan hit a perfect ball toward the far post, and there was Abby's head. The USA's celebration was tame, knowing full well there was a lot of time remaining.

In the 115ᵗʰ minute, Sawa played a ball behind the USA defenders to a sprinting Murayama. Solo charged hard as Murayama's touch slowly made its way toward the goal. Rampone, however, calmly cleared it out of danger. But Solo had collided with LePielbet and needed medical attention to her left knee. The medical staff checked her knee, flexing it over and over, and Solo got to her feet. But the USA was now facing a corner kick. During the injury stoppage, Sawa organized her team and sent Miyama to take the corner with instructions to hit it to the near post. Sawa then positioned herself 10 yards in front of the goal. Sawa took off on a sprint, meeting Miyama's corner at the near post, and with the outside of her foot, she directed the ball into the goal—2-2.

Certainly, there were heroic performances from players on both teams—Wambach, Morgan, Solo, Murayama, Sawa. But the play of the game was not one many people would remember. It occurred at the 120.14 mark. Carli Lloyd chipped a ball behind the Japanese defense into the path of Morgan. With an inch or two of a head start, Morgan got to the ball 20 yards in front of the Japanese goal. But defender Azusa Iwashimizu slid in to take Morgan down before she had a chance to go one-on-one with the goalkeeper. Considering the way Morgan had been playing, the accuracy of the shots she managed to take, and the likelihood that it was the last chance of the game, Iwashimizu most likely saved a goal and kept Japan's hopes alive. The price she paid—a red card for denying a goal-scoring opportunity—was, for all practical purposes, insignificant. Japan was reduced to 10 players for the two minutes of added time given by the referee. Carli Lloyd took the free kick from 19 yards and drove it low and hard to the far post where an attempt by Tobin Heath was blocked. The game moved on to penalty kicks.

Japan entered the PK shootout with poise and confidence. For USA fans, the shootout was painful, seemingly over before it started. In the huddle before the shootout, coach Norio Sasaki smiled. Japan had not been in a PK situation during the tournament. The USA, however, had, and Sasaki and his staff had studied it closely. Goalkeeper Ayumi Kaihori knew, for instance, which way Shannon Boxx, the USA's first kicker, would shoot. And she stopped it. Miyama made her shot, and Japan had a 1-0 lead. Then Lloyd uncharacteristically shot over the bar, but Solo stopped Japan's second shooter. Kaihori saved Tobin Heath's attempt, and the USA had come up empty with their first three shooters. Solo got a piece of Japan's third shot, but it trickled in, nonetheless. With Japan holding a 2-0 advantage, Wambach made her shot. Saki Kumagai, Japan's 21-year-old center back who frustrated the U.S. by barely beating Wambach to several solid crosses, sent Japan to the Gold medal platform for a celebration that had little to do with soccer.

But the American public didn't seem to mind the loss all that much. Some of the unlikeliest fans popped up on Twitter. Tom Hanks, LeBron James, and Aaron Rodgers were among the celebrities raving about the team. When they returned home, appearances on "Good Morning America" and the "Today Show," among others, were on the schedule, as was signing endorsement contracts and photo shoots and commercials.

Shannon Boxx
Photo by Andy Mead

PART V

U.S. VS. CANADA HEATS CUP

This time, the USA didn't mess around with qualifying for the 2012 Olympics that were to be held in Great Britain. Their three first-round opponents—the Dominican Republic, Guatemala, and Mexico—fell by a combined score of 31-0. Their closest game, a 4-0 win over Mexico, was over after nine minutes, thanks to an eighth-minute goal by Lloyd, the first of her three for the game, and a ninth-minute strike by O'Reilly. They disposed of the Dominican Republic 14-0, a game in which Amy Rodriguez scored five goals all in the second half. The Guatemala game ended 13-0, and it was Sydney LeRoux's turn to score five second-half goals.

LeRoux, a three-time All-American at UCLA under coach Jill Ellis, played only five minutes for the USA in 2011. In 2012, however, she played in 27 games all off the bench. She scored 14 goals. LeRoux terrorized opponents at the U20 level, scoring 24 goals in her 39 games —both USA records. She ended up at UCLA playing for then-coach Jill Ellis. But LeRoux's path to the U.S. National team was a bit different, and it started in 1999. LeRoux, a Canadian citizen, was nine years old and living in Vancouver, British Columbia, when she watched the 1999 USA-China final on television. She watched as Brandi Chastain scored the winning penalty kick and tore off her shirt in celebration in front of nearly 100,000 people at the Rose Bowl in Los Angeles.

As she continued through her promising soccer career, that image remained with her. Her African-American mom, a Canadian citizen, played third base for the Canadian National Softball team, and her white American dad, Ray Chadwick, played professional baseball. Her mother and father never married, and she was raised by her mother. As a 14-year-old Phenom, she played for Canada's Under-19 national team. She moved to Arizona with her mom shortly after that. She had played for the U.S. and Canada youth national teams and was still eligible to play for either country at the senior level. On January, 21, 2011, she came off the bench for the USA against China in the Four Nation's

Cup. Her choice was made. Apparently, unbeknownst to LeRoux, Canadian fans hated her for choosing the USA over Canada, and they made it clear with taunts and chants.

It started in 2012 during Olympic qualifying which was held in Canada. A week after scoring five goals against Guatemala, she came off the bench against Canada in the final in Vancouver. Every time she touched the ball, she was booed. She was 14 when she left and no one cared or tried to stop her. When she started scoring goals for the USA, all of a sudden it was a big deal.

They really seemed to care in 2013. During a friendly in Toronto, LeRoux came off the bench, a role she in which was excelling, and took a pass from Abby Wambach and scored the USA's third goal of the game, sealing a 3-0 win. As LeRoux celebrated, she tugged on the USA crest on her jersey. Fans spewed their venom, some extremely personal, some vulgar, and all designed to hurt and humiliate LeRoux. She put her fingers to her lips in a common "shush" motion. "Classless," was what a Canadian television commentator called her, and it was perhaps the nicest thing said about her. Twitter was much worse. The racial slurs may have bothered her more if not for a moment she had when an African-American girl came running up to her and said, "You look like me. I want to be like you."

# KEEP CALM AND CARRY ON

The U.S. had 373 days from the emotional end of the 2011 World Cup final to the start of the 2012 Olympics. To prepare, the U.S. traveled to Japan, Sweden, and Portugal in addition to playing a handful of domestic matches. As demonstrated during the Olympic qualifying tournament, the USA featured an explosive attack. Wambach was still producing goals at an impressive rate, but Alex Morgan built on her success at the World Cup and scored 17 goals in 15 games prior to the Olympic opener.

The Olympics consisted of 12 teams in three groups of four. The 2011 World Cup was used to determine Olympic qualifying, and Germany's loss to Japan in the quarterfinals knocked them out of the Olympics. Also missing was traditional powers Norway, China, Nigeria, and Australia. Paired with France, Colombia and North Korea in Group G, the USA began the Olympics in Glasgow, Scotland, on July 25th against France.

It took France 14 minutes to do something that had not happened in over a year—score two goals against the U.S. That's right, by the time the 15th-minute mark of the USA's first game rolled around, the team was trailing 2-0, the result of a span of two miserable minutes. A 25-yard strike by Gaetane Thinny that sailed away from Solo into the top corner got France going. Just as the public address announcer was getting around to announcing the first goal, France struck again. After a French corner kick ricocheted around the USA penalty area, Marie-Laure Delli smacked a loose ball past Solo from 12 yards. And two minutes later, Shannon Boxx went down with an injury and had to be replaced by Carli Lloyd.

Taking a cue from their British hosts, they USA kept calm and carried on. There were, after all, still 75 minutes to play. In the 19th minute, Megan Rapinoe lined up for the USA's first corner kick. She launched it to the far post, and guess what? Correct. There was Abby's head. Then in the 32nd minute, France was called offside deep in the USA end. With Alex Morgan flirting with the offside line at the other end, Solo sent an 80-yarder that Morgan finished off with a volley over the keeper's head. Now the USA could enter halftime tied 2-2 and figure out how to start the second 45 minutes better than they started the first. A Carli Lloyd goal in the 56th minute was the positive step they needed. Morgan scored her second of the game 10 minutes later, and the USA had escaped a nightmare start with a 4-2 win to get the all-important three points against what was considered their toughest competition of group play. Next up Colombia. The Colombians qualified out of South America with Brazil and lost their first game 3-0 to North Korea.

Here's something we haven't seen before. With the U.S. ahead 1-0 on a 32nd-minute goal by Rapinoe, the play was coming down the left flank toward in the USA's attacking end. Abby Wambach was running toward the Colombia goal halfway between Colombia's goal and the midfield line watching Rapinoe with the ball to her left. Lady Andrade, a skillful 20-year-old midfielder from Bogota, ran up along Wambach's right and punched her in the face. Not a little swat, by the way. She wound up and landed a punch to Wambach's left eye, which quickly swelled. The referee missed the whole thing. Television cameras, however, did not. After the game, Wambach and U.S. Soccer urged FIFA to review the play, which Andrade called "an accident," leading one to believe that perhaps she meant to punch her in the mouth not the eye. FIFA did review the play and suspended Andrade for Colombia's next match and the quarterfinal if they should advance. In reality, she was out of the tournament.

The USA went on to win 3-0. Wambach and her swollen eye scored in the 74th, and Lloyd finished it off on the 77th. Meanwhile, France pounded North Korea 5-0, so the U.S. was assured of advancing to the quarterfinals, regardless of the result over North Korea in the third group match. But Wambach got a goal 25 minutes in to give the USA a 1-0 win. They would meet New Zealand in the quarters. After three games in Glasgow, the Americans moved to England.

At this point in the tournament, it was doubtful New Zealand had many delusions of facing photographers on the medal stand. Featuring former Stanford University captain Ali Riley, New Zealand finished third in their group with a win over Cameroon and losses to Brazil and Great Britain. However, both losses were by 1-0 scores and New Zealand qualified for the quarterfinals as the second-best, third-place team. Canada moved on as the best third-place team. The USA, however, knew the New Zealanders were a stingy bunch defensively, having allowed just three goals in three games.

Morgan to Wambach produced the first goal and some breathing room for the USA in the 27th minute. LeRoux, the youngest player on the U.S. roster at 22-years-old, subbed in for Morgan in the 80th minute and scored her first Olympic goal seven minutes later. Canada was next in fabled Old Trafford Stadium in Manchester, England.

ONE, TWO, THREE, FOUR...

When Anson Dorrance took over the U.S. women's national team 26 years ago, way back in 1986, he was given the challenge to be competitive in CONCACAF. He took that to mean that they had to compete with Canada. Heading into the Olympic semifinals, the U.S. and Canada played 52 times. The USA won 43 and tied six. Now, when qualifying for major international events rolled around, it was always the same story. Canada and Mexico would fight it out for second place. The Canadians, long annoyed at the step-sister role they played to the USA in international women's soccer, had outstanding players over the years who received All-America honors playing for U.S. Colleges, most notably Charmain Hooper at N.C. State, Angela Kelly at UNC, Christine Latham at Nebraska, and several more recently who were in the process of making their marks. In 2012, the Canadians, however, had one thing no other team could claim—Christine Sinclair in her prime. At the University of Portland, Sinclair scored a remarkable 110 goals in 92 games, an NCAA Division I record. Twenty-five of her goals came in NCAA tournament games, also a record. As a senior, she scored 39 times, another record.

Entering the 2012 Olympic semifinals, Sinclair had scored 140 international goals in 189 games. By the end of the day, Sinclair would have 143. It would not be enough. Her team entered the semifinal match fresh off a solid 2-0 defeat of the hosts, Team Great Britain. The Canadians were talented, confident, and partial due to their new mental skills coach, they felt this would finally be their day. And it got started nicely for them. Sinclair scored just 22 minutes after kickoff, deftly navigating through two USA defenders and beating Hope Solo from 12 yards. Canada had a 1-0 lead at halftime.

Okay, so we have already seen Wambach get punched in the face. That's new. What else could these Olympics offer in the way of surprises? How about six goals after halftime? How about Canada taking the lead three times, and the USA tying it back up each time? How about someone scoring a hat trick against the Americans? How about someone curling a corner kick in at the near post?

That's what Rapinoe did in the 54th minute to tie the game. What's next? Sinclair scored in the 67th minute to make it 2-1, and Rapinoe responded in the 70th to tie it again. Sinclair again in the 73rd. And that's when it got even stranger.

With Canada holding a 3-2 lead late in the game, Abby Wambach felt Erin McLeod, the Canadian goalkeeper who played two years at Southern Methodist University before transferring to Penn State, was holding the ball too long. When the ball is in their hands, keepers are given six seconds in which to put the ball back in play. Rarely is the rule enforced. One of the few times it was called was in the 78th minute of the 2012 Olympic semifinal. Post-game reports indicated that McLeod held the ball once for 17 seconds and once for 13 seconds. On one occasion, she was verbally warned by the assistant referee. When McLeod had the ball late in the game, Wambach began counting out loud, making sure she was within earshot of referee Christina Pedersen of Norway. In the 78th minute, Wambach started counting, using her fingers, either for emphasis or so she wouldn't lose her place. One, two, three, four… She reached 10 when Pedersen blew the whistle. "I have never seen that call," said U.S. coach Pia Sundhage after the game.

The U.S. was awarded an indirect free kick just inside the penalty area. Tobin Heath tapped the ball to Carli Lloyd who drilled a line drive, elbow high, toward the Canadian goal. It hit Canadian defender Marie-Eve Nault, a former University of Tennessee standout, in the arm. Pedersen blew the whistle again, and the USA had a penalty kick, a chance to tie. The Canadians were irate as Wambach buried the penalty, and the game was headed to overtime, again.

One last thing. Have you ever seen a last-second goal on a header in overtime in a major international competition? Oh, that's right. It happened a year ago when Abby Wambach nailed a header on what was, in effect, the very last play of the game of the World Cup quarterfinals. Well, the USA did it again. Heather O'Reilly, who had made a career out of relentlessly pursuing balls on the flank and whipping them into the box, launched a cross that Alex Morgan finished off with a header in the 123rd minute. Final: USA 4, Canada 3.

Have you ever seen someone score a hat trick, let alone a hat trick in an Olympic semifinal and never crack a smile? That's how focused Christine Sinclair was. She had all three of her goals equalized by the team she wanted to beat the most. She had to watch as the ref gave that team an indirect kick and a penalty kick in a span of two minutes. It meant nothing that she scored more goals against Hope Solo than all of the previous four U.S. opponents combined. She had, by anyone's standards, done quite enough to be able to walk away with a win. Instead, she was livid. "It's a shame in a game like that, a game that was so important, the ref decided the result before it started," Sinclair told reporters after the game.

Carli Lloyd
Photo by Andy Mead

THE DIFFERENCE-MAKER

Poor Carli Lloyd. There she was, cruising along and having a great career for herself. She was recognized as one of the top players in the country, and she even advanced to play for her country's national team. On July 5, 2015, her Twitter and Facebook accounts started to blow up. Not again, she thought.

Carli Ellen Lloyd, is a volleyball player, and she admits she doesn't really know that much about soccer. Carli Anne Lloyd is, of course, really famous now. Carli Ellen first realized she shared a name with the U.S. soccer star when she started receiving congratulations from random people on Facebook and Twitter during the 2012 Olympics. "People always talk about her when they hear my name, so I feel like she's in my daily life," Carli Ellen told the United States Olympic Committee website. "It's like, yeah, but I don't know her at all. I've watched her success, and she is such a baller. I'm awful at soccer. I don't really even understand the sport that well. But I watch her fire, and it's cool."

Raising your level is another one of those clichés that provide an easy, yet incomplete, answer to a complex question. What exactly does mean, raising your level? Playing harder? Running more? Being better with the ball? Sure, all of those fit. But there's more, isn't there? There's what Carli Lloyd did against Japan in the 2012 Olympic final in front of 80,000 fans in London's Wembley Stadium.

There was a moment eight minutes into the Gold Medal match that served two purposes. First, it gave the USA a 1-0 lead over Japan. Second, it showed something about Carli Lloyd that should have been a gigantic hint of things to come. Kelly O'Hara, playing at left back, fed Tobin Heath down the line. Heath's cross was met by Morgan, whose touch got a bit away from her. But she tracked down the ball before it went over the end line, seemingly like no one else could, and hooked a cross toward the far post. Waiting at the far post, of course, was Abby Wambach, already positioning herself to drive home a header. But as soon as Morgan got to the ball, Lloyd, 14 yards in front of the goal, took off on a sprint.

There are points in games when it appears there are 21 players on the field all playing at the same pace. Then there is one player, someone who has decided to flick a switch, who seems to be in fast-forward mode. That was Lloyd. Nine players were in front of Japan's goal when Morgan crossed the ball. Eight of them were pretty much stationary. One decided that the ball belonged to her. Lloyd, crashing toward the goal, stuck her head between Wambach and a Japanese defender, both swinging at the ball. She met the ball perfectly, leaving no doubt where the ball would end up.

Then, nine minutes into the second half, Lloyd, inside the center circle, took a pass from Rapinoe and did what she does best. We can assume she had one thing on her mind. Lloyd headed toward the Japanese goal. Thirty yards and nine seconds after receiving the ball, Lloyd cracked a right-footed shot that Japan's keeper Miho Fukimoto had no hope of stopping. "Today, I was trying to be the person to make the difference," Lloyd told ESPN cameras after the game.

"I think I was in a little bit of shock in 2008 that I scored such a big goal," Lloyd continued, referring to her 96th-minute goal in the 1-0 win over Brazil in the Olympic Gold medal match four years ago. "I think right now, I am at a place where I think I played well and was consistent throughout the tournament. Today, I was stepping up. I was leading."

Yuki Ogimi brought the game to 2-1 in the 63rd minute, but solid defending and some spectacular moments from Hope Solo preserved the U.S. win and third straight Olympic Gold. "You can't go without saying that Hope saved the day, literally, five times," said Wambach told reporters after the game.

Back in June, Lloyd was not a starter for the USA. In a June 16th game in Sweden, she began the game against the Swedes on the bench. After starting 40 of 42 games dating back to July 19, 2009, she found herself watching. It wasn't until the Olympic match against Colombia, the USA's second of the tournament, that she was in the starting lineup.

"When someone tells me I can't do something, I'm going to prove them wrong," Lloyd said in a post-game release. "Coming in, I was coming off the bench, and I didn't know what to expect. I prepared harder than anyone. I don't think there is anyone who trains harder than I do. I was ready for the moment, and I took it game-by-game. I focused, and I kept on it every single day. I fought harder, dug deeper, and I wanted to make all those doubters out there wrong, and that's what I did. Hard work pays off."

Sundhage, it turns out, enjoys being proven wrong. "The thing with Carli Lloyd is we didn't have her in the starting lineup before the Olympics," she told media after the game. "She has proven that I was wrong. Today, I think she was one of the best players. I'm so proud of her because she played so many games, and all of a sudden, I thought she wasn't good enough. Then she just comes back and helps the team tremendously, and she proved that I was wrong. I love that."

The Olympic Games added women's soccer in 1996, creating a two-year period in which the Olympics and the World Cup would be played in succession. Since then, no nation has been able to win a World Cup and an Olympic Gold in back-to-back years. In 1995-96, Norway won the World Cup and the U.S. won the Olympics. In 1999-2000, the USA won the World Cup and Norway won the Olympics. The 2003-04 time-frame saw Germany win the World Cup and the USA win the Olympics. In 2007-08, Germany won their second World Cup and the USA won their third Olympic Gold medal. Then 2011-12 saw Japan take the World Cup title and the USA grabbed the Olympic championship.

In the World Cup, the USA had never finished lower than third place, a feat most countries would point to as an enormous success. They also had four Olympic crowns. Still, in the minds of the players, it felt incomplete. The team seemed to have an annoying habit of finishing third in the World Cup then winning the Olympics. Immediately after the win over Japan in Wembley, that was on the mind of at least one U.S. player.

"We all know I broke my leg in 2008, and this team went on to win gold," Abby Wambach told reporters after the game. "That was obviously very hard for me. It's been eight years since I've been a champion of the world. Yes, my team won, but I wasn't a part of it, so that's a totally different feeling. We came so close to winning a World Cup, which I've not yet done. That in and of itself was devastating."

TWENTY-SIX STATES IN
TWENTY-SIX MONTHS

The USA's well-deserved break lasted all of 29 days. They were back in action on September 1, 2012, with an 8-0 win over Costa Rica in Rochester. It was also the day Sundhage announced she was stepping down as national team coach. She would be replaced by Jill Ellis on an interim basis until October 30th when U.S. Soccer hired Tom Sermanni.

Sermanni, popular among players, administrators, and most all soccer folks, is a native of Scotland who had coached the Australian women's national team from 1994 to 1997 and again from 2004 to 2007. He started coaching in the U.S. when Ian Sawyers, the husband of Julie Foudy, brought him on as an assistant coach for the San Jose CyberRays in the WUSA in 2001. He then coached the New York Power in 2002.

On October 15, 2014, the U.S. would begin the qualifying tournament, which for the first time, would be held at home. By that time, Sermanni would be gone, though, and Ellis would be the head coach, the team's eighth all time. A month after Ellis was hired, Mike Ryan, the guy who got the whole thing started back in 1985, died. He was 77 years old and enjoyed a coaching career that spanned seven decades.

Between the end of the Olympics and the beginning of World Cup qualifying, a span of 26 months, the national team played in 26 states. There were the old standbys—Los Angeles, Hartford, Portland, Dallas, Columbus, Washington, D.C., Orlando, Cary, Rochester. But U.S. Soccer brought the team to some new venues, places like San Antonio, Detroit, Nashville, Atlanta, and San Francisco. The team would also travel twice each to Portugal and Canada as well as once to Germany and once to Holland.

Ellis's first task was to look at the player pool. In the USA, finding and evaluating talent has always been difficult, if for no other reason because of the sheer size of the United States. "This isn't a country," U.S. Soccer staff coaches often said. "It's a continent." However, the youth and college systems have always produced national team-level players. In 2014, however, there were more quality players than ever before. Becky Sauerbrunn and Sydney LeRoux had been on were on the Olympic roster and were now pushing hard for playing time. But Ellis also had to figure out where some newcomers, namely Christen Press, Meghan Klingenberg, Morgan Brian, and Julie Johnston, might fit in.

International debuts don't usually tell much about a player. Understandably nervous about seeing a lifelong dream realized and perhaps trying too hard to impress, players usually are tight and error prone. Usually, their first performance, if they are lucky, is okay. The opposite was the case for Press. The all-time leading scorer in Stanford women's soccer history and a standout on U.S. youth national teams, Press had also played professionally for two years in Sweden. In 41 games over two seasons with two Swedish clubs, Press scored 40 goals. With all that experience, she made her national team debut at age 26 on February 9, 2013, in Jacksonville, Florida, against Scotland. The U.S. won 4-1. Press scored the first two goals and assisted on the third. She scored in her next game, as well, becoming the first player in women's national team history to score three goals in her first two games.

How about a five-foot, two-inch defender? Before you pass, consider she is a black belt in Tai Kwon Do who grew up outside Pittsburgh where she and her brother, who played at Penn State, battled almost daily in the basement, battles their parents always had to break up before a hospital visit was needed. That's what you got with Meghan Klingenberg, a four-year starter at UNC.

There's also a two-time NCAA Player of the Year out of the University of Virginia who played for the U.S. Under-17 National Team as a 15-year-old. Morgan Brian made her debut with the senior national team in June of 2013 as a 20-year-old coming on as a sub for Lauren (Cheney) Holiday. "Morgan impressed me the first day she came to our camp," Holiday told *ESPNW.* "There's not a lot of people that come into camp with so much confidence. Alex Morgan is one of them, and Morgan Brian is another. They both are people who have come in and owned the position and owned the camp that they came into."

What about this Julie Johnston kid from Arizona who had a great career at Santa Clara? Her dad, David, was a kicker on the LSU football team. Apparently, when she was little, she used to cry every time she fell down on the soccer field, but that, of course, soon stopped. Then she got good. Then she captained the U20 team to the Under-20 World Cup title in 2012. Then she was named the U.S. Soccer Young Athlete of the Year the same year. And in 2013, she earned her first cap with the national team.

QUESTIONS

I n 1997, Bill Clinton was president of the United States, Mother Theresa and Princess Diana both died, Steve Jobs returned to Apple, *Titanic* and *Good Will Hunting* were the top movies, and Christie Pearce received a fax from U.S. Soccer.

Pearce, a junior at Monmouth College in New Jersey, thought the fax containing an invitation to a women's national team training camp was a mistake, or worse yet, a joke. The national team? Really? She was the starting point guard on the school's basketball team and held the career record for steals. She also played on the Monmouth soccer team and scored 79 goals as a forward. What she was unaware of, though, was that one day, the national team coach Tony DiCicco was urged by a friend to watch a player on a team that Monmouth was playing. What DiCicco found was Pearce, who could possibly be the greatest athlete ever to play for the USA.

Seventeen years later, at age 39, Christie (Pearce) Rampone, the team's captain, was a veteran of four World Cups and four Olympic Games. She had been on the field for over 380 hours for the USA and had 298 caps, more than any male or female player in the world except Kristine Lilly. When the World Cup kicked off in 2015, she would be 40. She still had the speed that helped her become an all-state track star in high school. Fitness for Rampone, the mother of two daughters age 10 and five, would not be, and never was, an issue. Would Rampone be able to play at a level high enough for a team seemingly exploding with new, young, talented players? Especially young defenders like Sauerbrunn, Johnston, and Klingenberg?

Then there was the question of whether Alex Morgan would stop suffering ankle injuries. Twice between the Olympic Gold Medal match and World Cup qualifying, Morgan was sidelined with ankle problems.

The U.S. played just 16 games in 2013 and 24 in 2014. They won 29, lost eight, and tied three. Wambach, now 33 years old, was still scoring goals at an above-normal rate, tallying a team-high 11 in 2013, as well as 13 in 2014, but it was time to starting asking the question—is the USA better with her in the lineup or coming off the bench? Pia Sundhage, the now head coach of Sweden, stirred up some controversy with comments she made in an interview with the *New York Times* prior to the 2015 World Cup. She said Wambach would be a sub if she was still coaching the team. A really good sub, she added, but still a sub.

Owning what might as well have been the most talented roster in U.S. history, Ellis had to answer a big question, a nice question, but one that needed to be answered nonetheless. What was her best lineup? Who were her best backs? Where do Carli Lloyd and Lauren Holiday fit into the midfield? Who are the best flank players? Who can she count on to consistently produce goals? She had plenty of choices. Qualifying would produce the answers, maybe.

Ellis used various combinations of Sauerbrunn, Rampone, and Whitney Engen as her center back pair in the qualifying tournament, during which the USA outscored their opponents 21-0. In the center of midfield, Lloyd, with her five goals during qualifying, and Holiday were consistently used in the middle of a 4-4-2, while Heath, Rapinoe, O'Reilly, and Press split the time in the wide spots. Wambach, who scored seven times in the tournament, and Morgan appeared to be emerging as the go-to pairing at forward, while LeRoux and Press also saw action at striker.

On the outside looking in was Julie Johnston. She didn't make the roster for qualifying and said she "was lost" at that time in her life. She started to think that maybe her time would come in four years. Johnston called it one the hardest moments of her life. She didn't know where she fit in. She didn't know when or how she could realize her dream of being a world champ. She used the time wisely, though. She re-focused and went to work. Carli Lloyd knew the answer to Johnston's questions. Lloyd was training under the eye of James Galanis in Lumberton, New Jersey, a 40-minute drive from Philadelphia where Johnston was living. Lloyd invited her to come train with them. Johnston jumped at the chance.

Meanwhile, Crystal Dunn, a versatile defender/midfielder/forward out of UNC, suffered an injury, and Ellis needed to find a replacement. Johnston received the invitation to be a reserve on the team for qualifying. She jumped at the chance, and her dream was alive again.

The first 54 minutes of the USA World Cup qualifying match had that "Not Again" feeling about it. Matched up with a vastly improved Trinidad and Tobago on October 15th in Kansas City, the U.S. could not find the net for what seemed like an eternity. But Wambach scored in the 55th minute, and the USA escaped with a 1-0 win and three points. They moved on to Chicago two days later, and Tobin Heath made sure her team didn't suffer through another frightening match. She scored twice against Guatemala that day, her first just seven minutes in, jump-starting the USA attack into a 5-0 win. On October 20th, the team wrapped up group play with a 6-0 pounding of Haiti to win their group. Wambach scored twice Lloyd, Press, Klingenberg, and Brian added a goal each.

In the other qualifying group, Costa Rica defeated Mexico and outlasted Trinidad and Tobago in semifinals, winning on penalty kicks when the first three T&T shooters missed. The U.S. played Mexico in the semifinals in Philadelphia next. Lloyd's two first-half goals were enough, but Press added a 56th-minute strike for the 3-0 final score line.

October 26th was one of those days when Abby Wambach was going to make sure her team won. She wanted to make sure there was no doubt in anyone's mind that the USA was, at the very least, a strong contender for the 2015 World Cup championship. The USA would take on Costa Rica in Philadelphia that day, and just four minutes after kickoff, Wambach put the USA in the lead. Lloyd scored 14 minutes later to make it 2-0. Then Wambach scored three more times before the 71st minute, and Sydney LeRoux capped off the 6-0 win with a 73rd-minute goal.

Christie Rampone
Photo by Tony Quinn

PART VI

OUT OF THE SHADOW

It's interesting. When it comes to being the best, Americans are rarely satisfied with past success. Being a four-time Olympic champion and having won three Golds in a row was now a footnote on the national team's resume. Been there, done that. There was never a World Cup awards ceremony that did not include the Americans. They had never finished lower than third place in any World Cup, but the last time they were champions was 16 years ago. And that was all that seemed to matter.

Of the current team, only Christie Rampone was on that '99 team. Morgan Brian and Julie Johnston, who were closer in age to Rampone's 10-year-old daughter than they were to Christie, were only six and seven years old, respectively. Jill Ellis was starting her first Division I college head-coaching job at the University of Illinois and was working as a scout for U.S. Soccer. Hope Solo was a freshman at the University of Washington, Carli Lloyd was at Rutgers, and it would be 11 more years before Alex Morgan would score her first goal in a USA uniform.

Abby Wambach was in college at Florida. She recalled the impact that win had on the country and young women and girls everywhere. "I can still picture them with their gold medals and seeing the pride and the sense of fulfillment," Wambach said. "I have won Olympic Gold medals and I cherish them, and now I want to win a World Cup more than anything. It is time for the U.S. to win it again."

Their competition was stiffer than ever, though. There were still the major obstacles of the recent past, like Japan and Brazil and Germany. There were the traditional powers like Norway and a recently re-vitalized Chinese program, as well as a Swedish team coached by Pia Sundhage. Then there were the teams that more recently rose to the upper-echelon of women's soccer like France and England. And, of course, there was Canada, who had had just about enough of the USA.

The USA's road to winning the 2015 World Cup would begin with Australia on June 8th in Vancouver, British Colombia. Rapinoe gave the Americans a 1-0 lead 12 minutes in, but Australia tied it up 15 minutes later. Christen Press, starting at forward with Wambach, scored in the 61st, and Rapinoe sealed it with a 78th-minute goal. The 3-1 score line was a bit deceiving, though. The USA never got a corner kick, while the Aussies had three. The USA's had six shots on target, three went in, while Australia had seven attempts at Solo.

"I don't think we played particularly well in the first half," said Ellis after the game. "But I was pleased that we grew in the game. Our players settled in during the second half, which was much better. That's something we can build upon."

There was something missing, something fans, writers, and commentators could not quite pinpoint. But they certainly tried. Far from a dominating performance everyone anticipated, the game at times seemed tame and lacking energy, enthusiasm, and urgency. Somehow, style now mattered. But, as Ellis said, the team grew during the game. The next game would be better, was the prevailing opinion. It wasn't.

In 1996, when the USA played Sweden in a crucial group-play match, then-coach Tony DiCicco said, "The last thing you want to do is play Sweden when their backs are against the wall." And that's where Sweden's backs were on June 12th in Winnipeg. Having battled to a thrilling 3-3 tie with Nigeria in their opening match, the Swedes needed three points to keep their hopes of advancement alive.

The U.S. made a change to the starting lineup, putting Wambach on the bench and starting LeRoux and Press as forwards. Ellis said the game was like "two heavyweights going at it." The teams traded punches, but neither one could land a knockout blow, and the game ended 0-0. Frustration continued from the fans and media. In fact, the voices were now becoming louder. Regardless, style points were not needed for the U.S. to win Group D and advance to the round of 16.

FRUSTRATION

The talent of the all the players in the tournament had vastly improved over the years. The individual technical ability was impressive. The speed at which the team played was outstanding, and the entertainment value was great. Every aspect of the women's game had increased rapidly in the second half of the decade, including expectations from U.S. fans.

Perhaps the biggest change in the U.S. soccer culture was in the area of fan support. With the introduction of social media, fans could keep up with players through photos, videos, and messages via Twitter, Instagram and Facebook. Fans began interacting with each other regardless of geography. Soon, they became organized and supporter's groups were formed in cities and towns across the country, and many were all organized under the banner of American Outlaws. The Outlaws attended games—MLS, NWSL, and national teams. Songs about fan favorites were written and sung at games, and watch parties were held where hundreds, maybe thousands depending on the size of the place showing the game, of fans gathered to cheer on the women. Parades of fans marched in unison to the stadium on game days dressed in red, white, and blue, wearing the jerseys of their favorite player. And the 2015 World Cup was held in Canada, close enough for American fans to consider it a collection of home games.

All that attention combined with the average American's increased knowledge of soccer led to frustration when the USA could not put on dazzling displays of dominance in each game. Ellis, who later said she was in somewhat of a self-imposed media blackout, was determined to go about her business and stick to her plan. Ellis, after all, knew her team and her players better than anyone. She knew the World Cup was a marathon, not a sprint, and she remained quietly confident in not only her team, but herself.

Colombia, perhaps the tournament's biggest surprise along with Cameroon, was the USA's round-of-16 opponent. Colombia advanced as one of the best third-place teams in group play. If anyone believed the U.S. would walk over the

Colombians, they needed only to look at a 2-0 victory over France, who many considered the best team in the tournament. Against France, Lady Andrade scored the game-winner and didn't punch anyone.

Catalina Perez, a junior at the University of Miami, grew up in Boca Raton, Florida, dreaming of playing against the USA. She got her wish in front of nearly 20,000 people on June 22nd in Edmonton, Alberta. Born in Bogota, Colombia, Perez got her first start of the tournament, stepping in for Sandra Sepulveda, who was red-carded in Colombia's previous game, a 2-1 loss to England. Perez was forced to make two outstanding saves in the first 15 minutes. But, as soon as Colombia settled down, they started to play. In fact, they were the better team for the first 45 minutes, showing individual skill and moments of flair, possessing the ball and frustrating the Americans. And, in the biggest surprise of all, Colombia was the aggressor.

Playing with Morgan and Wambach up front and Lloyd, Holiday, Rapinoe, and Heath behind them in midfield, the U.S. just could not click. They appeared mechanical compared to Colombia's creativity. With Colombia's near-relentless pressure and a determination not previously seen from the South Americans, the U.S. struggled to link passes together and generate a cohesive attack. To add to the USA's first-half troubles, both Lauren Holiday and Megan Rapinoe received yellow cards, meaning they would have to sit out of their next game if the U.S. advanced. And, at this point, advancing looked to be very difficult.

Perez's dream game turned into a nightmare just 1:30 into the second half. Rapinoe sent Alex Morgan racing toward goal. Morgan, as she is likely to do, reached the ball first and touched it around Perez at the top of the penalty area. Sliding out, Perez stuck out her leg and clipped Morgan just inside the penalty area. And just like that, the USA was in control. Colombia, had not only given up a penalty kick, but Perez was red-carded. Colombia had to play with 10 players, one of which would be a brand new keeper. It is hard enough for a keeper to come into a game cold. It's measurably worse facing a penalty kick immediately. That's what greeted Stefany Castano, a 21-year-old Bogota native who played collegiately at Graceland University in Lamoni, Iowa. But Abby Wambach missed wide of the net. Castano and Colombia were off the hook, for now.

Down a player and under significant pressure from a suddenly tenacious bunch of Americans, Colombia struggled to get out of their own half. In the 66th minute, Rapinoe was taken down in the box with a hip check, and the USA was awarded another penalty. Having missed a penalty earlier in the half, Wambach told Lloyd to take this one. Lloyd, who had yet to score a goal in the tournament, later admitted that to that point in the event, she felt she was not playing well at all. Her confidence was sagging, and she was unsure if she could keep her spot in the starting lineup. A turning point, she said, was when Wambach told her to take the penalty against Colombia. Wambach had no way of knowing at the time, but she had just created a monster.

With a very difficult 2-0 win behind them, the USA moved on to the quarterfinals, where they were joined by England, France, Japan, Canada, China, Australia, who were surprise winners over Brazil, and Germany, who thumped Sweden 4-1. Without Holiday and Rapinoe, two of the team's most important players, the U.S. would face China, whose only loss of the tournament to date was a group-round match to Canada, 1-0. And after a period of time when the Chinese government scaled back funding for the women's program, China was making a comeback on the world stage.

With increased exposure comes increased attention, and not all of it was positive. The U.S. was coming under criticism for the way they had been playing. Colombia, critics said, were the better team with better players. The U.S., they said, looked lost; they lacked skill and flair. There was definitely something lacking.

With Rapinoe and Holiday sidelined, Ellis needed to make two changes to her lineup. She made three. Morgan Brian came in to play a holding midfielder role. Kelly O'Hara was inserted on the right flank, and Amy Rodriguez replaced Wambach up front. In O'Hara and Rodriguez, the U.S. added speed and grit. Brian's job was to be disciplined, play in front of the back four, and enable Lloyd to concentrate more on attacking, a role in which she thrives. The U.S. jumped on a young Chinese team, who were visibly rattled by the swarming pressure the U.S. employed.

Rodriguez missed a solid opportunity just one minute into the game, and China desperately tried to play out of their early nervousness. As China settled down, so did the game. But the U.S. moved the ball quickly, ran with the ball, and seemed to be playing with a freedom that was lacking in earlier games. It took 51 minutes for the USA to score. Julie Johnston launched a 50-yard ball into the Chinese penalty area, where Lloyd, her training partner, standing 12 yards from the goal, headed it down to the corner of the goal. It was Carli Lloyd's second goal of the tournament.

In case you haven't noticed, and people were just starting to take note, the USA's back four—Krieger, Johnston, Sauerbrunn, and Klingenberg -- were virtually unbeatable. Sauerbrunn, who Klingenberg called "The most underrated player on our team," was perhaps the best defender in the tournament. On the uncommon occasion a team was able to get behind them, they were met by Solo. By the end of the China game, the U.S. had not allowed a goal since Australia scored in the 27th minute of the opener, 423 minutes ago.

THE USA MENTALITY

The China game was a big improvement, but there was still something missing. The missing element was not a formation change, changes to the personnel, or a tactical adjustment. It was not anything that could be drawn up on a white board or seen in a video. It was something simple yet so intricate, something that had to be pulled out by each individual because they cared deeply for the group. It was the USA Mentality.

The USA Mentality is what happens to athletes just after they examine themselves and find an extra supply of will and a reservoir of courage and then decide there is no way they are going to lose. It's not bluster. It has to be sincere. The USA Mentality has no time for egos. Far too busy for that, busy chasing down balls, turning 50-50 tackles into 75-25 opportunities. It's making the game uncomfortable for the opponent. It's playing the game at a pace and with a fury that can't be matched. It's putting your body at risk during a play that seems meaningless to the average person. Anson Dorrance, when coaching the USA and UNC, wanted other teams to stop and count the number of players on the field, certain they were playing against 12 or 13 players. He called it 90 minutes of hell.

But that's not all. The USA Mentality factors in all of the best qualities of elite American athletes, the grit, the athleticism, the pride and the ridiculously high fitness levels. And it counts heavily on all the characteristics that make American women strong. It depends on players who grew up never taking no for an answer, or settling for anything simply because they were girls. And it greatly depends on the willingness of a bunch of women to fight for a cause, for each other, and to cover each other's backs. The USA Mentality relies on those women to work as a team to accomplish something great. The USA Mentality was about to make its debut.

Germany, ranked number one in the world, entered the semifinals having scored 20 goals, including 10 against the Ivory Coast in their opener. They defeated Sweden in the round of 16 and eliminated France in penalties in the quarterfinals. The U.S. now had Holiday and Rapinoe back, but Brian stayed in the lineup with the idea to give Holiday and Lloyd freedom. After a brief early flurry by the Germans, the U.S. took over, applying relentless pressure, deftly moving the ball, and, at times, getting behind the German defense. Nadine Angerer, considered the one of the top two goalkeepers in the world, however, was able to turn away two solid chances to keep the score 0-0 through the first half.

In the second half, boosted by their best performance of the tournament, the USA continued hounding the Germans, who appeared rattled and fragmented, even confused, at times. But in the 59th minute, Julie Johnston, facing her own goal 17 yards out, struggled with a bouncing ball. A German attacker slipped past her, and Johnston yanked her down by her shoulder. Germany had a penalty kick. There is so little a goalkeeper can do on a penalty, but Solo did everything she could to take control of the situation. A drink of water, a little stroll around the box, a scan of the crowd, a stretch of her injured shoulder, she did anything but stand in the goal. Celia Sakic, with five goals already in the tournament, two on PKs, waited. She looked around, spoke to a teammate, anything to kill time, except, that is, look at Solo or the ball. When the referee blew the whistle, Sakic immediate approached the ball. She struck it wide. The U.S. received a boost.

Eight minutes later, Alex Morgan attacked the German backline, dribbling at speed at defender Annike Krahn, a 30-year-old veteran of 123 international games. Krahn knocked Morgan to the turf—PK for the U.S. From the point the referee gave Carli Lloyd the ball to the time she kicked it, a tense 1:10 elapsed. Lloyd spent the entire time staring at the ball. She beat Angerer cleanly to the right side. USA 1, Germany 0. Twenty minutes to play.

It wasn't so much the fact that the USA scored a second goal that made the players so happy, it was more who scored the second goal. Kelly O'Hara battled back from total reconstructive ankle surgery, and her work ethic earned her admiration from teammates and coaches. Then, she played a huge role in the quarterfinals against China, filling in for the suspended Rapinoe and adding much-needed energy to the lineup. That energy and work rate helped set the tone for a rejuvenated USA performance. So when O'Hara crashed the net in the 84th minute to get the outside of her right foot on the end of a Carli Lloyd cross from the end line for the second U.S. goal, her teammates mauled her. When the final whistle blew, the entire U.S. bench mauled her again.

The USA mentality had defeated the Germans. The U.S. defense had extended its streak of extreme stinginess to 513 minutes of not allowing a goal. And, most important of all, Carli Lloyd, a streaky scorer, had three goals in her last three games.

Carli Lloyd
Photo by Tony Quinn

# I BELIEVE THAT WE WILL... OH MY

The chant used by the American Outlaws went viral. It progressed from "I" to "I Believe" to "I Believe That" … all the way through, culminating with a boisterous "I Believe That We Will Win." The crowd of over 53,000 in Vancouver on hand to see the USA and Japan play for the World Cup title barely had time to settle in, let alone start chanting. That's because two-and-a-half minutes after kickoff, the Carli Lloyd Show had begun. Morgan Brian won a corner kick on the right side. Megan Rapinoe, celebrating her 30th birthday in the best of all possible ways, took the corner. Lloyd meandered around the top of the penalty area "trying to act disinterested." Before the game, Lloyd, as she always does, called her personal trainer, James Galanis. She told him, the first corner is going to be hers. Galanis told her not to make the first corner hers, but make all the corners hers. Oh. Okay, thought Lloyd.

Rapinoe drove a low, hard ball into a gap between Japanese defenders. Lloyd, no longer acting disinterested, flew to the ball. She timed it perfectly, redirecting it with her left foot for the shocking 1-0 lead. Lloyd sprinted to the corner and began her celebration in front of the American Outlaw section as her teammates swarmed her. It was the fastest goal in Women's World Cup history.

Wait. Don't sit down. Just two minutes later, Lloyd struck again. As Lauren Holiday lined up a free kick from the right flank, Lloyd again loitered around the top of the box as Holiday drilled another low ball into the box. Carli busted to the goal. Julie Johnston kept the ball alive with a clever little flick that deflected off a Japanese player. Lloyd, once again appearing to be playing at a different speed than the other 21 players on the field, knocked it home. And with 4:51 elapsed off the clock, the USA had a 2-0 lead. The pro-American crowd was in a frenzy, finding it hard to believe what they had just witnessed. The USA had already equaled the most goals scored by any one team in a Women's World Cup final, and one player had them both.

There is a saying about those people who tend to score goals on a regular basis. It is sometimes used almost a dismissive explanation. It's sometimes an attempt to say the player is rather lucky. They say the player "is just at the right place the right time." What that explanation is missing, though, is that the player didn't just wander into that right place and the ball happened to bounce off them. They had to know what the right place was going to be, didn't they? They had to know what exactly the right time would be. And, they had to have the determination, confidence, and guts to get there.

Japan huddled again. There's still plenty of time, they must have been telling each other. We still have time. But the USA seemed to be in quite the hurry. Swarming the ball, moving it quickly, and attacking at every opportunity, the Americans were far from satisfied with the 2-0 score. Still fresh in their minds was the 2011 World Cup when Japan came back twice and ended up winning on penalties. The USA stepped up the pressure, making sure any doubt the Japanese players had only grew bigger. In the 16th minute, Holiday chased a long ball to the penalty area. A Japanese defender attempted to clear it but instead headed it straight up in the air. Holiday's eyes got huge, like she had just been given the best present of her life. She accelerated and drove a volley that Japan's goalkeeper Ayumi Kaihori could only wave at. Fourteen minutes gone. USA 3, Japan 0.

What happened next proved that, without a doubt, the day belonged to the Americans. And, of course, to Carli Lloyd. Lloyd collected the ball in her own half, inside the center circle. She took a touch toward the Japanese end and glanced up at the goal. Kaihori was off her line. Why not? Carli had actually practiced shooting the ball from midfield in her workouts with Galanis. She rarely made one. But when you are having a day like Carli Lloyd was having, here's what happens: The ball travels 54 yards in the air, while the keeper frantically backpedals. Just to make it more dramatic, Kaihori, in a desperate attempt to steer the ball anywhere but where it is headed, gets a hand on it. And when your day is going like Lloyd's is going, of course the ball is going to bounce off the inside of the post, not the outside, and go over the line as Kaihori helplessly watches. That was in the 16th minute. "I was just on a mission," Lloyd said after the game. "A mission to help my team win."

Trailing 4-0 and just having faced an offensive onslaught unequaled in Women's World Cup history, Japan managed to score in the 27th minute. It was the first goal the U.S. had allowed in nine hours of World Cup soccer. The half would end 4-1. Japan was shocked but encouraged by their ability to score. An early goal for Japan in the second half, and the momentum would swing, right— that was the optimistic thinking. They went to the locker room to regroup. The USA was determined to not only avoid letdowns but to keep their foot on the gas and put Japan away. Japan pulled it to 4-2 in the 52nd minute when a ball into the box, glanced off Johnston's head, and changed direction just enough to avoid Solo.

But Tobin Heath got into the act. Counted on mainly for her ability to keep the ball and use her creativity to help the U.S. in possession, Heath slammed home a pass from Brian in the 54th minute.

"After 15 minutes, I had to pinch myself to make sure I wasn't dreaming," said Ellis in a post-game press conference. "We wanted to put them under pressure right from the start, and everything fell into place perfectly. To be honest, I couldn't really have imagined things turning out better. However, I did know that my players were capable of doing something exceptional. That's what they were born to do. The greater the pressure on their shoulders, the more they perform at a higher level. My backroom staff also did a fantastic job. We have a lot of respect for Japan, but tonight we were completely focused and were able to adapt our style of play perfectly."

# I BELIEVE THAT WE JUST WON

With Heath's goal, it was over. For the first time in 16 years, the USA was World Cup Champions. All that was left to do, other than making triple sure nothing dramatic would happen, was to celebrate. And to add a couple of instances of class and a nod to history to a thrilling day. First, Jill Ellis decided that the ending would not be appropriate without Abby Wambach, whose mother, Judy, spent the morning of the final praying and lighting candles in the Holy Rosary Cathedral a couple of blocks from her hotel in Vancouver. Abby accepted her role on the 2015 with grace and spent her time on the bench doing whatever she possibly could to help her team through each game.

To roars from the crowd, Abby entered the game for Heath in the 79th minute. Japan's Homare Sawa, who entered the game for Japan as a sub in the 33rd minute, came over and high-fived Wambach. Sawa, playing in her sixth World Cup, had been Wambach's teammate in Washington, D.C., and she wanted to honor her friend. Then, Carli Lloyd, serving as captain for the game, came over to Wambach and put the captain's armband on her. Then, in the 86th minute, Ellis put Christie Rampone in the game. Rampone, who was replaced in the starting lineup by Johnston for the World Cup, was 40 years old and the only member of the 2015 who had previously played on a World Cup winner. Ellis made sure, Rampone and Wambach, both invaluable pieces of the USA team for over a decade, were on the field when the final whistle blew, when the USA became the only country to win three Women's World Cups.

There were tears from both teams as the players wandered around the field, either congratulating or consoling each other. U.S. players searched the crowds to wave or blow kisses to family, friends, and loved ones. Ellis, with a huge grin, hugged all her players, and Wambach wrapped herself in an American flag having achieved the one title that had eluded her for so long.

"I can't even believe this is real life," Abby told the media after the game. "I am just so happy I can't even tell you. Finally, I am a world champion."

Abby got her World Cup, but it was, without a doubt, Carli Lloyd's spotlight. A hat trick in the World Cup final! All in the first half! All in 16 minutes! Six goals in the last four games of the tournament! "I was not in a good place the first three games," Lloyd, who had scored the winning goals in the 2008 and 2012 Olympic Gold medal games, told *USA Today*. "You come into a tournament like this, and you expect you're going to be firing on all cylinders all the time. And I'm my own worst critic. If I under-perform, I'm not happy. I just wasn't doing what comes naturally, what I can do to have an impact."

Life exploded for Lloyd and her teammates. Appearances, talk shows, new celebrity friends—all the things champions enjoy. A trip to the White House where President Barack Obama said, "This team taught all America's children that playing like a girl means you're a badass. Playing like a girl means being the best. It means drawing the largest TV audience for a soccer match—men or women's—in American history. It means wearing our nation's crest on your jersey, taking yourself and your country to the top of the world. That's what American women do. That's what American girls do. That's why we celebrate this team. They've done it with class. They've done it with the right way. They've done it with excitement. They've done with style. We are very, very proud of them."

And there were a couple interesting reactions to the USA's win. A farmer in California reportedly shaped a cornfield in the shape of Megan Rapinoe's face. Someone changed Carli Lloyd's Wikipedia page to list her as "President of the United States." The team got to join Taylor Swift on stage during a concert. And they were honored with a ticker-tape parade in front of an astonishingly large crowd through New York City's Canyon of Heroes.

"We've had a lot of amazing experiences," said Abby Wambach at the Canyon of Heroes. "But this actually will go down as the best thing I have ever been a part of in my life."

Among the signs held by fans along the parade route was one by a 13-year-old girl that simply said, "Thank you for letting me dream."

Heather O'Reilly
Photo by Andy Mead

THREE STARS

Let's go into room 606. It's where Mr. Thomas's Spanish class meets. But school's over for the day, and the boys' varsity soccer team from Westchester Country Day School in High Point, North Carolina, are in room 606 waiting for their coach. They had a state playoff game last night and won in overtime. Today is a recovery day, and they're going to watch a movie. That's what they've been told, anyway.

The Wildcats' coach, Adam Schwartz had other ideas, though. The school, you see, has two state titles to its credit, and the team wears two stars on their training jerseys, one for each title. The mission of the team all year is to add a third star. Their chance would come in a couple days, right outside Mr. Thomas's window on their home soccer field. So his team will sit in room 606 and watch an inspirational movie, or maybe coach Swartz could think of something else. Maybe he could bring in a speaker who could talk about what it takes to add the third star.

As the boys sit and wait, Coach Schwartz comes in and announces, "I have a guest for you today." That's when Heather O'Reilly comes in and the boys' jaws hit the desk. Even with jeans and a t-shirt replacing the USA kit, and her hair not in a ponytail, the boys had no problem recognizing her. The reaction, however, was not as dramatic as it was from the two 11-year-old soccer players who met Heather as she entered the building, their mothers part of a well-kept secret. Gasps and little screeches from the girls accompanied Heather's arrival.

Back in room 606, after telling the boys she spent yesterday at the White House, Heather passed her World Cup medal around the room. She's begun talking about that third star, the elusive third championship, the one that left no doubt as to which was the premier women's soccer program in the world. "I think it's great that you have set such a big goal," she told the team. "It's a very bold and powerful thing to do to set out to win and say you want to win."

O'Reilly knows a bit about winning. She won a high school state championship, an Under-19 World Championship, two NCAA titles at the University of North Carolina, three Olympic Gold medals, two championships with her professional teams, and now a World Cup title. Never, she said, did any of her teams set goals of making it out of group play, or reaching the semifinals. Nope. Win it all or bust. "It's a pretty cool way to live your life," she said with a smile.

The boys are paying attention. She has their attention when she talks about the bubble that needs to be created around the team, a way of insulating themselves from outside pressures and anything else that will take the focus off their mission. And she tells them to trust their training. "Believe in what you are doing every day. You will become so well-oiled that you don't have to count on that finger-crossed miracle to get you through."

The boys pay attention when she talks about roles and how each player on the 2015 World Cup roster had a role. She told them that it was important that each player not only accept their role but thrive in that role. She explained that how well each player performed in their role was critical to any success they were going to have in the World Cup.

There are two such roles she wants to talk about. The first is the part Abby Wambach played in the USA's 2015 World Cup win. "It was all about putting your ego aside and help the team win," she explained. "Here's someone who has scored more international goals than anyone in the world, and she has been pretty much responsible for carrying the team on her shoulders for about 10 years. But her role was to start some games and come off the bench some games. She accepted it and put everything she had into it. If Abby approached that tournament any differently, if she wasn't so awesome, who knows what would have happened."

"Everyone had a role," she continued. "My role was to be a reserve. My job was to push the starters to make them play as well as they could. I tried to do everything and anything I could come up with to help the team."

It's been 16 years since Heather, a New Jersey native, went to Giants Stadium in East Rutherford and watched the USA beat Denmark on June 19th in the 1999 World Cup opener. There have been three more World Cups since 14-year-old Heather and her youth soccer teammates eagerly awaited June 19th to arrive. "I remember going to the game with my club team, and we were all pumped up to get to the game, but it wasn't so much to see the game but to see Justin Timberlake perform before it. Then I saw Mia score that awesome goal, and I said, 'I want that to me.'"

In 2002, at the first-ever U17 Women's World Cup, O'Reilly had the type of performance that earns you a chance with the senior team, scoring four goals and dishing out seven assists to help the USA win the title. In the final against Canada on September 1st, she gave a glimpse of what fans, teammates, and coaches would come to expect from her—pure hard work to get to the far post in overtime and keep the ball in play and set up Lindsay Tarpley's Golden Goal. She made her first appearance with the full team six months later under coach April Heinrichs. She came on as a sub for Shannon MacMillan in a 1-1 draw with Sweden in Portugal. That was 224 international appearances ago. Some of the most important lessons she learned, however, came early.

"My first trip with the team was kind of memorable," said Heather. "I was late for breakfast one day, but nobody said anything to me. I thought they didn't notice that the 17-year-old kid wasn't there. They didn't care. That's what I thought anyway. Then at practice the next day, Julie (Foudy) called us all together and said, 'Some of the players have been late for meals and team meetings. I want to get back to the standards this team has always had. So as a result, tomorrow we are going to run fitness.' It was a day before the game and we would never run fitness the day before a game, but I didn't put two and two together. So we all lined up on the goal line to run fitness. Speed is one of my strengths, so I thought I was going to make up for it by being awesome at fitness. I lined up with everyone else, and April was down at the other end to start us. When she put her hand down to start us, I busted out as fast as I could go. I went about 50 yards. I looked to my right. I looked to my left. Nobody was near me. I thought I was flying. I turned around and no one had even left the line. They were all rolling around laughing. Me and my 17-year-old gullible self was the only one running. Kelly Wilson was the only other one to run. But she went about five yards before she figured it out. I went 50."

And she's been running ever since. Gifted with speed and grit, she was tough to ignore when coaches chose teams. Heinrichs could not resist the possibility of having O'Reilly come off her bench at the 2004 Olympics in Greece, even though she had appeared in just 12 matches all year, started none, and scored just once. However, none of that matter when a game was on the line. In a tense semifinal against Germany, a game that saw the U.S. take a 1-0 lead 33 minutes in on a goal from Kristine Lilly, only for Germany to tie it two minutes into injury time. O'Reilly replaced Tarpley in the 75th minute and scored the game winner in the 99th minute.

She's famous now, famous enough to have been to the White House and on stage with Taylor Swift and to have a "very pregnant woman" ask her to sign her belly. She drew the line at that one. Now, at 31, having played in three Olympics and three World Cups, Heather plays with the energy and enthusiasm of a 17-year-old but speaks with the wisdom of a seasoned veteran. And people listen, especially the boys at Westchester Country Day. They are listening when she tells them to approach their upcoming playoff match as if it was 90 one-minute games, and that they should always train the way they want to play, have the same intensity in training as you do in games. But they are really listening when she talks about the third star.

"That third star is something really special," she said. "For ever and ever, we can look at that third star and say, 'That was us.'"

MEANWHILE...

O n September 9, 2015, two months after the World Cup final, the New York University men's soccer team defeated City College of New York in a NCAA Division III men's soccer game. So what's the big deal? The NYU men's team featured the only female head coach in NCAA men's soccer. The coach of the NYU team is Kim Wyant, the college teammate of Michelle Akers at the University of Central Florida and a member of the 1985 Women's national team that went to Jesolo, Italy. Wyant played goalkeeper for the U.S., making 16 international appearances.

First, Lauren Holiday. Then Shannon Boxx. Then Abby Wambach. They all retired in 2015. Combined, they played 894 games for the USA and were among the most impactful players in the history of the program, and what they helped establish, the foundation for the future, was on solid ground.

Carli Lloyd and Becky Sauerbrunn were named as the team's new captains 1996. They would become the 13th and 14th captains in national team's 30-year history, joining the short and elite list that includes April Heinrichs, Carla Overbeck, Julie Foudy, Kristine Lilly and Christie Rampone.

In another in a long line of firsts *Sports Illustrated* put the U.S. team on its cover. That, in itself, is not a first, but creating a different cover for each of the 23 players and one of Jill Ellis is definitely new. That's 24 unique covers, counting the main cover featuring Carli Lloyd and the World Cup trophy.

For the first time ever, a professional women's soccer league was set to enter its fourth consecutive season. The National Women's Soccer League started modestly in 2013 with eight teams. It had the backing of U.S. Soccer in cooperation with the national federations from Mexico and Canada. After two solid years, which included tremendous fan support, most notably an average of 15,000 per game in Portland, the league has expanded to 10 teams. Every non-collegiate national team player and national team hopeful now has a club with which to play.

Carli Lloyd sat behind Cristiano Ronaldo in Zurich at the Balon D'Or Award Ceremonies, and later, as the winner of the FIFA Women's Player of the

Year, she sat on stage with Lionel Messi. She called it the most humbling and most tremendous experience of her career. Jill Ellis was given the FIFA Female Coach of the Year award. "This certainly represents a whole lot of people," Ellis said on stage. "So, certainly to my players, our captains, the staff back in the U.S. right now, it's my sincere gratitude for your commitment and your effort and your belief in this team. And I really, truly believe this is a team award."

Today in Memphis, Tenn., you have to travel on Cindy Parlow Drive to get into the Mike Rose Soccer Complex. Cindy is married to John Cone and living in Chapel Hill, North Carolina. She coaches youth soccer, and in fact, one of her recent players is Carson Overbeck, daughter of Carla and Greg. Cindy's husband is a certified sports scientist, an A-licensed soccer coach, and the only American to hold the prestigious Fitness Trainers Award from the English Football Association. They are starting a company called ImVere, which is developing a device that measures athlete's head impact and the rotation of the head. Parlow and Brandi Chastain have teamed up with the Sports Legacy Institute and the Santa Clara Institute of Sports Law and Ethics for a campaign called "Parents and Pros for Safer Soccer." And she is the face of an initiative called "Safer Soccer" by the Concussion Legacy Foundation, which has campaigned to raise the minimum age of heading the ball from 10 years old to 14.

In early 2016, the Los Angeles Football Club, which will begin playing in Major League Soccer in 2018, announced their ownership team. The owners include Magic Johnson, Will Ferrell, and Mia Hamm and her husband, former Major League Baseball great Nomar Garciapara. The Mia Hamm Foundation is still thriving. And on those occasions when she wears the baseball cap, it no longer has to be pulled so low. She's a mom of three and likes the role. "My kids will have a lot of coaches in their lives, but the will only have one mom," she says.

Carin Gabarra is the head coach at the U.S. Naval Academy and has been since 1993. Julie Foudy works for ESPN and, as always, is vocal about women's sports issues. Michelle Akers operates a horse rescue ranch in Georgia. Carla Overbeck is entering her 24th year as assistant coach at Duke University. April Heinrichs and Tracey Leone still work as coaches and advisors for U.S. Soccer. Angela Hucles is president of the Women's Sports Foundation.

And, at a soccer camp outside of Boston in mid-July of 2015, the instructor split a bunch of nine and 10 year-old boys into two teams and asked them to name their teams. "Typically, they yell Brazil, or Germany, or Barcelona or any other one of the top-flight professional or national teams," said the instructor, Scott Benjamin. "Today when I asked them, they all yelled, 'USA Women! Then they began to say, 'I'm Abby Wambach,' 'I'm Carli Lloyd,' 'I'm Alex Morgan.' They wanted to emulate champions. They didn't care if they were men or women."

Abby Wambach
Photo by Jeff McCrum

TO BE CONTINUED...

In the late 1990s, Lauren Gregg, the long-time assistant coach for the United States Women's National Team, related a story about how the national team often used the example of the four-minute mile as motivation. The four-minute mile was a barrier every elite distance runner eyed as a measure of greatness. For a period of time, it was believed that no one could do it. The thinking was that humans were not physically capable of running a mile in less than four minutes. Then, On May 6, 1954, Englishman Roger Bannister became the first person to do it. Two months later, Bannister and Australia's John Landy both broke the barrier in the same race. Then the mile was run in 3:50, then 3:45. In 1964, an American runner named Jim Ryun became the first high school runner to run a sub-four-minute mile. In 1994, a 40-year-old named Eamonn Coghlan did it. Fifty years after Bannister broke the barrier, 17 seconds had been shaved off the mark.

The message the coaches were sending was that the four-minute mile was a just a psychological barrier, not an unattainable physical feat. All that was needed was someone to show it could be done. In American society, the women who break down barriers are the ones who ignore limits that have been imposed upon them.

After she had finally won her World Cup and had decided to retire, Abby Wambach was able to look back and reflect on all the barriers—psychological, cultural, and societal—the U.S. women's soccer program had been able to break. It was the four-minute mile over and over and over. In 2015, the USA needed to break the barrier again. Now, when it comes time to set goals, things that have not yet been accomplished will certainly be somewhere on the list. And they will have to be accomplished without Abby Wambach.

You must have seen it by now. That emotional Gatorade commercial with Abby Wambach telling the audience to "forget her."

"I challenge everybody who is currently on this team or will ever be on this team to keep this culture alive, to keep looking and searching for something more," she begins. "More quality, more happiness, more truth, more trust, and just that unwavering desire to be the best. If everybody keeps doing that, this team will always be on top.

"Forget me. Forget my number, forget my name, forget I ever existed," the two-time Olympic gold medalist and 2012 FIFA World Player of the Year says in the commercial while sitting in front of a locker with her nameplate in her hand. "Forget the medals won, records broken, and the sacrifices made. I want to leave a legacy where the ball keeps rolling forward. Where the next generation accomplishes things so great that I am no longer remembered. So, forget me. Because the day I'm forgotten is the day we will succeed."[ii]

Maybe someday. Maybe with time, Abby Wambach will be forgotten. But for now, it could not be more important for everyone to remember the now-retired icon. There is some torch-passing that needs to be done first, and that has not been done all that often in the first 30 years of the program. It went from Heinrichs to Foudy and Overbeck. When Foudy and Overbeck were gone, though, Kristine Lilly was still around. Wambach was next, and she had the benefit of watching and learning. Who has been watching and learning from Abby? Who is going to accept Abby's very public challenge to "Keep this culture alive, to keep looking and searching for something more."

"I think that Alex Morgan will be a star for a long time," said Heather O'Reilly whose career overlapped with pieces from every generation. "She gets it. She knows what it takes. I think that Tobin Heath is a winner and is a special glue to the team, and I think that is important for players to see. I also think that Crystal Dunn is a promising young star that has the unselfish, blue collar mentality from Carolina that is needed at that level."

So for now, Abby will be remembered. But what does she remember? When she looks back at it all, what will be the most important moments? Certainly, the World Cup title, the Olympic Gold medals, the records she broke, the adulation, the applause. Nope. She said she will miss being with her teammates. She will miss being able to stay up late and chatting, or watching movies with them, travelling with them. "I have had the best life," she said. "I have literally grown up on this team, and my teammates have helped me through all of it. I have been extremely fortunate to have been able to share the field with truly extraordinary women."

That's what was important to her. In fact, that's what's been important to all of the players who came before her. Why? Look back at the first paragraph of this book.

It's not the glory that's lasting. It's the journey that mattered.

U.S. WOMEN'S NATIONAL TEAM ALL-TIME ROSTER (THROUGH 2015 WORLD CUP FINAL)

(Name – Caps – Goals – Years)

Adams, Danesha -- 1—0—2006

Akers, Michelle—153—105—1985-2000

Aldama, Heather–5–0–1998-2000

Allmann, Amy–24–0–1987-1991

Averbuch, Yael–26–1–2007-2013

Baggett, Samantha–2–1–1998-1999

Barnhart, Nicole–54–0–2004-2013

Bates, Tracey–29–5–1987-1991

Batista, Tami–1–0–1993

Baumgardt, Justi–16–3–1993-1998

Beene, Lakeysia–18–0–2000-2003

Belkin, Debbie–50–2–1986-1991

Bell, Keisha–2–0–2001

Bender, Denise–4–0–1985

Benson, Jenny–8–0–2001-2003

Berry, Angela–2–0–1992-1993

Billett, Jackie–1–0–1992

Bivens, Kylie–17–0–2002-2004

Borgman, Danielle–2–0–1997-2000

Boxx, Shannon–186–27–2003-2013

Boyer-Murdoch,

    Denise– 7–1–1985-1987

Branam, Jen–6–0–2000-2006

Brian, Morgan–19–3–2013-2014

Brooks, Amber–1–0–2013

Bryan, Thori

    (Staples)–64–1–1993-2003

Buckley, Tara–2–0–1985

Bueter, Sheri–1–0–1998

Bush, Susan–10–3–1998-2000

Bylin, Laurie–4–0–1985

Cassella, Gina–2–1–1992

Chalupny, Lori–95–8–2001-2014

Chastain, Brandi–192–30–1988-2004

Clemens, Mandy–5–0–1999-2002

Cobb, Suzy–1–0–1986

Cole, Lisa–2–0–1990

Confer, Robin–8–1–1996-1998

Connors, Kerry–4–0–1997

Conway, Kim–4–0–1993

Cook, Ann–1–0–1998

Cornell, Pam (Baughman)–4–1–1985-1986

Cox, Stephanie (Lopez)–89–0–2005-2014

Cramer, Aleisha–19–0–1998-2002

Cromwell, Amanda–55–1–1991-1998

Cunningham, Colette–2–0–1992

Dalmy, Marian–11–0–2007-2009

Daws, Cindy–2–0–1997

Demko, Michelle–1–0–1997

DeVert, Kristi–4–1–1997

DiMartino, Tina–5–1–2008-2009

Drambour, Betsy–7–0–1986-1987

Ducar, Tracy (Noonan)–24–0–1996-1999

Dunlap-Seivold, Joan–4–1–1986

Dunn, Crystal–12–0–2013-2014

Egan, Danielle–6–1–1993

Ellertson, Tina

    (Frimpong)–34–1–2005-2008

Engen, Whitney–23–3–2011-2014

Enos, Stacey–10–0–1985-1986

Fair, Lorrie–120–7–1996-2005

Fair, Ronnie–3–0–1997-1998

Fawcett, Joy (Biefeld)–239–27–1987-2004

Ferguson, Karen–2–0–1992-1993

Figgins, Lorraine–1–0–1986

Fischer, Jessica–2–0–1993

Fletcher, Kendall–1–0–2009

Florance, Meredith–3–0–1999-2001

Fotopoulos, Danielle
(Garrett)–35–16–1996-2005

Foudy, Julie–272–45–1988-2004

French, Michelle–14–0–1997-2001

Gabarra, Carin
(Jennings)–117–53–1987-1996

Gancitano, Linda–2–0–1985

Gebauer, Wendy–26–10–1987-1991

Gegg, Gretchen–2–0–1986-1990

Gmitter, Lisa–12–3–1986-1987

Gordon, Cindy–13–0–1985-1988

Gregg, Lauren–1–0–1986

Grubb, Jen–12–2 1995-19999

Hagen, Sarah–2–0–2014

Hamilton, Linda–71–1–1987-1995

Hamm, Mia–275–158–1987-2004

Harker, Ruth–2–0–1985

Harris, Ashlyn–4–0–2013-2014

Harvey, Mary–27–0–1989-1996

Hawkins, Devvyn–9–1–2001-2003

Healy, Tuca–3–0–1985

Heath, Tobin–85–11–2008-2014

Heinrichs, April–46–35–1986-1991

Hellmuth, Holly–1–0–1990

Henry, Lori–41–3–1985-1991

Higgins, Shannon–51–4–1987-1991

Holiday, Lauren–114–23–2007-2014

Horan, Lindsey–2–0–2013

Hucles, Angela–109–13–2002-2009

Huffman, Sarah–1–0–2010

Huie, Lindsey–1–0–2005

Irizarry, Patty–2–0–1987-1988

Jobson, Marci
(Miller)–17–0–2005-2007

Johnston, Julie–5–0–2013-2014

Jones, Laura–1–0–1992

Kai, Natasha–67–24–2006-2009

Kaufman, Christina–2–1–1993

Keller, Beth–1–1–1999

Keller, Debbie–46–18–1995-1998

Kester, Sherrill–3–3–2000

Klingenberg, Meghan–24–1–2011-2014

Kluegel, Jena–24–1–2000-2003

Kramarz, Nancy–6–1–1993

Kraus, Anna–6–0–2000-2001

Krieger, Ali–57–1–2008-2014

Lalor, Jennifer–23–2–1992-2001

LePeilbet, Amy–84–0–2004-2012

Leroux, Sydney–64–33–2011-2014

Lilly, Kristine–352–130–1987-2010

Lindsey, Kelly–4–0–2000-2002

Lindsey, Lori–31–1–2005-2013

Lloyd, Carli–185–61–2005-2014

Lohman, Joanna–9–0–2001-2007

Long, Allie–4–0–2014

Loyden, Jill–10–0–2010-2014

Luckenbill, Kristin–14–0–2004

MacMillan, Shannon–176–60–1993-2005

Manthei, Holly–22–0–1995-1997

Markgraf, Kate
(Sobrero)–201–1–1998-2010

Marquand, Ally–4–1–2001

Masar, Ella–1–0–2009

McDermott, Marcia–7–4–1986-1988

Mead, Jen–6–0–1993-1997

McCarthy, Megan–42–0–1987-1994

Mewis, Kristie–15–1–2013-2014

Mewis, Samantha–3–0–2014

Milbrett, Tiffeny–204–100–1991-2005

Mitts, Heather–137–2–1999-2012

Monroe, Mary-Frances–9–0–2000-2001

Morgan, Alex–77–49–2010-2014

Mullinix, Siri–45–0–1999-2004

Naeher, Alyssa–1–0–2014

Nairn, Christine–2–1–2009
Neaton, Natalie–5–4–1995-1998
Nogueira, Casey–5–0–2007-2010
Oakes, Jill–1–0–2005
Oleksiuk, Emily–2–0–2001
O'Hara, Kelley–52–0–2010-2014
O'Reilly, Heather–215–41–2002-2014
Orlandos, Lauren–1–0–2001
Orrison, Ann–5–0–1985-1986
Osborne, Leslie–61–3–2002-2009
Overbeck, Carla (Werden)
    168–7–1988-2000
Pagliarulo, Jaime–3–0–1997-2001
Parlow, Cindy–158–75–1996-2004
Pearman, Tammy–9–1–1995-1997
Pickering, Emily–15–2–1985-1992
Poore, Lou Ellen–2–0–1992
Press, Christen–35–19–2013-2014
Pryce, Nandi–8–0–2000
Putz, Caroline–1–1–2000
Rafanelli, Sarah–34–8–1992-1995
Rampone, Christie
    (Pearce)–304–4–1997-2014
Ramsey, Alyssa–8–0–2000-2001
Randolph, Sara–2–0–2001
Rapinoe, Megan–96–29–2006-2014
Raygor, Keri (Sanchez)–13–0–1991-2001
Remer, Sharon
    (McMurtry)–6–0–1985-1986
Ridgewell, Kathy–3–0–1985-1987
Rigamat, Stephanie–7–1–2001
Roberts, Tiffany–110–7–1994-2004
Robinson, Leigh Ann–2–0–2013
Rodriguez, Amy–114–28–2004-2014
Rohbock, Shauna–1–0–1998
Rowe, Christy–1–0–1996
Rutten, Jill–1–0–1998
Sauerbrunn, Becky–71–0–2008-2014
Schmedes, Kelly
    (Wilson)–4–1–2002-2005

Schnur, Meghan–6–0–2010
Schott, Laura–5–1–2001
Schwoy, Laurie–4–0–1997-1999
Scurry, Briana–173–0–1994-2008
Serlenga, Nikki–30–6–2000-2001
Slaton, Danielle–43–1–1999-2003
Smith, Gayle–2–0–1992
Steadman, Amy–4–0–2001
Stewart, Jill–2–0–1997
Strong, Jennifer–1–0–1992
Szpara, Janine–6–0–1986-1987
Tarpley, Lindsay–125–32–2003-2011
Taylor, Brittany–2–0–2010-2011
Tomek, Chris–12–0–1986-1987
Tower, Rita–6–0–1993-1994
Trotter, India–2–0–2006-2007
Tymrak, Erika–3–1–2013-2014
Van Hollebeke, Rachel (Buehler)
    112–5–2008-2014
Venturini, Tisha–132–44–1992-2000
Wagner, Aly–131–21–1998-2008
Walbert, Kelly–1–0–1994
Wambach, Abby–232–177–2001-2014
Ward, Marcie–3–0–2001
Webber, Saskia–28–0–1992-2000
Weiss, Kristen–4–0–2001
Welsh, Christie–39–20–2000-2006
Whalen, Sara–65–7–1997-2000
White, Kacey–18–0–2006-2009
Whitehill, Cat
    (Reddick)–134–11–2000-2010
Wilson, Staci–14–0–1995-1996
Woznuk, Angie–10–2–2005-2009
Wyant, Kim–9–0–1985-1993
Zepeda, Veronica–5–1–1998-2000

ENDNOTES

i   Information about Hope Solo's childhood is from her book with Ann Kilion, *Solo, A Memoir of Hope*, Harper Collins, 2012

ii   Abby Wambach, Gatorade commercial. Gatorade, 2015.

ABOUT THE AUTHOR

Tim Nash previously co-authored three books on women's soccer – Training Soccer Champions, by Anson Dorrance; Standing Fast, by Michelle Akers; and The Champion Within, by Lauren Gregg. Tim spent 17 years covering soccer in the United States. He covered the 1996 Olympics, 1999 Women's World Cup, the 2000 Olympics and the 2003 Women's World Cup. He served as Senior Editor of internetsoccer.com, collegesoccer.com, womenssoccer.com, and provided content for six WUSA teams as well as WUSA.com. He also published Soccer News, a national soccer monthly. He has covered 17 Women's College Cups and 13 Men's College Cups. His soccer articles have appeared in several major newspapers, including USA Today, the Detroit Free Press, San Jose Mercury News, the Raleigh News & Observer, the Memphis Commercial Appeal, and the Greensboro News & Record, as well as the NSCAA Journal, Soccer Jr., and Southern Living.

Today, Tim is a freelance writer living in Graham, N.C., with his wife Cheri, daughter Allison and son Ian. He has coached girls' soccer teams from U12 to U18 and is currently coaching U12 girls in Greensboro. To contact Tim, email 56thminute@gmail.com